'This is the fit-for-right-now, caring, scalable approach we desperately need for the AI age. A triumph.'
Kerri O'Neill, Chief People Officer, Ipsos UK

'In this much-needed wake-up call, Laura Overton and Michelle Ockers provide powerful principles for L&D to navigate a changing world. For anyone planning a future in the field, this is essential reading.'
Donald H Taylor, Lead Researcher, L&D Global Sentiment Survey

'Nestled in deep research and storytelling, this is the ultimate playbook for the entire spectrum of L&D professionals, giving us the scaffolding to do our best work.'
Lori Niles-Hofmann, AI transformation strategist and Founder of 8Levers

'The quintessential guide for any aspiring or current leader. This is not just a compelling read, it is a comprehensive "how to" for any serious L&D leader.'
Damien Woods, Chapter Lead (GM), Learning and Growth

'By advocating for leadership that is comfortable with ambiguity and change, *The L&D Leader* provides an indispensable guide for L&D professionals seeking to remain relevant and effective in an AI-driven world. What a great book!'
Marc Ramos, Global Head, Learning strategy and Innovation, ServiceNow

'Practical, flexible and deeply human, this book is a call to action for anyone shaping learning in complex times.'
Stella Lee, AI literacy architect and Founder of Paradox Learning

'This is about remaining relevant in a world being turned upside down – nothing could be more important in this brittle age of turbulence and bewilderment.'
Nigel Paine, learning strategist, author and broadcaster

'Grounded in real-world application, the book empowers L&D professionals to ask the right questions, challenge assumptions and experiment with new approaches to drive genuine value.'
Marie Daniels, APAC L&D leader

'This excellent book takes the reader on a voyage of discovery. It provides a robust set of principles for any HR, talent or L&D leader looking to navigate today's fast-moving and increasingly technology-supported world.'
Charles Jennings, Director, Duntroon Consultants

'Packed with tried-and-tested advice from two stalwarts of the profession. The authors use real case studies to illustrate how we can shift from band-aid reactions to strategic solutions.'
Ryan Tracey, senior L&D leader

'A book packed with valuable principles that are evidence-based and grounded in research and pragmatic experience. They unify diverse and complex ideas with a wonderful navigational story that resonates, bringing an unexpected magic to the book.'
Stella Collins, learning strategist

'Written by recognized sector leaders, the book offers both seasoned professionals and emerging leaders a roadmap for driving organizational capability in today's complex learning landscape.'
Ben Campbell, CEO, Australian Institute of Training and Development

'Working in a large, complex organization, I recognize the challenges and opportunities that Laura Overton and Michelle Ockers have captured so perfectly. The book addresses those challenges and helps L&D professionals navigate the continuously changing waters in order to make a real difference and shape organizational future.'
Vickie Roberts OBE, Head of Skills, HMRC

'*The L&D Leader* is different because it delves into rich data collected over two decades and then gets creative about finding a way forward. This framework is both broad enough to allow agility and focused enough to provide a valuable navigation tool for any aspiring L&D leader.'
Piers Lea, Chief Strategy Officer, Learning Technologies Group

'Each chapter's inclusion of "what gets in our way?" points provide a realistic view of the work ahead for the L&D leader, and the built-in Field Notebooks provide great opportunities for reflection and review.'
Jane Bozarth, Director of Research, The Learning Guild

'Every time I sat down to read *The L&D Leader* it helped create a still place to think. I'm in awe of the wisdom that Laura Overton and Michelle Ockers have generated and brought to life in this book.'
Darryn Gray, learning designer and Founder of the Crackin' LnD (Down Under) community

'Outlines the cross-sector learning principles our profession desperately needs to shape the future of workplace learning together.'
Martin Baker, CEO, The Charity Learning Consortium

'Kudos to the authors for tackling how our professional mindset influences our impact – without this reset, we're simply putting new tools in the same broken toolbox that keeps us reactive instead of strategic.'
Shannon Tipton, Learning Rebels

'This is a masterclass in how learning can truly make a difference, from two of the most thoughtful and respected voices in the field.'
Drew McGuire, Director, Capability Group

'*The L&D Leader* is both a clarion call for BOLD change in the L&D function and a blueprint for successful navigation of the new norm. It is a must-read for savvy learning leaders who want to shape the future of the field.'
Sandra Loughlin, Chief Learning Scientist, EPAM Systems

'Laura Overton and Michelle Ockers have delivered more than just another theoretical framework – TRI and be BOLD is the dynamic navigation system we need to develop commercially aware, strategically minded leaders who can align learning with business priorities.'
Cathy Hoy, Co-founder and CEO, CLO100

'This book is both a rallying cry and a reliable guide for L&D leaders who know they're meant for more than taking orders and delivering training.'
David James, Chief Learning Officer, 360Learning

'This is an extraordinary and innovative approach to helping L&D professionals and wider senior teams make the decisions of where they want people to go and, crucially, the strategic map of how to get there.'
Jo Cook, Editor, *Training Journal*

The L&D Leader

*Principles and practice
for delivering business value*

Laura Overton
Michelle Ockers

KoganPage

Publisher's note
Every possible effort has been made to ensure that the information contained in this book is accurate at the time of going to press, and the publishers and authors cannot accept responsibility for any errors or omissions, however caused. No responsibility for loss or damage occasioned to any person acting, or refraining from action, as a result of the material in this publication can be accepted by the editor, the publisher or the authors.

First published in Great Britain and the United States in 2026 by Kogan Page Limited

Kogan Page
Kogan Page Ltd, 2nd Floor, 45 Gee Street, London EC1V 3RS, United Kingdom
Kogan Page Inc, 8 W 38th Street, Suite 902, New York, NY 10018, USA
www.koganpage.com

EU Representative (GPSR)
Authorised Rep Compliance Ltd, Ground Floor, 71 Baggot Street Lower, Dublin D02 P593, Ireland
www.arccompliance.com

Kogan Page books are printed on paper from sustainable forests.

ISBNs
Hardback   978 1 3986 2032 2
Paperback   978 1 3986 2027 8
Ebook   978 1 3986 2031 5

British Library Cataloguing-in-Publication Data
A CIP record for this book is available from the British Library.

Library of Congress Control Number
2025029865

Typeset by Integra Software Services, Pondicherry
Printed and bound by CPI Group (UK) Ltd, Croydon CR0 4YY

CONTENTS

List of figures and tables xii
About the authors xiv
Foreword xv
Acknowledgements xvii
The structure of the book xx
How to use this book xxiii
Why we wrote this book xxviii

Introduction: A navigator's tale 1

PART ONE
What got us here won't get us there... or will it?

1 Calling all L&D leaders 11
What does value look like? 14
The disruption advantage 18
Navigating continual changing 21
Dreaming big together 23
Notes 25

2 Looking back to look forward 28
Why do we do what we do? 28
Looking back, to look forward 29
Abundance and overwhelm 30
Success leaves clues: Revisiting the evidence 30
The learning maturity data trail 33
Navigating our way to success: Getting back to basics 35
Be BOLD 40
Notes 41

PART TWO

Equipped: Navigation principles

3   **Tuning In** 45

Launching the start of something different at Barnardo's 45
Tuning In: What the data reveals 46
Navigation fundamentals 1: Tuning In 47
What gets in our way? 49
Success leaves clues: Unpacking the principle of Tuning In 50
Tuning In at a glance 59
Practical ideas to improve Tuning In 59
Moving forward to Responding 64
Notes 65

4   **Responding** 67

Designing the complete journey: Evidence-informed choices
    at Sydney Trains 67
Responding: What the data reveals 68
Navigation fundamentals 2: Responding 69
What gets in our way? 71
Success leaves clues: Unpacking the principle of Responding 72
Responding at a glance 83
Practical ideas to improve Responding 84
Moving forward to Improving 89
Notes 89

5   **Improving** 92

From proving to Improving at a global eye-care company 92
Improving: What the data reveals 93
Navigation fundamentals 3: Improving 95
What gets in our way? 97
Success leaves clues: Unpacking the principle of Improving 98
Improving at a glance 106
Practical ideas to improve Improving 106
Moving forward to TRI principles in action 112
Notes 113

6 Integrating TRI: AstraZeneca's learning transformation 114

AstraZeneca: Transforming learning to create business value 116
TRI principles in action at AstraZeneca 119
BOLD mindset: A preview 120
From understanding to application: The path ahead 121
Notes 121

PART THREE
Charting your course

7 Navigating safe waters: Equipped for today 125

The familiar waters of today 126
TRI stepping back to get control 128
Multiplex: Re-shaping compliance training in the construction
   industry 129
Multiplex: Principles in action 132
Vitality: Supporting frontline performance in real-time 134
Vitality: Principles in action 138
Tailoring TRI to different contexts today 140
TRI streamlining and scaling to equip people for today 141
Get your bearings: Equipping people for today 142
Distance covered 144
Notes 145

8 Beyond the horizon: Ready for tomorrow 146

Readiness for an accelerating horizon 147
TRI enabling continuous adapting 150
McKinsey: Receive to Grow – fuelling continuous adapting 151
McKinsey: Principles in action 154
EPAM: Skills and learning culture 157
EPAM: Principles in action 160
TRI building adaptability 162
Get your bearings: Enabling continuous adapting 164
Distance covered 166
Notes 167

9   **Journeying together** 168

The landscape of today 169
It's a journey, not a race 170
TRI journeying together from tensions to trust 171
Coles and Liberate Learning: Partnering to innovate 173
Coles/Liberate Learning: Principles in action 176
Open University and North Yorkshire Police: Forging a new path in policing 178
OU/NYP partnership: Principles in action 182
TRI journeying from partnership tensions to success 183
Get your bearings: Building higher-value partnerships 186
Distance covered 188
Notes 189

PART FOUR
Ready: The BOLD navigator

10   **Mindset matters** 193

A moment of clarity 193
When we become our own barrier to success 194
Navigating through the fog 195
From blame to navigation 195
Understanding our internal navigation instruments 197
How cognitive bias impacts our work 200
Caught in the doldrums: The impact of limiting beliefs 201
Recalibrating our navigation instruments 202
Amplifying our L&D professional superpowers 203
From mindset to action: Preparing to be BOLD 210
Notes 211

11   **Calibrating our BOLD compass** 212

An eye for business value 212
Our internal compass 213
BOLD learning leaders 215
Recognizing our thinking habits 216
BOLD in action: Navigating the edge of innovation 223
Knowing when to turn around 225

Becoming BOLDER: Your safety net 227
Using your BOLD compass to chart your path 229
Notes 230

PART FIVE

Shaping the future

12 L&D: Equipped and ready 233

Get your bearings 234
L&D's own navigation challenges 235
TRI as a navigation system for growth 237
Navigating together 251
Notes 251

13 Shaping our future 253

Over the horizon: Getting ready 253
A future of building business value 254
TRI and be BOLD: Navigating forward 256
AI: The disruption advantage 257
Shaping our future together 259
Shaping the future of L&D: A renaissance 263
Notes 265

Appendix 1: Learning Performance Benchmark 267
Appendix 2: Tool to build your matrix of models 273
Appendix 3: Learning science checklist 283
Appendix 4: L&D thinking habits continuum 285
Appendix 5: L&D Sail Plan 287
Index 290

LIST OF FIGURES AND TABLES

FIGURES

Figure 1.1   The L&D Value Spectrum 15

Figure 1.2   The L&D Value Landscape 18

Figure 2.1   The L&D performance gap 31

Figure 2.2   The Transformation Curve Maturity Model 32

Figure 2.3   The TRI principles 37

Figure 3.1   How are L&D leaders Tuning In? Shifts in practice 2018–23 47

Figure 4.1   How are L&D leaders Responding? Shifts in practice 2018–23 69

Figure 4.2   Supporting the learning process with technology 76

Figure 5.1   How are L&D leaders Improving? Shifts in practice 2018–23 94

Figure 9.1   PCDA student journey 180

Figure 10.1   Honing our professional superpowers 207

Figure 11.1   BOLD L&D compass 217

Figure 11.2   Thinking about value 218

Figure 11.3   Thinking about our role 219

Figure 11.4   Thinking about our relationships 219

Figure 11.5   Thinking about technology 220

Figure 11.6   Thinking about timeframes 221

Figure 11.7   Thinking about risk and innovation 221

Figure 11.8   Thinking about decisions 222

Figure 11.9   Thinking about our influence 222

Figure 11.10   BOLD safety net 228

Figure 12.1   L&D skills: What L&D pros say 243

Figure 13.1   The Learning Value Landscape 255

Figure 13.2   L&D Value Cycle 263

Figure A2.1   5 Moments of Need 274

Figure A2.2   5Di© model 276

Figure A2.3   12 Levers of Transfer Effectiveness 277

Figure A4.1   L&D thinking habits continuum 286
Figure A5.1   L&D Sail Plan prompters 288
Figure A5.2   L&D Sail Plan 289

TABLES
Table 3.1   Tuning In to create opportunities 61
Table 4.1   Reacting versus Responding 70
Table 4.2   Responding to create opportunities 85
Table 5.1   Indicators of value across the L&D Value Spectrum 99
Table 5.2   Benchmarks and consequences 104
Table 5.3   Using the Improving principle to create opportunities 107
Table 7.1   Using TRI to tackle challenges 141
Table 7.2   Experiments to simplify learning 143
Table 7.3   Experiments for enhancing solutions 144
Table 8.1   Using TRI to overcome roadblocks to adaptability 163
Table 8.2   Experiments to improve adaptability 165
Table 8.3   Experiments for strengthening your adaptive ecosystem 166
Table 9.1   Applying TRI principles to build stronger partnerships 184
Table 9.2   Small experiments to build stronger partnerships 187
Table 9.3   Experiments for strategic partnership growth 188
Table 10.1   Learning science insights used in L&D practice 198
Table 10.2   Cognitive biases 201
Table 11.1   Signals to turn around 225
Table 12.1   Tuning In tips 241
Table 12.2   Responding tips 245
Table 12.3   Improving tips 249
Table A1.1   Timeline of key reports in the Benchmark series 268
Table A2.1   Model alignment with principles: originator's view 278
Table A3.1   Learning science checklist 283

ABOUT THE AUTHORS

Laura Overton is an award-winning learning analyst dedicated to uncovering effective practices in learning innovation that drive business value. With 35 years of practical experience, Laura has authored over 70 reports and hundreds of articles based on her commitment to supporting evidence-based learning decisions. She established Learning Changemakers and is a co-founder of Emerging Stronger – global initiatives supporting the changing world of workplace learning. As the founder and original CEO of Towards Maturity, Laura led a 15-year longitudinal study (2004–19) with thousands of learning leaders worldwide to uncover strategies that lead to business success. She is an Academic Fellow of the CIPD, contributing to and leading their Learning at Work study. As a result of her research, keynote speaking and facilitation, Laura has been consistently recognized as a significant global influencer of workplace learning trends since 2012.

Michelle on Laura: 'Laura is one of the most curious people I've ever met. She combines this with clarity – grounded in research and driven by a desire to understand – she sees patterns others miss and helps make sense of complexity in ways we can actually use.'

Michelle Ockers helps organizations build high-impact learning functions through strategic consulting, mentoring and capability development. As founder and Chief Learning Strategist at Learning Uncut, Michelle partners with learning and development (L&D) teams to design modern learning strategies, facilitate learning transformation and mentors both aspiring and seasoned L&D leaders. Since 2018, she has hosted the popular Learning Uncut podcast, sharing real learning solution case studies from around the globe. Michelle is a co-founder of Emerging Stronger. Previously, Michelle held senior L&D roles in large organizations across multiple industries, bringing a wealth of hands-on experience to her work. Her contributions to the field have been recognized with the 2019 Australian Institute of Training and Development's Learning Professional of the Year award and the 2019 Internet Time Alliance Jay Cross Memorial Award for contribution to informal learning.

Laura on Michelle: 'Michelle cares. She cares about the impact of the strategies she helps others to navigate. She cares about her podcast interviewees and listeners, surfacing and celebrating what's worked in the past to inspire success in the future. She cares enough to encourage, to challenge and to build, harnessing her wide industry experience with humility.'

FOREWORD

In the learning and development world, we see a lot about transformation. We discuss how L&D needs to evolve, how we must become more strategic, more data-driven, more aligned with business outcomes. Yet despite years of conversation, our research at RedThread shows a concerning trend: L&D's involvement in business strategy discussions has dropped by 50 per cent in just two years.

Hope, as we've said, isn't a plan.

This is why Laura Overton and Michelle Ockers' book comes at such a critical time. While many voices call for change in our profession, few have spent decades meticulously gathering the evidence needed to chart a viable path forward. Even fewer have done so while fostering genuine community and connection across the global L&D landscape.

We first encountered Laura's work through the Learning Performance Benchmark research years ago. What struck us then – and continues to impress us now – is her commitment to letting the data speak, even when it challenges our long-held assumptions. Similarly, Michelle's Learning Uncut podcast has cut through industry noise to capture stories of what works in different organizational contexts. Together, they bring something our field desperately needs: the marriage of rigorous research with practical application.

What makes this book different from other L&D texts crowding the marketplace? Three things stand out to us.

First, Laura and Michelle don't offer yet another rigid model. In our research at RedThread, we've consistently found that the most successful L&D functions don't blindly adopt frameworks – they adapt principles to their unique contexts. The Tuning In, Responding, Improving (TRI) principles presented here provide that flexible foundation, allowing you to navigate your specific organizational waters rather than following someone else's predetermined route.

We're particularly struck by how the TRI framework helps transform L&D professionals from producers of learning to enablers of learning. This shift – from creating courses to facilitating development wherever and however it happens – represents exactly the kind of evolution our research indicates is needed for L&D to increase its strategic value. What's especially powerful is that these principles apply regardless of where you are in your

L&D journey. Whether you're just starting out or leading a sophisticated learning organization, these navigation tools will help you chart your course.

Second, this book acknowledges something our research repeatedly confirms: L&D cannot operate in isolation. The most innovative L&D functions are deeply integrated with other organizational systems. They collaborate across boundaries, share data and co-create solutions. This book's emphasis on 'journeying together' isn't just inspirational language – it's a business imperative backed by evidence.

Third, we appreciate how this book addresses both the external and internal aspects of L&D transformation. At RedThread, we've found that systems, processes and technologies matter enormously – but they're only part of the equation. The BOLD compass Laura and Michelle introduce acknowledges that our mindsets, attitudes and personal leadership qualities are equally crucial to navigating today's complex environments.

As researchers who have spent years studying what makes HR and L&D functions effective, we find this book refreshingly honest about L&D's challenges while remaining genuinely hopeful about its potential. Laura and Michelle have something here beyond the typical L&D guidebook – they've drawn on their decades of wisdom and turned it into actionable principles that can guide us through the uncertainty ahead.

In a field that often chases the next shiny object, this book calls us back to fundamentals while still pushing us forward. It reinforces that L&D's value doesn't come from delivering courses but from ensuring individuals, teams and organizations have the right skills for whatever lies ahead.

Most importantly, it reminds us that we're not alone in this journey. The collective wisdom gathered within these pages – from benchmark data to practitioner stories – demonstrates the power of community and connection. That's something we at RedThread deeply believe in as well.

We invite you to approach this book not as a prescription but as a compass. Let it help you find your bearings, adjust your course and navigate toward the business impact your organization needs. The waters may be choppy, but with these principles as your guide, you're well-equipped for the journey ahead – regardless of where you are in your L&D career.

Dani Johnson
Co-founder and Principal Analyst
RedThread Research

ACKNOWLEDGEMENTS

This book draws inspiration from the remarkable journey and wisdom of the Polynesian Voyaging Society, celebrating its 50th anniversary in 2025, the year of our book's publication.

The story of Mau Pilaug, Nainoa Thompson and their journey with the Hōkūle'a to revive traditional wayfinding practices has profoundly shaped our thinking about navigating complexity in uncertain times. We approach this cultural treasure as learners, humble recipients of knowledge that has been captured throughout the ages and now generously shared through books, interviews and documented voyages.

We wish to express our deepest respect for the navigators past and present whose connection to the stars, ocean and natural world demonstrates that the ability to lead through true navigation requires more than tools and technology – it demands attunement, presence and responsibility to those we serve.

The mana'o (wisdom) shared within these pages is offered in the spirit of pono (righteousness) and panna (reciprocity), with the understanding that we are all on a journey of discovery together.

> Hōkūle'a embodies the mana, the spiritual power and wisdom of all who sailed aboard her or laid their caring hands on her. Our great teacher told us always to travel with serum, with the light. He taught us that voyaging aboard Hōkūle'a was a kuleana, both a privilege and responsibility: that a voyager sets out to discover new worlds and new values to bring them home and nourish the spirit of his people.

SOURCE Nainoa Thompson, 2025

We would like to express our profound gratitude to everyone who has supported us on the journey of creating this book.

First and foremost, we thank the many learning and development professionals who generously shared their real-world examples, stories, frameworks, insights and experiences with us. Your willingness to open your work to others helps us all learn, grow and navigate the complexities of our field. As the saying goes, 'A rising tide lifts all boats.' By sharing knowledge, we elevate not only ourselves but the entire profession. Thank you for your contributions to shaping the future of learning and development.

We would like to thank the editorial team at Kogan Page for their trust in us, patience and support as we crafted the book.

Mahalo to Tim Ohai for his support and insight on respecting culture in our sharing of the story of the Polynesian navigators and Polynesian Voyaging Society. Any remaining cultural oversights are our responsibility alone.

While this book represents our shared vision, we each brought distinct perspectives and expertise to the collaboration.

Michelle would like to acknowledge Laura as the original creator of the frameworks we've introduced in this book. Her benchmarking research and thoughtful analysis of the data gathered through it laid the foundation for the TRI principles, while her interpretation of our shared Emerging Stronger research led to the development of the thinking habits and the BOLD Compass. I'm grateful to Laura for inviting me to co-author this book with her – it's been a privilege to work alongside someone whose generosity, curiosity and rigour continue to influence our field in such meaningful ways.

Laura would like to acknowledge Michelle for her exceptional skill in gathering and curating real-world stories through the Learning Uncut podcast. Her ability to draw out authentic, practical insights from professionals across the globe has brought these principles to life and grounded our work in the reality of everyday L&D practice.

Michelle would also like to thank Karen Moloney and Amanda Ashby for starting the Learning Uncut podcast with her in 2018, and agreeing that she should continue it solo after 18 months. Special thanks to Mark Schenk for teaching her how to craft and share stories that resonate in business contexts and communicate ideas with greater impact. She'd also like to thank everyone who has encouraged and supported her in being bold in her professional life over the past decade – particularly Shai Desai, Arun Pradhan, Emma Weber, Donald H Taylor, Nigel Paine and Jane Hart.

Laura would also like to add her thanks to these and other mentors and allies who are continually challenging and shaping her thinking. Thank you to Mark Fenna-Roberts not only for introducing her to the world of 'technology-based training' but, 30-plus years later, for giving her the nudge she needed to start this book. To the thousands of participants gifting their data to the benchmark process, the Towards Maturity Ambassadors and the curious minds of Dr Genny Dixon and Dr Gent Ahmetaj, thank you for exploring the data with her over 20 years. To Professor Kate McGuire and her cohort of Dprof candidates at Middlesex University who have challenged her to go deeper still as she looks back on the past to surface new ways to navigate the future.

We both thank Shannon Tipton, co-founder of Emerging Stronger, for her friendship and insight and for all our Emerging Stronger community who turned the pandemic chaos into a deeply insightful moment in time for us.

To our families and friends who supported us through the intensive writing process, particularly during those times when we disappeared into our work for hours on end – thank you for your understanding, encouragement and patience. Michelle is especially grateful to Mark and her daughter Jessica, who believe in and encourage her. Laura is equally thankful to her husband Nigel and personal champions Mike and Jean who do the same.

Finally, to you, our readers – whether aspiring or seasoned L&D leaders – thank you for joining us on this voyage. We hope the principles and insights shared here will help you navigate your own unique path to creating greater business value through learning and development.

THE STRUCTURE OF THE BOOK

We're inviting you on a journey to discover how to navigate the continuously changing workplace as an L&D professional. Our goal is to equip you with practical, evidence-informed principles to design your own pathway to business value. Whether you're new to L&D or an experienced professional, this book will help you steer yourself, your people and organization to success in an increasingly complex landscape.

Part One: What got us here won't get us there… or will it?

In this part, we map the changing landscape of work and L&D. We explore why relying on past successes or outdated models isn't enough to navigate today's ambiguities and complexities to deliver meaningful business value.

- Chapter 1: Calling all L&D leaders. Explores today's landscape of continuous changing and why L&D professionals need to shift their approach to help organizations thrive.
- Chapter 2: Looking back to look forward. Reflects how evidence from the the past can guide us towards future business value creation.

Part Two: Equipped: Navigation principles

With an understanding of today's landscape and the value of evidence, we introduce TRI, practical navigation principles that will help you chart your course toward business value. This part creates space to go back to first principles of effective L&D professional practice. These TRIed and tested principles will help you navigate through today's noisy, messy landscape.

- Chapter 3: Tuning In. Focuses on developing awareness through aligning with organizational goals, understanding your people and grounding your work in your organizational context.

- Chapter 4: Responding. Shows how to respond professionally and effectively to the needs of your organization and people using evidence-informed approaches and learning science.
- Chapter 5: Improving. Explores how to use data and feedback to refine efforts and stay on course through continuous adjustment.
- Chapter 6: Integrating TRI – AstraZeneca's learning transformation. Demonstrates how the TRI principles work together in a real-world transformation of learning at AstraZeneca.

Part Three: Charting your course

Armed with these principles, it's time to put them into practice. Through real-world examples, you'll see how L&D professionals demonstrate the TRI principles in action across various contexts to equip people to perform today and be ready for tomorrow, ultimately driving business value.

- Chapter 7: Navigating safe waters: Equipped for today. Using the TRI principles as a lens, examines how to help equip people to perform effectively in their current roles, addressing the 'everyday' L&D tasks of compliance, onboarding and role-readiness.
- Chapter 8: Beyond the horizon: Ready for tomorrow. Addresses how to prepare your organization and people for an accelerating future, keeping pace with emerging skills through building a learning culture.
- Chapter 9: Journeying together. Shows how to apply TRI principles to build stronger partnerships between L&D teams and external partners.

Part Four: Ready: The BOLD navigator

Now we focus on you – the aspiring or seasoned L&D leader. Navigating new landscapes takes courage, and your mindset is key to becoming a bold navigator. This section introduces the BOLD principles to help you adopt the thinking habits of high-performing L&D leaders who consistently deliver business value.

- Chapter 10: Mindset matters. Explores how thinking habits shape professional decisions and examines biases that can prevent action and the superpowers releasing success.

- Chapter 11: Calibrating our BOLD compass. Introduces a tool to navigate uncertainty, discovering what it means to think **Business-First**, be **Open Minded,** adopt a **Leading and Learning** mindset and take **Deliberate** action.

Part Five: Shaping the future

Having explored how to apply the TRI principles to create business value for others, we now focus on applying these same principles to your own professional journey and that of your team. You'll discover how to use TRI for personal development, build resilience for bold action, and position yourself to navigate and shape the future of learning to create business value in a continuously changing workplace

- Chapter 12: L&D: Equipped and ready. Applies the TRI principles to your own professional growth and team development, creating a personal navigation system to help you step into your potential as an L&D leader.
- Chapter 13: Shaping our future. Brings together everything you've learned to help you thrive amid disruption and actively shape the future of L&D and business value.

HOW TO USE THIS BOOK

Whether you're new to L&D, transitioning from another field or a seasoned professional, this book offers evidence-informed principles to help you navigate continuous changing in the workplace. Drawing inspiration from the Polynesian Voyaging Society – whose story we urge you to read before you dive into the rest of the book – we provide tools to help you chart your course through complexity to business value with confidence and purpose.

Reading approaches

- **Sequential reading:** We recommend reading the book from start to finish to build understanding of both the TRI principles and the BOLD compass.

- **Mindset first:** If particularly interested in thinking habits, explore Part Four first before returning to practice principles.

- **Targeted use:** After your initial read, dip back into specific chapters when facing particular challenges or looking for inspiration.

For readers at different stages

- **Aspiring L&D leaders:** You'll find structured reflection questions and clear starting points for observation and experiments.

- **Seasoned L&D leaders:** These same elements offer opportunities to challenge assumptions and adapt principles to complex situations. We've included more advanced application ideas to develop your practice.

- **Teams:** Consider reading and discussing chapters together to enrich learning through diverse perspectives.

Your Field Notebook

Throughout this book, you'll notice this icon highlighting opportunities for reflection and application. Your Field Notebook – whether physical or digital – is more than just a place to jot down notes. Inspired by the practice of scientific field journals, it serves as a powerful thinking tool that will help you:

- capture observations and insights about your workplace challenges
- document your professional journey and track patterns over time
- generate new ideas through the act of writing itself
- create a record of experiments and their outcomes
- build self-awareness through regular reflection

As Charles Darwin demonstrated with his own field notebooks, writing and drawing about your observations improves thinking.[1] The simple act of putting pen to paper (or fingers to keyboard) forces you to discriminate, judge and select – all processes that sharpen your understanding.

As Dani Johnson advised in a Learning Uncut Emergent podcast, 'Keep a lab book… all your successes and your failures… You look at that stuff as data.'[2]

Your Field Notebook becomes a companion on your journey – one that will help you see connections, generate insights and track your growth as you apply the principles in this book.

Taking action

- Select just one or two ideas from each chapter to try out.
- Start with 'Trojan mice' – small, nimble experiments that test ideas with minimal risk.
- When exploring real-world examples, pause to consider applications in your context before reading our analysis.
- Keep track of your actions and what you learn in your Field Notebook.

To help you move from understanding principles to applying them effectively, we recommend using Stella Collins' GEAR model.[3]

GEAR model

The GEAR model is an evidence-based framework that helps bridge the gap between learning something new and applying it successfully at work. Developed by Stella Collins and grounded in neuroscience, it recognizes that meaningful learning requires consistent motivation, practice and repetition throughout the learning process.

GEAR stands for:

- **Guide:** Learn key concepts in manageable chunks.
- **Experiment:** Test and practise in a safe environment.
- **Apply:** Transfer skills to your workplace.
- **Retain:** Build habits that make learning stick.

This approach transforms knowledge into action, ensuring your learning leads to lasting change in your professional practice.

GUIDE

Just as a guide helps you navigate a new city, this book will guide you through essential concepts with real-world examples. You'll find reflective prompts throughout to help you engage actively with the material. Share your thoughts with colleagues and your network – these conversations will deepen your understanding and help you see how these ideas fit your unique context. Your Field Notebook is the perfect place to capture these insights and conversations.

EXPERIMENT

Learning thrives on experimentation. Involving others in your experiments allows you to learn together. As you start testing new ideas in your context, involve your team, peers or external network. Work together to design experiments and encourage input to shape your approach. Capture not only your own results but also insights from those you collaborate with, Use your Field Notebook to document hypotheses, track progress and gather feedback from others. By engaging others in your experiments, you'll gain different perspectives and refine your ideas faster.

APPLY

Now comes the time to apply the new skills, strategies and behaviours that you have practised in Experiment more broadly. Whether you're implementing successful approaches in current projects or reshaping your learning strategy, this is where you create lasting impact. Seeking support is also important, including opportunities to apply your learning, receiving continued feedback and gaining encouragement and recognition from colleagues and leaders.

This phase also involves working on yourself. Use the BOLD principles we introduce in Part Four to develop your leadership approach. Document your progress and personal insights in your Field Notebook as you put principles into practice.

RETAIN

Making your learning stick requires spaced practice and repetition to build strong neuronal connections, behaviours and habits. Use your Field Notebook as a tool for this by including retrieval prompts like 'How did I apply the Tuning In principle this week?' and conducting regular gap analyses to identify principles you haven't engaged with recently. These self-questioning exercises strengthen neural pathways each time you recall and apply what you've learned.

To truly embed these practices, you must test your learning regularly and maintain consistent habits. Connect with others on similar journeys to reinforce your progress, share experiences, exchange ideas and build a supportive network. This continuous cycle of spaced learning, testing and adapting will help you stay responsive to change while building a strong foundation for success.

Your unique path

This book is built on the collective wisdom of the global L&D community. It draws from stories, real-world examples and evidence to inspire and guide you. But, ultimately, your journey is your own.

This book will serve you in different ways, depending on your context:

- **For novices:** Take your first steps with confidence.
- **For experts:** Gain fresh perspectives and deeper insights to refine your craft.
- **For teams:** Foster shared understanding and alignment around principles that drive impact.

We invite you to use this book as a starting point – to experiment, adapt and build your own story. By applying these principles, you're not just navigating your own path to improving business value – you're shaping the future of L&D for your organization and beyond.

Notes

1 Darwin Online. Darwin's Beagle field notebooks (1831–1836), Darwin Online, nd. darwin-online.org.uk/EditorialIntroductions/Chancellor_fieldNotebooks.html
2 S Collins and D Johnson. The rise of technology and L&D – Stella Collins and Dani Johnson, Learning Uncut Emergent Series podcast, 15 September 2020
3 S Collins (2023) *Neuroscience for Learning and Development*, Kogan Page, London

WHY WE WROTE THIS BOOK

Laura's reflection

I was first asked to write this book back in 2019 and it seemed like a good idea at the time!

I had just completed a 15-year research journey exploring how learning innovation can contribute to business value. It was a journey that had taken me around the globe exploring data gifted by thousands of learning leaders. It was a voyage of connection and collaboration and celebrating the wisdom of the crowd. I was encouraged to stop and reflect and share my learnings with a wider audience and a book deal was signed.

But something didn't feel quite right.

At that moment in time, I could talk with confidence about the past, about lessons learned, models developed and organizations helped. But creating a book about lessons learned purely from the past just wasn't working for me. Most of my writing leading up to 2019 was about having the courage to let go – the world is changing around us and our old ways don't always prepare us for the future.

Writer's block was real – blocked by a fear of being locked into the past, of forever being known as the 'data queen' even though I had left my data legacy in the capable hands of a new research team. My research was originally known as Towards Maturity. In hindsight this name reflected something fundamental in my approach to work and life. It has always been about looking forward, towards a future where we are growing and learning together.

That 2019 book about looking back did not emerge.

Instead, the Covid-19 pandemic hit, and with it came new insight on the future. The first 15 years of my research history was peppered with references to change: around us, to us and with us. But 2020, for me, ushered in a different type of new normal – a recognition that the only certainty that we can prepare for is constant changing.

When Michelle asked me to join her and Shannon Tipton to co-host a series of podcasts exploring how we might emerge stronger from the pandemic, my curiosity kicked in and my research approach shifted from data to observation, conversation and immersion.

I was observing an industry flooded with opportunities to make a difference. And yet many in L&D were floundering and overwhelmed as new tools, new operating models and new technologies placed increasing demands and pressure.

For me, this journey has highlighted new questions over the last five years.

Now my questions are about how we prepare to shape our future. This was the future that I wanted to invest myself in, to explore and to write about. For the past two years I have been looking back to see if our past offers insight into how we can prepare for the future.

I have also been looking outside of our industry and many of the insights that have really set my skin tingling are from the other side of the globe.

I was deeply moved by the heroic story of the early Polynesian navigators who found pathways in the sea that no one could imagine, reaching islands and resources thousands of miles away to better serve their communities. The story of their heroic descendants became the ultimate inspiration for writing this book. I wanted to learn from the wisdom of those more recent heroes who revisited and reimagined the ancient journeys of their past in order to renew pride in their people and, as a result, shape a better world.

Michelle's reflection

I joined the Royal Australian Air Force (RAAF) when I left school and spent 16 years as a logistics officer. In the final eight years of this time, I worked on projects to introduce new aircraft to service. I thrived in this highly structured environment.

After leaving the RAAF in 2000 I used my project management skills to work in a range of sectors and roles. Clear process, structure and control remained the hallmarks of my approach. I was repeating what had brought me success in the past and finding settings where this worked.

Then, in 2011, I joined Coca-Cola Amatil (CCA) to set up and manage a Technical Academy in Supply Chain. CCA had adopted the '70:20:10 framework' which the Academy was expected to apply. I'd never heard of it, but the concept seemed straightforward. I guided my team to develop programmes using this framework. While they were good programmes, my instincts had still been to control and structure training.

In early 2014, at a conference in Sydney, I discovered Twitter as a professional development tool. The following week I enrolled in a Social Learning Practitioner programme. From this moment my professional development and career direction were radically transformed. I connected with L&D professionals around the world and discovered new perspectives and approaches to workplace learning.

One of these resources was the Towards Maturity Health Check, discovered in a Twitter chat where Laura was the expert guest. It was so useful that I have used it with the teams and clients I've worked with ever since.

I started the *Learning Uncut* podcast in 2018 to understand, through examples of real work in organizations, what was actually making a difference in helping people learn, change behaviour and improve performance. When Laura and Shannon Tipton joined me to co-host a special series during the pandemic, I realized my podcast conversations were a form of research and evidence-gathering too.

When Laura asked if I would join her as co-author, I knew immediately that it would be a great opportunity to do more with the real-world examples gathered through the podcast, examined through the lens of the principles derived from Laura's deep body of research.

Our approach together

We've written this book not because we are right, but because we are learning. We don't have all the answers to the question of how L&D leaders can navigate the complexities of today's world to have impact. However, we are deeply curious about this question and have some evidence-informed ideas that give us a starting point.

Our approach is rooted in our belief that the real value lies in the process of exploration, rather than in arriving at a definitive destination. This requires true leadership – the desire, motivation and belief that we can create positive change and the courage to take action even when the path ahead is not clear.

The metaphor of navigation felt fitting, not because we see ourselves as expert pilots, but because we are continually discovering the joys and challenges of wayfinding in the complex landscape of L&D.

We each bring our personal experiences and insights to this book, shaped by different contexts, industries and continents, untied by the common thread of navigating complexity. Together, we have chosen to lean into evidence, not to prove our points, but as a way to explore, to challenge our assumptions and continuously improve our practice.

All our voices matter

This book is not just about our voices. It reflects the voices of those we've spoken with, interviewed and learned from. Throughout the pages, you will hear from a diverse range of L&D professionals, each contributing their unique perspective on what it means to thrive in a constantly changing environment. We have aimed to give you examples of how the principles might be applied in a wide range of contexts rather than offer you prescriptive solutions, steps or models to follow.

More importantly, reader, this book also invites you to recognize and add your own voice. You may be new to the L&D sector or more experienced and wayfinding in a continually changing work environment. Either way, our goal is to empower you to design your own pathways to business value – in your context, based on your experience, with your voice.

We invite you to join us to shape the future of L&D together.

Introduction
A navigator's tale

Raising islands: The journey of the *Hōkūle'a*

When Captain James Cook first sailed through Polynesia in the 1770s, he encountered a vast civilization spread across a 'triangle' of ocean spanning over 10 million square miles – from Hawaii to New Zealand to Easter Island. Cook marvelled in his journals at how these islanders had accomplished what European sailors, with their advanced ships and navigation instruments, had only recently managed: the systematic settlement of the Pacific.[1]

For millennia, these ancient navigation techniques had been essential to survival. Traditional voyagers served as 'lifeboats… ferrying stricken islanders to temporary refuge on other atolls and bringing back saplings and seeds to replant gardens'.[2]

The distance from Hawaii to Tahiti – just one island within this triangle – is over 2,500 miles of open ocean. Imagine voyaging in one of those canoes – surrounded by an endless circle of water stretching to the horizon in every direction. No landmarks. No instruments. Only water meeting sky in a perfect, disorienting circle. Yet the ancient Polynesians had navigated these waters intentionally and repeatedly, using only their knowledge of stars, ocean swells, wind patterns and wildlife.

By the 1970s this profound navigational heritage had been largely lost. Western ways of knowing had disrupted traditional knowledge transmission. Modern technology had replaced traditional skills. The last practitioners of ancient navigation techniques were ageing, with few apprentices to carry their knowledge forward.[3]

More painfully, Western academics had dismissed these heroic achievements entirely. Some suggested Polynesians had merely stumbled upon islands accidentally – denying the intentional, skilful navigation that had been at the heart of Polynesian identity for millennia.[4]

A vision takes shape

In 1973, at a time when native Hawaiians were actively countering negative stereotypes by celebrating cultural identity, three visionaries – Ben Finney, Herb Kane and Tommy Holmes – founded the Polynesian Voyaging Society. They had an audacious dream: build a traditional double-hulled voyaging canoe and sail it from Hawaii to Tahiti using only ancient non-instrumental navigation techniques.[5]

They named the canoe *Hōkūle'a*, 'Star of Gladness'. But who would help them navigate it?

Their search led them to Mau Piailug, one of the last master navigators from the tiny island of Satawal. Mau recognized in this project something deeper than adventure – he had watched 'not only the demise of the art of navigation but the death of his way of life'.[6]

In 1976, *Hōkūle'a* successfully approached Tahiti, which first appeared on the horizon as a dot, and then slowly rose from the ocean before them. This process of 'raising Tahiti' from the vast ocean confirmed that thousands of tiny observations, adjustments and calculations had led them to this moment.

Over 20,000 Tahitians gathered to welcome the canoe, many overcome with emotion. One crew member recalled: 'We weren't prepared for that reception. Suddenly we realized this wasn't just about proving a point to academics – this was about reconnecting a people with their heritage.'[7]

Nainoa Thompson, only 20 at the time, was inspired by the vision of the *Hōkūle'a* and eager to learn from Mau. But Mau decided not to continue after the initial voyage. In Mau's tradition, navigation was a sacred responsibility tied to community survival – connecting islands, maintaining trade and ensuring his people's sustenance. Learning non-instrumental navigation to prove it could be done rather than as a living practice serving community needs did not sit well for him.[8]

Learning through adversity

Mau's departure was devastating for Nainoa. But adversity became a catalyst. Without access to traditional oral teachings and lifelong immersion in these techniques, he had to develop his own approach to learning navigation that bridged traditional and modern methods.

In 1978, tragedy struck when the *Hōkūle'a* capsized and Eddie Aikau, a legendary Hawaiian lifeguard who embodied the spirit of the cultural revival, set out on his rescue board to find help and was never seen again. This loss was felt deeply by Nainoa and by the nation.

From this tragedy emerged renewed determination. Nainoa's father Myron 'Pinky' Thompson provided crucial inspiration: 'Before our ancestors set out to find a new island, they had to have a vision of that island over the horizon. They made a plan for achieving that vision. They prepared themselves physically and mentally and were willing to experiment, to try new things. They took risks. And on the voyage, they bound each other with aloha so they could together overcome the risks and achieve their vision.'[9]

The inner compass

Mau recognized Nainoa's vision and when he returned to work with him, he asked a simple yet penetrating question: 'Can you see Tahiti?' When Nainoa admitted he couldn't but that he could see it in his head, Mau replied, 'Don't ever lose that image or you will be lost. A navigator knows where the land is inside of him even when he can't see it.'[10]

This wasn't about physical sight but about holding the destination so clearly in the navigator's mind that it guides every decision, every adjustment, every response to changing conditions.

Nainoa's breakthrough came through developing the Hawaiian Star Compass – a mental model that divided the horizon into 32 houses aligned with the rising and setting points of key stars.

Imagine standing on a canoe, ocean stretching endlessly around you. In this mental model, you are literally at the centre – the fixed point in a revolving world. As Nainoa explained, 'In wayfinding, you are always at the centre of the ocean.'[11] This perspective transforms abstract celestial mechanics into a personal, intuitive system.

To develop his system, Nainoa blended modern knowledge with traditional wisdom. He spent countless nights studying the stars, asking questions, exploring anomalies and tracking star movements to allow patterns to emerge. As he described it: 'The more I learn, the more I understand; the more I understand, the more I know how complicated the heavens are.'[12]

One night, Nainoa experienced what his mentor described as 'insight favoring the prepared mind'[13] – a sudden comprehension of how everything connected. This hybrid approach – honouring tradition while adapting methods – became characteristic of the entire project.

Yet when Nainoa reunited with Mau, he recognized the limits of his academic approach: 'Nainoa knew more about the stars than Mau, but what he got from Mau was a sense of the sea, of weather and ocean swells.'[14] Technical knowledge alone wasn't enough.

The sail plan

Preparation was key to achieving their vision. Pinky reminded Nainoa: 'The only way you will succeed is if you have a powerful vision. You need to know the path, where you are going and why you are going there. You need to define the values that will guide you on the path... Ninety per cent of success is in preparing for it. Accepting the risk of failure was part of preparing for success.'[15]

Their sail plan began with this inner vision – a clear image of their destination that remained constant even as the path adjusted to wind, current and weather. Yet a sail plan isn't static – it's a framework for continuous adaptation. As Nainoa described his first voyage as navigator: 'The conditions were not perfect, but it was good enough.'[16]

This journey was inherently collective. While Western navigation often focuses on a single captain, Polynesian voyaging emphasizes community. Each crew member plays a vital role, contributing observations and supporting the navigator. This collective awareness creates resilience – when one person misses something, others notice.

The 'awa ceremony before departure marked another vital aspect of preparation – psychological and spiritual readiness. It 'signified they were about to travel',[17] marking a transition from planning to action.

A renaissance in the making

From the first voyage of the *Hōkūle'a*, the Polynesian Voyaging Society's mission shifted from proving ancient capabilities to playing a significant role in the Hawaiian renaissance. In 2023, they initiated a journey to circumnavigate the Pacific – a journey of 43,000 nautical miles over 47 months – to ignite a movement of 10 million planetary navigators to amplify the importance of nature, science and indigenous wisdom.

At the earliest point of his journey, Nainoa declared, 'I'm going to navigate to learn.'[18] This careful phrasing revealed his strategy – positioning himself not as a leader or expert, but as a student dedicated to restoring what had been lost. As he later explained, 'Being afraid of social expectation translates to being afraid to learn.'[19]

Despite decades of experience, he remains a student: 'Science and math had given me some grounding to go out and understand the world, but as I got more experience, I became more trusting of my instinct. It's always there, but I didn't trust it at first.'[20] This integration of analytical knowledge with developed intuition represents the highest form of mastery.

Over the last 50 years, the Polynesian Voyaging Society has brought the wisdom of the ancient culture forward while embracing possibilities for the future. Female navigators now play crucial roles in the movement.[21] Modern technology complements traditional methods – GPS is carried for safety but sealed in cases for use only in emergencies.

Modern voyages of the *Hōkūle'a* maintain traditional protocols while incorporating new elements. Each journey begins with ceremony, acknowledging both ancient spiritual practices and current educational objectives.

This evolution reflects the deeper purpose that eventually drew Mau back to the project. Navigation isn't just about raising islands – it's about connecting communities, maintaining cultural knowledge and ensuring human survival.

Perhaps most importantly, this cultural renaissance reminds us that seemingly lost wisdom can be recovered and reimagined for new generations.

And so the journey continues. The Polynesian Voyaging society's mission perpetuates ancient traditions and the spirit of exploration in order to 'inspire their students and their communities to respect and care for themselves, each other, and their natural and cultural environments'.[22]

Today, each voyage builds capacity not just for navigation but for facing humanity's greatest challenges with wisdom, courage and collective action.[23]

In 2025, the Polynesian Voyaging Society celebrated its 50th anniversary.

The birthday is such an important moment for us to dream again and believe again and have courage to let go of the lines. *Nainoa Thompson*[24]

From ocean to organization

Like these Hawaiian navigators, today's L&D leaders face seas of continuous change where old maps no longer serve us. For us, business value is the island we seek to raise on the horizon. By developing our own internal compass – a clear vision of our destination and the ability to read the environment – we can guide our organizations through complexity and disruption. Just as the *Hōkūle'a*'s journey wasn't just about reaching Tahiti but revitalizing a culture, our work isn't just about delivering learning – it's about creating lasting impact and meaningful transformation.

This is where our journey begins.

> If your actions create a legacy that inspires others to dream more, learn more, do more and become more, then, you are an excellent leader. *Dolly Parton*[25]

Notes

1 National Museum of Australia. Cook's journal, NMA, nd. www.nma.gov.au/exhibitions/endeavour-voyage/cooks-journal (archived at https://perma.cc/T4SK-FY85)

2 Mau Piailug Society. The navigators: Pathfinders of the Pacific, YouTube, 2012. youtu.be/uxgUjyqN7FU?si=arHr1k8mncH_s6Ep (archived at https://perma.cc/5M4N-ZRMY)

3 Mau Piailug Society. The navigators: Pathfinders of the Pacific, YouTube, 2012. youtu.be/uxgUjyqN7FU?si=arHr1k8mncH_s6Ep (archived at https://perma.cc/F2KW-QHP8)

4 National Museum of Australia. Cook's journal, NMA, nd. www.nma.gov.au/exhibitions/endeavour-voyage/cooks-journal (archived at https://perma.cc/WV5P-2L7Q)

5 Hokulea Archive. Twenty-Five Years of Voyageing, 1975–2000, Hokulea Archive, nd. archive.hokulea.com/holokai/nainoa_twenty_five_years.html (archived at https://perma.cc/TS4G-LTGH)

6 Mau Piailug Society. The navigators: Pathfinders of the Pacific, YouTube, 2012. youtu.be/uxgUjyqN7FU?si=arHr1k8mncH_s6Ep (archived at https://perma.cc/NB4C-JF7K)

7 S Low (2019) *Hawaiki Rising: Hōkūle'a, Nainoa Thompson, and the Hawaiian Renaissance*, University of Hawai'i Press, Honolulu.

8 S Low (2019) *Hawaiki Rising: Hōkūle'a, Nainoa Thompson, and the Hawaiian Renaissance*, University of Hawai'i Press, Honolulu.

9 S Low (2019) *Hawaiki Rising: Hōkūle'a, Nainoa Thompson, and the Hawaiian Renaissance*, University of Hawai'i Press, Honolulu.

10 S Low (2019) *Hawaiki Rising: Hōkūle'a, Nainoa Thompson, and the Hawaiian Renaissance*, University of Hawai'i Press, Honolulu.

11 W Kyselka (1987) *An Ocean in Mind*, University of Hawai'i Press, Honolulu.

12 W Kyselka (1987) *An Ocean in Mind*, University of Hawai'i Press, Honolulu.

13 W Kyselka (1987) *An Ocean in Mind*, University of Hawai'i Press, Honolulu.

14 W Kyselka (1987) *An Ocean in Mind*, University of Hawai'i Press, Honolulu.

15 S Low (2019) *Hawaiki Rising: Hōkūle'a, Nainoa Thompson, and the Hawaiian Renaissance*, University of Hawai'i Press, Honolulu.

16 S Low (2019) *Hawaiki Rising: Hōkūle'a, Nainoa Thompson, and the Hawaiian Renaissance*, University of Hawai'i Press, Honolulu.

17 S Low (2019) *Hawaiki Rising: Hōkūle'a, Nainoa Thompson, and the Hawaiian Renaissance*, University of Hawai'i Press, Honolulu.

18 W Kyselka (1987) *An Ocean in Mind*, University of Hawai'i Press, Honolulu.

19 W Kyselka (1987) *An Ocean in Mind*, University of Hawai'i Press, Honolulu.

20 W Kyselka (1987) *An Ocean in Mind*, University of Hawai'i Press, Honolulu.

21 J Salama. This woman navigated a 3,000-mile Pacific voyage without maps or technology, *National Geographic*, 18 May 2022. https://www.nationalgeographic.com/history/article/woman-navigated-3000-mile-pacific-voyage-without-maps-technology (archived at https://perma.cc/QK75-TREQ)

22 Polynesian Voyaging Society *Hōkūle'a*. About, *Hōkūle'a*, nd. hokulea.com/about (archived at https://perma.cc/5WNF-2D7Z)

23 Polynesian Voyaging Society *Hōkūle'a*. About, *Hōkūle'a*, nd. hokulea.com/about (archived at https://perma.cc/3HEW-KYRY)

24 Hokuleacrew. Hokulea is 50, Instagram, 15 March 2025. www.instagram.com/reel/DDv0VybxRCE (archived at https://perma.cc/87FK-NMF9)

25 Quoted in L Adraine (1997) *The Most Important Thing I Know*, Andrews McMeel Publishing, Kansas City.

PART ONE

What got us here won't get us there... or will it?

1

Calling all L&D leaders

If your actions create a legacy that inspires others to dream more, learn more, do more and become more, then, you are an excellent leader.

DOLLY PARTON[1]

Learning and development (L&D) has long attracted individuals who are passionate about helping others 'learn more, do more and become more'. If your work inspires this in others, you're not just supporting learning – you are a leader.

You may be new to your L&D role – an aspiring leader in our industry. You may be a seasoned leader, leading a team and looking for more. For all of us, our working world today is one of constant change.

Organizations no longer operate in predictable environments with clear, proven pathways to success. The rapid advancement of AI, generational shifts, the way we trade and provide services all impact the way that organizations are run, teams are formed and individuals contribute. **The stakes are higher than ever.** Organizations that can't quickly adapt to change are failing at unprecedented rates. Those that can navigate through disruption are capturing market share, attracting top talent and creating sustainable value. The difference often comes down to whether their people are equipped and ready to adapt with them – even when the path ahead isn't as clear as it used to be.

We believe that people who can navigate this new world of work to help others perform today and be ready for the new tomorrow are more essential than ever.

We are calling all L&D leaders around the globe – your organization needs you!

To all L&D leaders – whether in corporate, public service, non-profit or volunteer settings – your organization needs you. It needs your commitment to support others to perform today. It needs your insights to build the new skills they will depend upon tomorrow. It needs your ability to take others on a journey that will help them to change and adapt, creating the agility needed for individuals, teams and organizations to thrive in the face of continuous change. Your capacity to read signals, plot clear courses and guide others through their personal transformation directly impacts bottom-line results.

To L&D leaders working with vendors or as consultants – our industry needs your capacity to innovate, to lead by example and bring others with you. Your unique position working with a range of organizations gives you a broad perspective on the evolving challenges of the modern workplace. We need your ability to 'read the room', share with integrity and help others navigate their way to success.

To seasoned L&D leaders – our industry needs your wealth of experi-ence. We also need your openness to explore new pathways helping your team and your organization as they are continually learning and adapting in new and exciting ways.

To aspiring L&D leaders – you are our breath of fresh air. We need your open minds, inspiration and energy to help drive us forward. If you are joining us from other fields we need your fresh perspective to challenge the status quo and introduce new approaches.

As we work and learn together we will adapt together. We all play a significant role in shaping the future of L&D.

For years we've heard the call to shift from being order-takers to strategic partners, from delivering courses to providing resources and from training to performance. But disruption continually raises the stakes. We believe that the future of L&D is no longer about evolving our professional identity – it's about stepping into our vital role of enabling organizational survival and success in a business landscape.

TO LEAD IS TO NAVIGATE

Unlike traditional leadership books aimed at the few at the top, this book is for everyone in the L&D profession who understands that the environment in which we work is interwoven and often messy. Navigating our way to business success requires a different definition of what it is to lead. Like Polynesian wayfinders who guided their communities across vast oceans:

- We lead by charting paths when stakeholders need to reach their goals.

- We lead by making small daily decision to keep us on track.

- We lead by inspiring others to follow new routes.

- We lead by creating value, and with it, a vision of what is possible.

This book is for all L&D leaders who recognize that, while continual changing is our business context, we are responsible to not only navigate that change but to lead others to do the same.

To navigate is to lead. To lead is to create value. And creating value is how L&D not only secures but shapes its future.

This sounds so easy – but our stakeholders don't always align to our vision.

Are our business leaders calling out for more learning?

No, but they are calling out for organizational transformation to remain relevant in a shifting world where artificial intelligence is causing them to question the way that work is done.

And the top barriers to that transformation are skills gaps in the labour market, organizational culture and resistance to change, outdated regulatory frameworks that need to be changed.[2]

Are leaders calling out for more courses and programmes? No, but they are calling out for workforce strategies that include upskilling the workforce, accelerating the automation of processes and tasks, hiring staff with new skills, augmenting the workforce with new technologies and transitioning existing staff to address growing roles.[3]

All of the shifts that are important to business leaders – changing processes, changing roles, changing jobs or changing skills – involve changing the behaviour of people in the business. They require support and interventions that help individuals and teams become competent and perform in their new tasks and roles.

If this does not create opportunities for a new generation of L&D leaders to help drive business value then what else can?

Who among us doesn't dream of a bold and courageous L&D profession, one that is known and respected for the value it brings to business? Don't we all envision an L&D profession that makes a meaningful difference to individuals, teams and organizations – contributing to business performance, success and agility?

These dreams drew your authors, Laura and Michelle, together from opposite sides of the globe, driven by a shared curiosity: **how can L&D truly create business value?**

Get your Field Notebook ready!

Throughout this book, you'll find reflection points like the one coming up. Your Field Notebook is a tool to support your curiosity – a space to capture insights, plan experiments and track your progress. If you haven't already, check the Introduction for more guidance on using your Field Notebook effectively.

What does value look like?

HOW DO YOU DESCRIBE L&D SUCCESS?

Before we go any further, take a moment and reflect on how you think and talk about the value L&D provides to your organization. To make this more concrete you may want to consider how you've described the success of a recent L&D initiative to others.

When you describe a successful L&D initiative, what do you emphasize? In your Field Notebook, make a brief list of what you typically say or highlight. This honest reflection will provide useful context as we explore different perspectives on L&D value.

In 2002 Laura began to question why some L&D teams were reporting more impact from their investments in technology-enabled learning than others. From that point onwards her research focused on finding out how learning innovation might contribute business value. Over the years, millions of data points were collected from thousands of L&D leaders taking part in the Learning Performance Benchmark (originally known as the Towards Maturity Benchmark) in pursuit of the answer.[4]

From the beginning, it was clear that those who reported more bottom line benefits didn't just talk about helping their business to retain staff, drive revenue, improve customer service – the pursuit of business value was their guiding star. It influenced their conversations, their actions and interactions and continual iteration of their business. During the next 15 years, various hypotheses were tested as new technologies and learning models came (and went) and economic conditions fluctuated.

However, one critical factor underpinned the work of the high-performing teams. No matter what the world threw at them – the aftermath of 9/11, the 2007 global recession, the Covid pandemic – their focus on creating business value was the bedrock of their success.

The L&D Value Spectrum

So back to your reflection point. How **do you** describe your value to others? We've asked this question of L&D leaders many times, and we've reviewed hundreds of awards submissions where L&D teams talk about their successes.

The L&D Value Spectrum (Figure 1.1) illustrates the range of language that we use when we discuss the value that L&D brings to business. What we celebrate (highlight on our dashboards, share in our awards submissions) often reflects our comfort point on the L&D Value Spectrum.

Many of us in L&D celebrate indicators of learning value – talking about activity surrounding our programmes: hours, engagement and efficiency. Our dashboards proudly showcase savings and reach, highlighting those

FIGURE 1.1 The L&D Value Spectrum

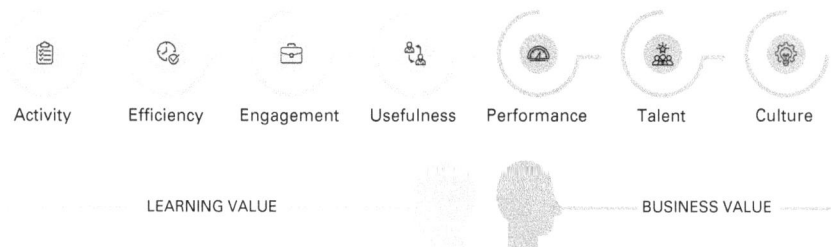

| Activity | Efficiency | Engagement | Usefulness | Performance | Talent | Culture |

LEARNING VALUE   BUSINESS VALUE

SOURCE L Overton. Introducing the L&D Value Spectrum, Learning Changemakers, 2024. www.learningchangemakers.com/introducing-ld-value-spectrum

who complete or rate our offerings. More recently, and importantly, we've started to see our value being discussed in terms of the usefulness of our offerings, including learner reflections of relevance and intent to apply. Learning value provides us with a great indicator about how our learning interventions are being received and used.

At the opposite end of the spectrum is business value – where L&D value is determined by the impact we make on the goals that matter to business. High-performing L&D teams consistently use business value as their guiding star. They seek to understand the key outcomes that matter in their organization, such as customer satisfaction, revenue, productivity, quality or patient care. These teams also help build healthy organizational cultures that support innovation and agility.

The Learning Performance Benchmark consistently asked participants what their goals were. Over the years 80–90 per cent of the sample would say their goals were to improve revenue or customer service or overall productivity. Fewer than half reported that they had achieved their goals and fewer still could put a number on the level of improvement. The number who did mounted up over time, with those measurable results highlighting an average 14 per cent increase in productivity, 21 per cent uplift in customer satisfaction and 28 per cent improvement in the speed of implementing new initiatives.[5]

One concrete example is the 2019 redesign of contact centre training at National Australia Bank (NAB).[6] Damien Woods, then General Manager of Learning at NAB, spent time observing the bank's contact centre staff. He listened to customer calls, saw how employees juggled multiple systems and identified the challenges they faced. Armed with this insight, he approached the business manager and suggested they work together to reduce time to proficiency and increase retention. They replaced a 17-day face-to-face induction with a four-day blended learning approach. This resulted in employees reaching proficiency 30 per cent faster, with call escalations by new starters reduced by 80 per cent and average call handling times cut by over 60 seconds.[7] By focusing on business outcomes, NAB improved efficiency and demonstrated the true potential of aligning L&D with business goals.

L&D practitioners operating at the learning value end of the spectrum operate from a place of familiarity – success is determined by how well we deliver a service and the perception of that service – we are in control. But driving business value requires us to step into new territory, where success is measured by how well we contribute to solving real business problems. While it might feel more like stepping onto shifting sands than standing on bedrock, this book will go on to show that L&D teams with a business value mindset consistently deliver stronger results.

When hoping isn't enough

Most L&D practitioners hope to drive business value but struggle to achieve this, limiting our vision as we spend our time operating at the learning value end of the spectrum. Our aspirations can also be limited by the expectations of the organizations we serve.

Robert Brinkerhoff, an international expert in learning effectiveness and evaluation, provided a wonderful example of this.[8] He asked a manager what they'd expected from the training that his direct reports had just completed. They said, 'I didn't expect a damn thing, and that's exactly what I got, not a damn thing. So why should I waste my time supporting training that doesn't do a damn bit of good?' … *ouch*!

Of course, there may have been a number of reasons for that response. It could have just been a bad day for that manager. Or it could be that the manager expected miracles from L&D to completely shift the behaviour of their team within the confines of the classroom. Or it could be that the L&D team were operating at the learning value end of the spectrum and the manager genuinely couldn't see the relevance.

For whatever reason, when business leaders expect us to add business value and we are driven by sharing our learning value – L&D teams are in the **Danger Zone** (see Figure 1.2). The upside of being in the Danger Zone is that we often feel the friction and may have an opportunity to do something about it. The downside, as the Bytedance Talent team at Bytedance found out, is that our team could be ruthlessly eliminated in a five-minute town hall meeting because our managers believe that we have 'limited practical value'.[9]

The bigger challenge is when both our business leaders and L&D teams are very happy working at the learning value end of the spectrum. We create programmes that people respond well to and our leaders love us for it. It's in this **Comfort Zone** that we are most exposed. Our business leaders may have no expectations beyond delivering a programme of courses, content and curricula. But when the organization needs to change quickly will they come to us for support and leadership on how to help the people adapt their skills and behaviour to accelerate that change? It is unlikely.

When leaders believe that their L&D teams can make a significant difference to business outcomes and have seen evidence of how they do that they are more inclined to seek out advice and work out ways to move forward together to co-create value. The high-performing teams over the last two decades show us what it is like to operate in this **Co-creator Zone**.

FIGURE 1.2 The L&D Value Landscape

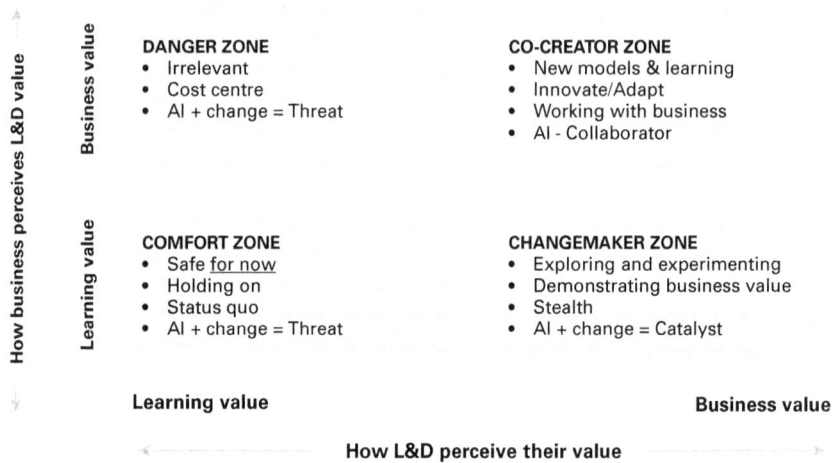

DANGER ZONE
- Irrelevant
- Cost centre
- AI + change = Threat

CO-CREATOR ZONE
- New models & learning
- Innovate/Adapt
- Working with business
- AI - Collaborator

COMFORT ZONE
- Safe for now
- Holding on
- Status quo
- AI + change = Threat

CHANGEMAKER ZONE
- Exploring and experimenting
- Demonstrating business value
- Stealth
- AI + change = Catalyst

Business value

Learning value

How business perceives L&D value

Learning value   Business value

How L&D perceive their value

When we see ourselves as business value creators but the business sees us as course creators we can feel frustrated. Smart L&D leaders, however, will see this as the **Changemaker Zone** – the space where we harness friction to make a difference. Changemakers spot opportunities to do things differently, exploring, experimenting, taking action. They take small steps and big chances to turn the heads of the business leaders around them. Changemaking is about finding paths to better business value, breaking the mould of how learning is seen in the business, one step at a time.

Being a changemaker is not easy but disruption can help!

The disruption advantage

While it was a time of tragedy, the Covid pandemic created a unique opportunity for many L&D professionals who stepped up alongside colleagues across their organizations to meet the urgent need to adapt to the rapid unexpected change. L&D became essential, helping teams manage short-term upheaval and helping businesses through uncertainty. This period showed just how vital our work can be in a moment of crisis.

The pandemic brought a significant shift for L&D. In 2020/21 L&D teams became more strategically aligned with their organizations than ever before. The CIPD's *Learning and Skills at Work Survey 2021* found that, while L&D resources were stretched, the crisis provided an opportunity to align learning strategies with business priorities.[10] Most organizations in this study reported that senior leaders now valued learning more highly than before. This was echoed by LinkedIn's *2022 Workplace Learning Report*, where 72 per cent of L&D professionals agreed that their role had become more strategic.[11]

According to the *2022 Workplace Learning Report*, the percentage of learning professionals reporting their function had a seat at the executive table grew further from 53 per cent in 2022 to 58 per cent in 2024.[12] L&D became a key strategic player in many organizations.

However, the CIPD study also showed that the expanded role has brought new pressures. L&D teams are expected to deliver faster results on a larger scale, particularly in response to the increased demand for upskilling and reskilling to drive workforce agility. This surge in responsibility left many L&D professionals stretched thin, with limited time to focus on their own development. Fluctuating downturns in budget and team allocation increase the pressure further.

Despite being valued, L&D continues to face challenges. Budgets per employee have shrunk over the past seven years, and L&D professionals still encounter cultural barriers. Employees are perceived to lack the skills to manage their own learning, and it can be difficult to get managers to prioritize learning in their teams.[13] L&D teams must find ways to thrive in this tough environment.

Education technology expert Peter Shea suggested that historians might one day debate whether the pandemic or generative AI caused the most disruption.[14] While the pandemic was sudden, AI has been building in the background for years, quietly reshaping industries and workflows.

The pandemic forced a sudden transformation of work and learning environments. Almost overnight, organizations moved to remote work. Employees adapted to new technologies and ways of collaborating, and leaders scrambled to maintain engagement and productivity across dispersed teams. This digital acceleration pushed businesses to fast track transformation agendas at unprecedented scale.

For L&D this crisis was an opportunity to rethink collaboration, embrace digital technologies and support employee reskilling and redeployment. Fosway's 2020 survey showed that 94 per cent of L&D professionals made significant changes to their strategy within the first few months of the pandemic.[15] Digital learning surged, with increased activity on both internal and external platforms. This shift allowed L&D teams to become more agile and better aligned with organizational priorities.

The pandemic lowered many traditional barriers and sparked innovation under pressure. L&D teams embraced new approaches and delivered large-scale learning initiatives to address the shifting needs of the workforce. This period showed just how quickly L&D can drive meaningful change when disruption hits.

AI: The next disruption wave

Generative AI represents a different kind of disruption, which is ushering in a new era of automation and innovation, reshaping industries by automating tasks that once required human input. This promises to boost productivity and streamline operations, but it also raises significant concerns. The automation of tasks has prompted fears of job displacement, while issues around ethical AI use, data privacy and bias are gaining more attention.

In L&D AI is creating its own levels of disruption. We're seeing ripples of change as AI is being used to simplify content automation, personalized learning paths and intelligent resource curation. Like the technologies before them, these applications deliver clear efficiency gains by automating routine tasks.

Looking ahead, AI's potential is being explored in more sophisticated applications like AI agents in instructional design. These tools can support everything from role-play to coaching, data analysis to evaluation. Potentially liberating, the tools can also be emotionally challenging.

Trish Uhl explores this in her book *Adaptive Humans + AI Agents: Sink, swim, or swarm*:

> Even before the first interaction, the anticipation of collaborating with advanced AI agents can be fraught with emotion. Individuals often oscillate between curiosity and anxiety, forming expectations – sometimes inaccurate – about how these systems will reshape their work, their value, and even their identity. Fuelling this uncertainty is the exponential pace of development; AI capabilities are doubling roughly every 6–7 months, a pace noted by both industry leaders and specific research like Model Evaluation and Threat Research (METR). As AI moves from tool to collaborator, it doesn't just change tasks; it fundamentally disrupts established work patterns and expertise boundaries. This often triggers a period of disorientation and deep identity questioning for individuals, forcing them to renegotiate not just **how** they work, but who they are in the context of their profession.[16]

Unlike the pandemic's sudden impact, AI's influence is unfolding more gradually but will likely have an even greater effect on work and learning. To navigate this disruption successfully, we must embrace AI's benefits while addressing ethical concerns around bias, accuracy and appropriate human oversight.

Beyond AI, we face disruptions from geopolitical shifts, changing workforce expectations and sustainability imperatives. Each creates unpredictable consequences that demand adaptive responses from businesses and from us.

These converging disruptions have refocused business leaders on their people. Upskilling and reskilling have become top priorities as organizations recognize that success depends on an adaptable, creative workforce. This should place L&D at the centre of strategic conversations – our ability to equip individuals, teams and organizations for an uncertain future has never been more valuable.

This is why our organizations need **you** – L&D leaders at all stages of your careers – to respond well and in doing so shape the future of workplace learning.

Disruption, despite its challenges, creates the energy we need to realize our dreams and shape a future where we, and those we support, are equipped and ready for whatever comes next.

Navigating continual changing

If the post-pandemic years have taught us anything, it's that we will never again settle into a 'new normal' – a stable, fixed state. Instead, our 'new normal' is one of continual changing. In a continually changing workplace things don't always add up.

Our work with people is unpredictable – new behaviours emerge as organizations navigate novel situations. For instance, when Schneider Electric introduced a Talent Marketplace supported by a new talent philosophy, they encouraged a more fluid approach to career progression and empowered employees to manage their own development.[17] While many embraced this freedom, some line managers struggled with the speed at which staff began transitioning to new roles. They felt employees should stay longer in their positions to develop further, often with the best interests of their people in mind. This tension highlighted how difficult it can be to anticipate how individuals will respond to new initiatives, even when those initiatives are designed to empower them.

We are part of a bigger system – our work is interconnected. A small change in one part of the organization can trigger unexpected outcomes in other areas. This interconnectedness often involves multiple perspectives on the same challenge.

Organizations themselves are dynamic, constantly moving just to maintain the status quo. Whether responding to market shifts, regulatory changes or employee expectations, businesses must continually adjust.

L&D operates within this complex, messy, unpredictable environment. It's not just complicated – it's an interconnected, dynamic world where small changes in one area can lead to unexpected outcomes elsewhere. The pandemic, while a catalyst for change, was just a warm-up act. The new normal is thriving in a world where continual changing is the only constant.

The old world and the new normal

This dynamic environment can be disorienting, leading to frustration when our attempts to make a difference and drive impact don't seem to work. But it also creates momentum and opportunity. To harness this energy, L&D leaders must find ways to navigate continual changing.

The old world of work is gone – along with its clearly defined roles and set career paths. Traditional L&D tools such as Training Needs Analysis, learning design models, competency frameworks and evaluation frameworks were built in a more stable time. Our toolkit often feels rigid and formulaic, built for a world where following the process usually guaranteed a predictable outcome.

Just as traditional tools can feel rigid in today's dynamic environment, the 'best practice' case studies we hear at conferences or on podcasts don't translate seamlessly into our unique contexts. What works well for some is rarely best for all. One-size-fits-all approaches often falter when faced with the messy realities of our constantly evolving organizations. Aspiring to mimic others rarely leads to impact in our own organization.

Over the years we've been encouraged to embrace new approaches like e-learning, mobile learning, peer-to-peer learning, micro-learning, learning in the flow, user generated content – and more! As new technologies and approaches often promise more than they deliver, it is not surprising that many L&D teams find themselves overwhelmed in the new world and remain stuck, tied to models forged in more stable times that become increasingly ineffective during continual change.

Real value comes when learning is relevant and useful. We know that learning doesn't happen in the isolated world of our LMS, curricular or classrooms. For real growth to occur, individuals and teams need psychological safety and the freedom to experiment and apply new knowledge. Delivering knowledge alone isn't enough. People must connect that knowledge to the ever-changing context of their work, which is how true behavioural change happens.

Even the way that we describe our roles seems outdated in this new world of work. Over the 20 years explored by this book, learning professionals have shifted the way that we describe our role from training to learning and development, to capability, to performance, to... what's next? From 2025, **we believe that our essential focus should be ensuring that individuals, teams and organizations are equipped and ready, equipped to perform the tasks they need to do today and ready to perform in the unknown of tomorrow.**

In times of continual changing, plenty of voices (including ours) have called for change. Clark Quinn called us to a revolution in 2014.[18] In 2018 the Learning Performance Benchmark report spoke about the pivot point of change.[19] Charles Jennings called for a fundamentally different view of work, performance and learning.[20] In April 2025 Josh Bersin claimed that AI is blowing up the corporate L&D market – you can't get a bigger challenge than that.[21]

This is where **you** come in. Our organizations need bold L&D leaders actively shaping how learning happens in a continually changing world – our actions must encourage others to dream more, learn more, do more and become more.

Dreaming big together

In our work we have seen the potential, explored the data and heard the stories of those who are shaping the future. The boldest among us are creating their own pathways for success. They recognize that continual changing doesn't have to be a barrier; it can be a catalyst for bold, impactful action.

We are dreaming big for our profession – and we know that you are too.

This book is about harnessing collective wisdom, learning together and dreaming big together so that we can all confidently navigate this complex, evolving world of work. As L&D leaders, we have the opportunity not just to respond to change, but to drive it — empowering ourselves and those around us to thrive in a world where change is the only constant.

Destination success: Shaping the future together

Our traditional tools and models help us retrace known paths, but they falter when the landscape is constantly shifting. Disruption challenges the status quo, demanding different ways of thinking. To create our own pathways to business success we must return to first principles and rethink how we navigate the unknown with clarity and purpose to unlock business value.

We've written this book not because we have all the answers, but because we are learning too. Our aim is to offer some evidence-informed principles as a starting point – principles that capture our research findings, our insights and experiences along with those of people we've spoken with, worked with and learned from. By exploring real-world examples and insights from L&D leaders across different sectors, we hope to spark ideas that inspire you to bring your unique perspective and create your own path forward.

Our goal is not to offer another rigid model. Instead, we want to equip you with principles that you can apply to assess, adapt and apply to create your own way forward. Principles that are on the surface so simple that they can be practised daily and embedded as habits. Principles that are deeply embedded in rich evidence and have been honed through the fire of experience. **We don't want you to view other people's stories as a template to copy – but to inspire you to innovate and create your own story and contribute to shaping the future of L&D.**

That said, we know that as humans we crave stability and seek out its comfort. The principles that we draw on in the following pages will feel familiar and somewhat ageless. They have guided L&D through known territory and we want to share how they can continue to guide us through the unknown.

Success in an ever-changing landscape isn't something we achieve alone. While personal reflection and experimentation are essential, true success will come from learning together. Just as we, Laura and Michelle, have drawn upon each other's strengths and experiences and reached out to our networks, we encourage you to engage with others on your journey – within your organization, across your networks and within the broader L&D community. As you move from knowing to doing, collaborating with others and sharing insights will deepen your connections and foster shared success along the way.

We are all different but when we journey together, we learn together.

As you read this book, think about the bold steps you can take to drive meaningful change in your organization. What will your first step toward creating success in this constantly evolving landscape be?

IDENTIFY YOUR OPPORTUNITIES

Take out your Field Notebook. Reflect on your learning journey ahead:

1   Consider how you currently define L&D value versus how you think business leaders in your organization view it. Where do you see alignment or gaps between these perspectives?

2   What areas of complexity or continual changing are you experiencing in your workplace right now? How are these impacting your ability to deliver learning solutions?

3   Think about a recent situation where the path to success wasn't clear. What made it challenging to navigate, and what helped you find your way?

4   How do you feel about being called upon to be an L&D leader who shapes the future of learning in your organization? What excites or concerns you about this role?

Join us on the next step of the journey as we reflect on the lessons from past approaches, seeking to understand how models and frameworks have both succeeded and failed, and how we can better use evidence to inform our decisions moving forward. Models are maps, not the territory, and this distinction is key to applying principles that will guide future success.

Notes

1   Quoted in L Adraine (1997) *The Most Important Thing I Know*, Andrews McMeel Publishing, Kansas City.
2   World Economic Forum (2025) *Future of Jobs Report*, WEF, Figure 4.1.
3   World Economic Forum (2025) *Future of Jobs Report*, WEF, Figure 4.4.
4   Refer to Appendix 1 for information about the Benchmark initially developed by Towards Maturity when Laura Overton was the founder and director. Originally called the Towards Maturity Health Check, the Benchmark has been run by Mind Tools since 2019 and is now called the Learning Performance Benchmark.
5   L Overton, *The Transformation Journey*, Towards Maturity, 2019. www.learningchangemakers.com/wp-content/uploads/2019-The-Transformation-Journey-FINAL.pdf (archived at https://perma.cc/UU8P-9R5D)

6 D Woods. Business impact through design thinking – Damien Woods, Learning Uncut podcast, episode 38, 29 October 2019.

7 D Woods. Business impact through design thinking – Damien Woods, Learning Uncut podcast, episode 38, 29 October 2019. Improvement data as reported by Damien Woods.

8 R Brinkerhoff. Why managers are right not to support training, LinkedIn, 2025. www.linkedin.com/posts/robert-brinkerhoff-7b8a224_why-managers-are-right-not-to-support-training-activity-7313093627411386368-M19J (archived at https://perma.cc/J9R6-7BB2)

9 A Ng. TikTok owner ByteDance laid off a global HR team in December, CNBC, 2022. www.cnbc.com/2022/01/31/tiktok-owner-bytedance-laid-off-a-global-hr-team-in-december.html (archived at https://perma.cc/HJ3X-ETZU)

10 E Crowley and L Overton. *Learning and Skills at Work Survey 2021*, Chartered Institute of Personnel and Development, 2021. www.cipd.org/globalassets/media/comms/news/as2learning-skills-work-report-2021-1_tcm18-95433.pdf (archived at https://perma.cc/XUB5-3YWP)

11 LinkedIn Learning. *2022 Workplace Learning Report: The transformation of L&D*, LinkedIn, 2022. learning.linkedin.com/content/dam/me/learning/resources/pdfs/linkedIn-learning-workplace-learning-report-2022.pdf (archived at https://perma.cc/7SDM-XFRW)

12 LinkedIn Learning. *2024 Workplace Learning Report*, LinkedIn, 2024. learning.linkedin.com/content/dam/me/business/en-us/amp/learning-solutions/images/wlr-2024/LinkedIn-Workplace-Learning-Report-2024.pdf (archived at https://perma.cc/9LRL-KWER)

13 Based on data about budget and challenges in Mind Tools. Learning and development in organizations: Reflecting on 20 years of research, Mind Tools, 2023. www.mindtools.com/thought-leadership/reports/20-years-of-research (archived at https://perma.cc/Y777-5LXW)

14 P Shea. The resistance to AI in education isn't really about learning, Medium, 2024. medium.com/the-quantastic-journal/the-resistance-to-ai-in-education-isnt-really-about-learning-41d2d9cf4476 (archived at https://perma.cc/N7RK-WLSH)

15 Fosway Group. Covid-19 L&D research: First take, Fossway, nd. www.fosway.com/research/next-gen-learning/covid19-research (archived at https://perma.cc/PYD3-LDYG)

16 Paragraph adapted by Trish Uhl from T Uhl. *Adaptive Humans + AI Agents: Sink, swim, or swarm*, independently published, 2025. The statistic regarding the six– seven month doubling time for AI capabilities is drawn from industry observations and research such as T Kwa, et al. Measuring AI ability to complete long tasks, arXiv, 2025. arxiv.org/abs/2503.14499 (archived at https://perma.cc/B6F6-W2X2)

17 D Summlar. Talent marketplace at Schneider Electric – Dean Summlar, Learning Uncut podcast, episode 118, 21 March 2023.

18 C Quinn (2014) *Revolutionize Learning and Development: Performance and innovation strategy for the information age*, Pfeiffer, San Francisco.

19 L Overton. The transformation curve: The L&D journey to deliver lasting business impact, Towards Maturity, 2018. www.learningchangemakers.com/research_whitepapers/the-transformation-curve (archived at https://perma.cc/672E-MNRN)

20 J Arets, C Jennings and A Heijnen (2015) *702010 Towards 100% Performance*, Sutler Media, Maastricht.

21 J Bersin. How AI is blowing up the corporate learning market: The whole story, Josh Bersin Company, 12 April 2025. joshbersin.com/podcast/how-ai-is-blowing-up-the-corporate-learning-market-the-whole-story (archived at https://perma.cc/H5HV-PT8D)

2

Looking back to look forward

L&D professionals do not work in stable, predictable environments. We work with people who work with people who work in organizations that are constantly flexing just to keep stable. Recognizing this is the start of the journey.

In this ever-shifting landscape of workplace learning, L&D professionals often find themselves searching for the next new thing to guide and support their efforts. But what if the key to navigating this complex terrain lies not in finding the perfect technology, model or framework, but in honing our navigational instincts?

In this chapter we'll explore why we do what we do, establishing our destination for success and how success leaves clues. We'll also take a look at why traditional models may fall short in our rapidly changing world and introduce a set of principles that can help you chart your own course to business value.

Welcome to the journey of finding our way in the new world of learning and development.

Why do we do what we do?

There are many interpretations of what L&D professionals do and why we do it. Our definition of the purpose of **L&D is to ensure that individuals and the teams that they work in are equipped and ready.**

They must be equipped today to perform the tasks they need to do their jobs well and be ready for the new tasks, skills and jobs that they will need for tomorrow. This job of ensuring that humans are equipped and ready is more important in the new world of work, not less. Our human brains are uniquely powerful in the way that they connect, remember and make associations with stories. They have evolved to allow us to flex and continually adapt in messy and complex environments and also influence how we connect with others.

Despite all of the giant steps forward that AI has made in the last few years, experts agree that the technology continues to struggle with the dynamic, flexible adaptability of the human brain.[1]

As humans, we are continually learning, growing, adapting and changing – our ability to do this is unique to us. We are continually faced with novel or new situations where we need to take that journey from being a complete beginner to being able to demonstrate sufficient mastery to survive, evolve and grow.

In the workplace our job is to support that journey and make it as effective as possible in the context of the organizations that we support. It's a job that has changed significantly over the years.

Looking back, to look forward[2]

Would you believe that the training function as we know it didn't really exist until the late 1930s? It was World War II that truly kicked things into gear when the US government teamed up with industries to quickly prepare workers to ramp up military production.

Before that, knowledge was passed down quite simply from master to apprentice. As factories and assembly lines changed how we worked, companies needed more structured ways to get everyone on the same page.

After the war, businesses started embracing classroom training and on-the-job coaching to boost workforce efficiency. Companies like Ford were ahead of their time, creating departments dedicated to employee development – teaching everything from English to personal finance.

By the 1970s and 1980s, training departments had a clear mission: build specific job skills with measurable results. Success meant workers who could do their jobs safely and effectively.

When 'training' departments evolved into 'learning and development' late in the 20th century, it signalled a bigger shift – we weren't just preparing people for today's tasks, but investing in their growth for tomorrow's challenges. Each wave of new technology – from e-learning to mobile apps to social learning – has opened new doors for how we support people's development.

What began as straightforward training to get the job done has blossomed into something far richer – supporting individual growth, organizational agility and business transformation. We've moved from isolated training events to learning that's woven right into the fabric of work.

Abundance and overwhelm

Working in L&D today, we face a broader mandate than our predecessors – moving beyond job readiness to fostering personal growth, continuous learning and building cultures that support innovation and agility in constantly changing environments.

Our work is no longer simply 'This is the job you need to do, and this is how you do it.' We must ensure others are equipped and ready to navigate uncertainty whenever they face new tools, processes or responsibilities.

We have unprecedented access to resources that should make this easier. Research on how the brain learns is more accessible than ever. Technologies to capture expertise, share knowledge and support practice continue to multiply – from learning management systems that offered structure, to mobile learning that removed location constraints, to AI tools that personalize experiences at scale. We'll dig deeper into the science and technology in Chapter 4, but for now let's keep to the point – there is a lot to take in!

This abundance creates its own challenges. Our brief online search uncovered over 150 different models all promising to help L&D work smarter and drive impact.[3] From theories about how we learn to frameworks for needs analysis, design, facilitation, performance support and evaluation – the options became overwhelming after a while and we gave up looking!

In 2023, the Learning Performance Benchmark data confirmed that this sense of being '**overwhelmed and under-equipped**' was identified as one of the **top three challenges for L&D teams**.[4]

Here's the paradox – the very tools and models designed to help us serve business goals more effectively often leave us more overwhelmed than empowered. In trying to navigate this complexity of our own making, we can lose sight of our core purpose: ensuring others are equipped and ready.

Success leaves clues: Revisiting the evidence

Tony Robbins often says that 'success leaves clues'.[5] Laura Overton, founder of the Learning Performance Benchmark, has spent two decades following

FIGURE 2.1 The L&D performance gap

Enhanced organizational performance
22%   96%
                    ⟨ Performance Gap ⟩

Improved on-the-job productivity
22%   94%

Developed a continual learning culture
16%   93%

Built organizational capability to solve problems
16%   91%

Faciliated new ways of working
29%   91%

Increased employee retention
16%   90%

Managed risk successfully
32%   83%

% Wanting these goals in 2018   % achieving goals 5 years later (2023)

these clues to understand how we can effectively ensure others are equipped and ready.

The research began in 2003 with a fundamental question: what does e-learning success look like for learning teams, and how do they achieve it? From the start, success was defined as the difference learning makes to business priorities, including performance improvements, organizational agility and cultural transformation.

Despite 90 per cent of organizations consistently identifying these as important goals, fewer than a third were actually achieving them by 2023 (see Figure 2.1). Over time, the 'e-learning' was dropped but the persistent gap between aspiration and achievement became the research's driving question and ultimate indicator of learning maturity.[6]

FIGURE 2.2 The Transformation Curve Maturity Model

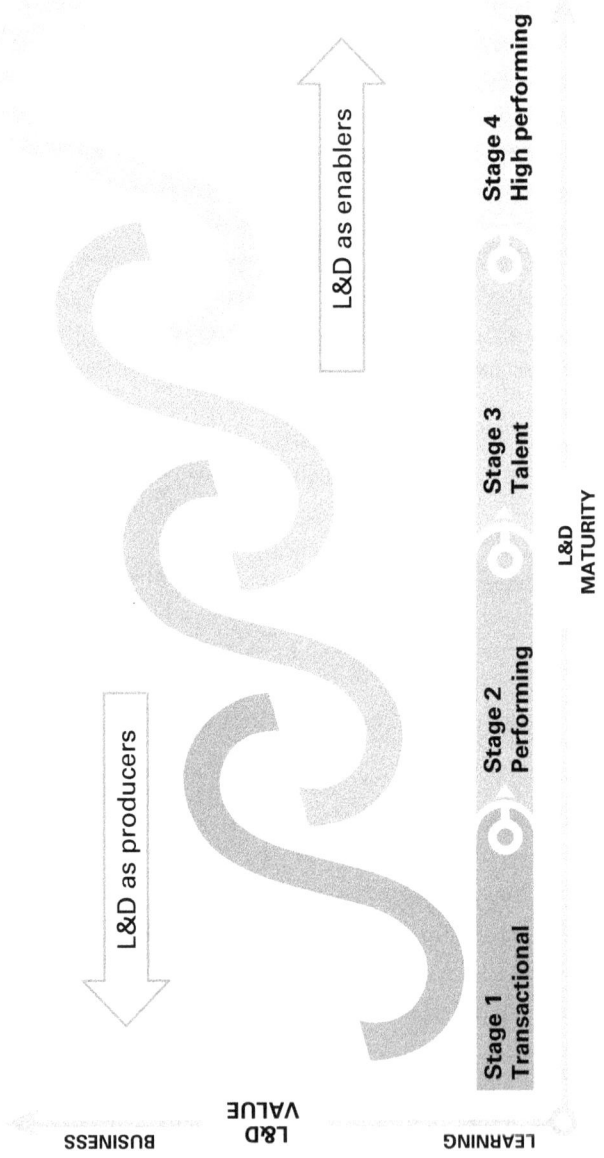

L&D as producers

L&D as enablers

BUSINESS

L&D
VALUE

LEARNING

Stage 1
Transactional

Stage 2
Performing

Stage 3
Talent

Stage 4
High performing

L&D
MATURITY

SOURCE L Overton. The transformation journey, Towards Maturity, 2019. www.learningchangemakers.com/wp-content/uploads/2019-The-Transformation-Journey-FINAL.pdf

The learning maturity data trail

What correlates with successful business impact? The study explored numerous variables – from technologies to skills – but the strongest correlations emerged in behaviours. The research deconstructed over 90 different work practices, revealing six behavioural patterns that consistently linked to business results that were called the Towards Maturity Index.

Letting go: A pivot point of change

By 2018, something wasn't adding up for Laura. Despite years of sharing insights and evidence, the data showed most organizations remained stuck in the early stages of maturity.

'I started to wonder if the index was working,' Laura recalls. 'There was so much talk in the industry about change and modernization but the data showed so little progress year on year. We were in danger of being stuck and caught in the headlights.'

This uncomfortable realization led Laura to question her own creation – the very maturity model she had built over 15 years. Working with researchers Gent Ahmetaj and Genny Dixon, she made the difficult decision to dismantle the established index, examining every component afresh with a single question in mind: what truly drives business impact?

This willingness to let go of her own established framework yielded the breakthrough insight of the Transformation Curve Maturity Model (Figure 2.2) – the understanding that L&D's journey follows a pattern where each stage delivers value but eventually plateaus, requiring a pivot to move forward.

The journey across the Transformation Curve

What emerged was a clear picture of how L&D functions evolve across four distinct stages:

- **Stage 1: Transactional.** Here, L&D focuses primarily on efficiency: delivering more for less, improving administration and expanding the course catalogue. Learning is seen as an 'event' rather than a process, with little involvement from managers or learners themselves. While well-intentioned, these teams often lack the technology skills and strategic alignment needed for broader impact.

- **Stage 2: Performing.** At this stage, L&D begins aligning with business goals and improving employee engagement. Their role shifts from 'taking orders' to 'taking control'. While technology use expands and manager involvement increases, there's still limited support for workplace learning and minimal use of data to drive decisions.

- **Stage 3: Talent.** The critical pivot point occurs here, where L&D's identity fundamentally shifts from content producer to learning enabler. Teams focus on integrating learning into daily work, supporting self-directed learners and recognizing learning as an organizational responsibility rather than an L&D function. Coaching, mentoring and performance support become priorities.

- **Stage 4: High performing.** At this maturity level, business and learning leaders share responsibility for how the organization learns and adapts. There's a shared vision of outcomes, managers actively create a culture of permission and individuals become connected contributors. Learning becomes embedded in the culture.

High-performing teams in the top stage were three times more likely to report improved growth, productivity and profitability, and four times more likely to contribute meaningfully to business transformation.

The comparison between high performers and average organizations isn't just an academic exercise – it's a map showing what's possible when L&D navigates successfully through these stages, letting go of comfortable practices to embrace new ways of creating value.

Laura's personal journey of questioning and ultimately letting go of her established framework mirrored exactly what successful L&D teams must do – release what's working today to create space for tomorrow's greater impact.

The map is not the territory

The maturity model contains signs of hope for many. Organizations at the highest stages achieve greater agility, productivity, engagement and stronger learning cultures. Importantly, these high performers aren't just teams with big budgets or cutting-edge technology – they're organizations like the ones that we all work in. The difference is that they have navigated the transformation journey successfully.

Yet most L&D functions remain at the early stages of this journey. The 2023 Learning Performance Benchmark revealed that over 74 per cent of organizations are still at stages 1 and 2.[7]

This persistent gap has led many in our industry to hunt for a silver bullet solution – the simple idea that will solve all of our learning impact and culture challenges. But in our complex, messy world, silver bullets only fly straight – and our path is anything but linear.

The L&D profession isn't at a crossroads with clear choices ahead – we've reached the shore of an ocean. As we gaze out to sea, there are no signposts or previously trodden paths. The Learning Performance Benchmark data points to consistent patterns of success, but each organization must chart its own course through uncharted waters.

Navigating our way to success: Getting back to basics

Trusted principles: Simplified, not simple

The human mind naturally makes mental models to help cope with complexity.[8] Perhaps this is why we're drawn to models – they create a sense of direction and control in changing environments, reducing our sense of risk and encouraging action.

L&D has accumulated countless models over decades, each breaking down aspects of our practice. But they often tend to reduce the process to simple steps rather than simplify our lives. There is a crucial distinction between two approaches to operating in complex and interwoven workplaces:[9]

- **Reductionism** dissects complex systems into individual pieces – like separate models for performance consulting, learning design and evaluation. While this provides detailed insights into specific processes, it often loses sight of how these elements work together in our messy reality.
- **Simplification**, by contrast, identifies essential patterns that make the whole system work. It's about understanding key principles rather than memorizing every detail of every model.

The Learning Performance Benchmark took a simplification approach. Rather than testing which models worked, it deconstructed the behaviours from popular models and analysed how they functioned in real organizations. By removing the predefined processes that we traditionally followed in steps (first we analyse, then we design etc.) we isolated the behaviours within those steps and asked participants to reflect on those behaviours. This granular approach provided a more holistic lens on how L&D teams create value and led us to the maturity model in Figure 2.2.

But, as we have already seen, knowing what a more mature, high-performing organization is doing doesn't guarantee that we will follow in their footsteps. It can even demoralize and limit us.

It was time to step back and look at the data again. Rather than focus on the characteristics of those driving the most business value, we revisited the individual behaviours that correlated to business impact. This helped us identify a set of foundational principles that consistently emerged in success-ful L&D practices, *and* could be followed by everyone, regardless of their stage of maturity.

In exploring the data for this book, we could clearly see principles of practice that correlated with business impact regardless of organization size, industry sector or economic conditions. These weren't just theoretical concepts but practical approaches proven to drive results through boom and bust cycles, technological disruptions and changing workplace dynamics.

The principles appeared as distilled wisdom rather than stripped-down formulas. As a lens they helped us make sense of the stories that Michelle was uncovering in the Learning Uncut podcast. They helped us explore which models are useful for our success and, moving forward, helps us explore our unique workplace landscapes to navigate to better business value.

Instead of blinding us with 90 behaviours or demoralizing us with a maturity model that made us feel that progress was unobtainable, we began to see these principles had the potential to:

- underpin the most useful models
- shape how we approach tools and technologies
- help us navigate our own unique dynamic, complex environments and improve business value

Introducing TRI principles

We've distilled these patterns into what we call the TRI principles – Tuning In, Responding and Improving (Figure 2.3).

We were conscious that as L&D leaders we operate in a world that doesn't stand still – it is continually changing, transforming, reacting. We saw these principles at work in our interviews and research, not as a one-off process but a continual cycle. So we took Dr Sharon Varney's advice. In her book

Leadership in Complexity and Change: For a world in constant motion, she talks about the importance of reminding ourselves that our work world is not static and predictable; it is dynamic and continually changing so in any process that we follow, she advises to 'remember to add the -ing'.[10]

FIGURE 2.3 The TRI principles

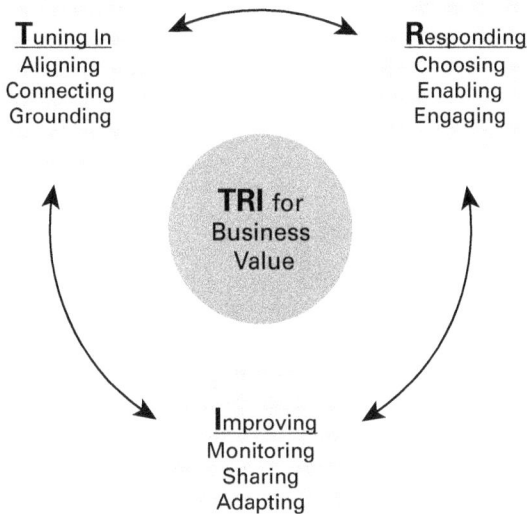

Tuning In is about awareness – truly understanding the landscape within our organization. It's how as L&D leaders at all stages of our career we gain clarity about what matters. What's happening on the factory floor, what tasks nurses and doctors are being asked to perform or what challenges your salespeople face daily. Tuning In helps us identify where we can make the most valuable contribution by understanding our surroundings and pinpointing a shared destination.

Responding represents the professional actions we decide to take as a result of Tuning In. It's how we draw on our expertise, knowledge and technologies to support, design and engage others. Responding involves making deliberate choices – about what approaches to maintain, what new experiments to try and what activities to stop because they distract us from reaching our destination.

Improving completes the cycle by establishing a continuous flow of insight and reflection. It's not just about evaluation in the traditional sense, but also about creating feedback loops that allow us to adapt our course, enhance our approach, and ultimately reach our destination of driving more business value more effectively.

The TRI principles form an interconnected cycle, with each element reinforcing the others. Think of them as distilled wisdom rather than stripped-down formulas. They help us recognize potential pathways to business value and navigate our unique organizational landscapes. These principles:

- consistently correlate to achieving business value
- underpin the most useful models
- help us evaluate which models will be useful – see Appendix 2
- shape how we approach tools and technologies
- help us navigate dynamic, complex environments

Common sense, but not common practice

These TRI principles may seem familiar – perhaps even obvious. After all, who wouldn't agree that understanding your context, taking appropriate action and continually improving are important? They're discussed at conferences, celebrated in awards and featured in countless articles. Yet you can pick up any of the Learning Performance Benchmarks from the last 20 years and you will see that they rarely translate into common practice.

So why this persistent gap between knowing and doing? Our observations point to several key factors:

- **Jargon:** How we describe things is always a challenge. New scientific findings, new models, new influencers all introduce new language to explain and differentiate approaches and service offerings. Inconsistent definitions cause confusion and power struggles.
- The hunt for the **silver bullet:** A continual search for a new thing to fix the problem means we are often willing to drop last week's best idea for this week's new one.
- **Churn:** A continually shifting industry – new people are coming into and experienced people leaving the profession, creating cycles of knowledge loss and rediscovery.
- **Disconnection:** Our piecemeal approach to learning what it means to be an L&D professional has not been helpful – do I learn to design, to use data, to evaluate, to consult, to market – yes all this and more! No wonder those new in the industry might feel overwhelmed.

- **Overwhelm:** Time, resources, industry noise – we've said it already and are repeating it here. This is real and our natural human response is to retreat to comfort in the face of overload.[11]
- **Historical precedent** is given more credence than current realities – the 'Not invented here' syndrome kicks in to protect the familiar.

Note that our evidence in the list above is based more on observation than independently verified data but we are advocates about making a note about what we notice as part of making sense of our world. What would you add to this list?

TRIed and tested

The TRI principles are trustworthy because:

1 They emerge from extensive analysis of actual L&D practices, with over 90 behaviours considered in the study.

2 They're validated by real outcomes and success metrics in L&D over a period of decades, not just months.

3 While they align with universal principles of handling complexity, they're specifically tailored to L&D challenges.

4 They represent patterns that emerged from the data rather than being imposed upon it.

5 They maintain the richness of L&D complexity while making it manageable.

What makes these principles particularly valuable is that they echo successful approaches across many organizational disciplines while being firmly grounded in L&D realities.

Agile development follows a similar cycle with sprint planning, sprint execution and retrospectives. The OODA loop (observe, orient, decide, act), originally developed by John Boyd for the military, has been adapted to decision-making across fields.[12] Design thinking includes empathizing and defining (Tuning In), ideating and prototyping (Responding), and testing and iterating (Improving).[13]

The concept of Tuning In recognizes the unique challenges of balancing business needs with individual needs within specific organizational contexts. Responding builds on evidence of what works in L&D interventions, accounting for diverse learning needs while reflecting practical constraints. Improving considers the unique challenges of co-creating value with stakeholders, celebrating success and sharing lessons learned.

In going back to first principles, we're not introducing new language but helping establish shared understanding. We're not offering another silver bullet but a holistic approach to make sense of the abundance of tools at our disposal. These principles help us reconnect with what's important, building a strong foundation for growth. They become a lens through which we can recognize and evaluate the influence of the past and use it to anticipate the future.

Be BOLD

TRI provides the principles to navigate to our business destination, but navigators need the right attitude to succeed.

When Nainoa asked Mau Piailug how he would find his way across thousands of miles of open ocean, Mau asked a simple yet profound question: 'Can you see Tahiti?' Though Nainoa couldn't physically see the island, he needed to hold it clearly in his mind to navigate successfully.

In the same way, L&D professionals who create lasting impact hold a clear vision of their destination – the business value they seek to create – even when it lies beyond the horizon. What guides them isn't just their understanding of principles or their technical skill, but also their internal compass – what Mau called knowing where the land is 'inside of him'.

We call this internal compass being BOLD – not the showy boldness that creates waves without direction, but the deep, considered boldness that allows us to apply the TRI principles effectively.

Our BOLD compass influences how we apply the TRI principles in our unique context. It gives language to our professional thinking habits that shape how we perceive opportunities, make decisions and respond to the changing conditions around us.

Throughout our research, we've observed that those who successfully navigate complexity to create value share certain thinking patterns – perspectives about business value, openness to diverse viewpoints, approaches to innovation and intentionality in their actions. These habits of mind aren't fixed traits but capabilities we can develop, just as Nainoa developed his navigational abilities through practice and mentorship.

As we journey into Part Two, we'll explore each of the TRI principles in depth. We'll examine how high-performing L&D teams apply these principles to navigate complexity and drive business impact.

Join us as we explore the navigation fundamentals that allow L&D professionals to create value in constantly changing conditions – starting with how we are Tuning In to our organizations.

Notes

1 S Varney (2021) *Leadership in Complexity and Change: For a world in constant motion*, De Gruyter, Berlin.

2 M R Chaudhuri, M Roy, N Mehrotra and P Talukdar. Emergence of training and development in organizations: A historical perspective, *New Applied Studies in Management, Economics and Accounting*, 2022, 5 (1), 7–15.

3 Survey of L&D models, unpublished internet research conducted by authors, June 2024.

4 MindTools. Megatrends reshaping the future: The crucial role of L&D in business transformation, Mind Tools, 2023. www.mindtools.com/thought-leadership/reports/megatrends-reshaping-the-future (archived at https://perma.cc/52S7-KKLK)

5 T Robbins. Success leaves clues, TonyRobbinsQuotes.com, 2020. tonyrobbinsquotes.com/success-leaves-clues (archived at https://perma.cc/7MST-2Y7F)

6 Source: Learning Performance Benchmark study, see Appendix 1.

7 Mind Tools. Unlocking excellence: The strategic business alignment blueprint for L&D, Mind Tools, 2023. www.mindtools.com/thought-leadership/reports/unlocking-excellence (archived at https://perma.cc/4DRF-4YP3)

8 P N Johnson-Laird (1983) *Mental Models: Towards a cognitive science of language, inference, and consciousness*, Cambridge University Press, Cambridge.

9 J Boulton (2024) *The Dao of Complexity: Making sense and making waves in turbulent times*, De Gruyter, Oxford.

10 S Varney (2021) *Leadership in Complexity and Change: For a world in constant motion*, De Gruyter, Berlin, p 13.

11 For example, B G da Silva Cezar and A C G Macada. Cognitive overload, anxiety, cognitive fatigue, avoidance behavior and data literacy in big data environments, *Information Processing and Management*, 2023, 60 (6).

12 Farnham Street. The OODA loop: How fighter pilots make fast and accurate decisions, FS, nd. fs.blog/ooda-loop (archived at https://perma.cc/DUD4-VQYN)

13 IdeoU. What is design thinking and why is it beneficial? IdeoU, nd. www.ideou.com/en-gb/blogs/inspiration/what-is-design-thinking (archived at https://perma.cc/B9QX-P5DU)

PART TWO

Equipped

Navigation principles

3

Tuning In

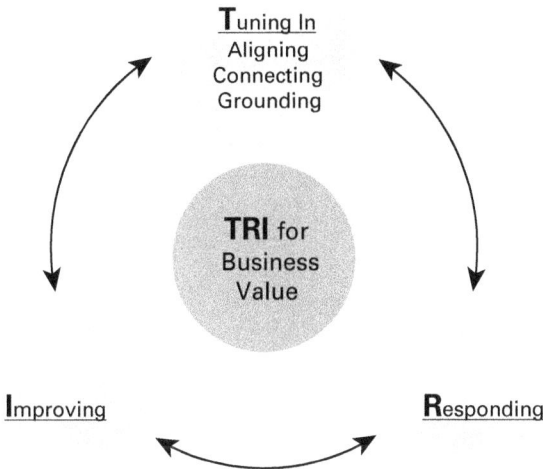

Tuning In
Aligning
Connecting
Grounding

TRI for
Business
Value

Improving

Responding

Launching the start of something different at Barnardo's

When Jodie Pritchard joined Barnardo's as Director of Learning and Development, she faced a difficult challenge: how do you ensure that the colleagues and volunteers of the largest children's charities in the UK are capable, safe and can deliver excellence?[1] How do you do this with an L&D team of just three people and a limited budget to support 25,500 learners?

Jodie's first year was spent tuning into the realities of working and learning at Barnardo's. Her arrival coincided with the release of a new organizational strategy, which she quickly leveraged to open new conversations with business directors about how L&D might support change.

The team spent time listening. Focus groups and conversations revealed an interest in learning: 'We were starting from a point of we want to learn, we want to share. We do some great stuff here.' This allowed Jodie and her team to build on successful practices and an open culture. They took a 'test and learn' approach to exploring ideas to address organizational needs.

While the L&D budget was limited, she found pockets of L&D excellence that already existed at the local level. Redeployment initiatives meant business professionals with an interest in learning could join the team, bringing organizational know-how to L&D. Budget constraints forced creative thinking – they could no longer solely rely on outside providers. Jodie introduced 'Alex', their name for ChatGPT, to support various tasks, demonstrating how resource constraints can drive innovation.

These insights informed a new learning strategy: a three-layer approach that made development accessible to everyone across the organization. The 'fundamentals' layer covers essential knowledge, the 'focus' layer addresses role-specific skills and the 'curious' layer opens up learning across disciplines. The latter addressed one of Jodie's biggest bugbears where organizations 'keep stuff a secret because it's not for you'. This structure provided clarity while opening up learning opportunities.

Looking ahead, Jodie emphasizes this is just the beginning: 'We've been really clear that this is a start of something. We're not launching a finished product. We are launching the start of something different.'

Tuning In: What the data reveals

The Learning Performance Benchmark research reveals a consistent pattern: organizations that excel at Tuning In to their environment achieve greater business impact, reporting improved productivity, revenue and organizational agility (Figure 3.1).[2] This pattern has persisted through changing economic conditions, technological revolutions and even a global pandemic.

When we observe high-performing learning teams through the benchmark data, we see they naturally prioritize understanding the organization's strategic direction – at every level of the entire L&D team. They've discovered ways to create adaptable learning strategies that shift as business priorities change, and they're twice as likely to maintain ongoing awareness of individual needs that influence both results and the journey to achieve them.

This pattern of awareness has been a consistent characteristic of effective learning teams across two decades of research. Yet, despite this evidence, just over half of learning professionals believe their teams understand their organization's strategic goals, and only a quarter maintain awareness of how their workforce actually learns what they need for their job. The high

FIGURE 3.1 How are L&D leaders Tuning In? Shifts in practice 2018–23

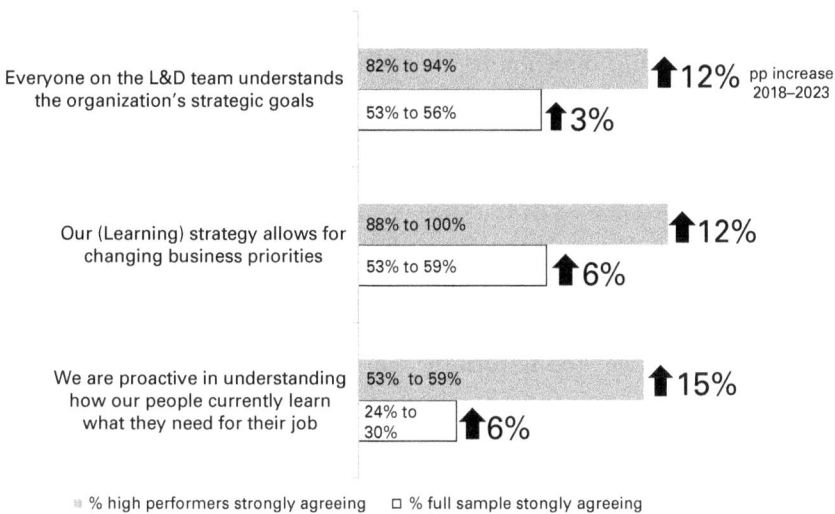

Everyone on the L&D team understands the organization's strategic goals

82% to 94% ↑12% pp increase 2018–2023

53% to 56% ↑3%

Our (Learning) strategy allows for changing business priorities

88% to 100% ↑12%

53% to 59% ↑6%

We are proactive in understanding how our people currently learn what they need for their job

53% to 59% ↑15%

24% to 30% ↑6%

▨ % high performers strongly agreeing   □ % full sample stongly agreeing

performers don't just recognize the importance of Tuning In to what is important, they're twice as likely to continually deepen this capability over time.

Navigation fundamentals 1: Tuning In

Tuning In is a continuous state of awareness that allows us to detect signals and patterns in our organization before choosing our course. You might recognize this pattern in other fields. Master navigators observe the stars, ocean swells and bird patterns to establish their course. Similarly, L&D professionals who consistently create impact have discovered ways to understand their organization's strategic priorities, individual motivations and cultural realities before designing and adapting solutions. This isn't about completing a data-gathering exercise; it's a habit of active listening and observation that reveals both stated and unstated needs.

Tuning In manifests as an ongoing connection to business goals, learner experiences and workplace realities. It shows up as being open to what's going on around us, rather than rushing to immediate solutions. The difference becomes apparent when we compare teams that react to training requests with those that first understand the deeper patterns and opportunities that enable true business impact.

Tuning In is an ongoing practice

In contrast to linear processes, Tuning In serves us as an ongoing practice that helps determine direction regardless of where you are in your journey or what you face. It looks different across different contexts, but certain elements remain consistent in successful L&D practice.

Traditional approaches like annual training plans or individual development planning capture goals at a single point in time, but they don't account for ongoing shifts due to the complex, dynamic factors that influence learning across organizations. Tuning In provides continuous awareness to help us navigate these complexities.

Consider how we used to turn the dial on a radio to find our favourite station. In a similar way, successful L&D professionals have discovered various methods to explore current business strategy and culture, and to listen to what matters to individuals in their organization. While the specific approaches vary widely, the underlying pattern of attuning to priorities remains consistent.

Jodie's approach at Barnardo's provides one example of how to Tune In. She prioritized listening and understanding before making decisions about how to support individual, team and organizational learning. By developing awareness first, she was able to make informed choices that aligned with both organizational strategy and the needs of the people she served.

What Tuning In isn't

Applying the principle of Tuning In differs from several common approaches. It's not:

- a data-gathering exercise designed to justify predetermined solutions
- a one-time analysis that you complete and file
- creating consensus around a good idea
- a process for gaining buy-in for solutions already decided upon

Rather, this principle involves discerning and maintaining awareness of multiple perspectives. Each person has their own lens on shared challenges and each viewpoint contributes to a richer understanding. Tuning In provides awareness of new perspectives, insights and opportunities to collaborate.

What gets in our way?

Even when we understand the importance of Tuning In – that continuous state of awareness that allows us to detect signals and patterns before taking action – many of us struggle to put it into practice. Like a navigator who knows they should check the stars but finds themselves too busy adjusting the sails, we often face barriers that prevent us from truly understanding our organizational context. By the time we look up we realize we are sailing in the wrong direction.

Here are the common barriers that get in the way of effective Tuning In:

- **The tyranny of time:** When deadlines loom and stakeholders demand immediate results, Tuning In can seem like a luxury. By skipping this essential work, we risk investing precious resources in solutions that don't address real needs. Effective L&D professionals have a habit of continuous awareness that informs every conversation, decision and action.

- **'Once and done' mindset:** Many of us conduct an annual training needs assessment, then consider our Tuning In complete. But organizations are living systems that constantly evolve. Creating lightweight, ongoing touchpoints keeps us connected to shifting priorities and emerging needs.

- **Action bias:** Our natural tendency to jump quickly to solutions often prevents us from seeing the complete picture. This solution-orientation intensifies under time pressure, creating a cycle of quick action, incomplete solutions and rework. Gathering multiple perspectives before designing solutions helps ensure they address real business needs.

- **Analysis paralysis:** Gathering so much data that we become overwhelmed and can't move forward. In complex organizations, perfect information is rarely possible, but high-performing L&D teams can identify the signals that matter most and focus on what really needs to be addressed.

- **Permission and pushback:** Stakeholders might expect immediate solutions rather than thoughtful exploration, or we find ourselves boxed into a traditional training role when we want to be more strategic. Demonstrating value through small wins can build the credibility needed to engage others with Tuning In.

- **Our blind spots:** Our professional expertise can create 'trained incapacity', where specialized knowledge limits our ability to see situations with fresh eyes. We might make assumptions based on past experiences or filter information through our preferred solutions. We'll explore this more fully in Chapter 10.

> As a consultant, I would always have a map of stakeholders and how to get things done. Now being inside the organization, I understand it's way more complicated. It's knowing five levels deeper of relationships that I wouldn't have known before, and that completely changes how I approach problems.
> *Arun Pradhan, L&D Leader, Financial Services*[3]

Identifying common barriers is the first step toward overcoming them. We'll now explore practical approaches to strengthen your Tuning In practice – ways to integrate awareness into your daily work, create ongoing connection to business needs, filter signals from noise, pause before jumping to solutions and build credibility for a more strategic approach.

Success leaves clues: Unpacking the principle of Tuning In

Tuning In consists of three key sub-principles that work together to create a comprehensive awareness of your organization's learning landscape. Each has a different focus. All are essential for understanding the complete picture before choosing how to respond.

1. Aligning Together

'Do you see Tahiti?' master navigator Mau Piailug asked Nainoa Thompson about their vision of their destination, over 2,000 miles away from Hawaii. He understood the power of visualizing a destination long before seeing it. The successful voyages on the *Hōkūle'a* were crewed by teams who shared the same vision of success – they want to raise Tahiti from the ocean.

This powerful question establishes a common destination and purpose for any journey. It encapsulates the essence of our first sub principle in Tuning In – Aligning Together on common goals.

In today's shifting landscape, Aligning Together provides a shared reference point for everyone on the journey. While waves of change may buffet us, this alignment ensures we sail with others across the organization. In a continually changing environment, business goals often provide a relatively stable destination.

This isn't just about mapping courses and programmes to KPIs. It's about keeping our ear to the ground, noticing what matters and focusing on real impact. We recognize this dimension through three key behaviours.

(A) ESTABLISHING A COMMON DIRECTION

When we align to common goals, we take a critical step toward tightly integrating our learning strategy with our business strategy. This means our team's activities continually synchronize with strategic business goals. It's not just understanding the direction; it's embodying it. The emphasis is on 'shared' – it works both ways.

The Learning Performance Benchmark shows that high-performing L&D teams consistently outperform others in this area. While only half of L&D leaders feel their teams' activity aligns with business strategy (52 per cent in 2018 and 2023), high performers are far more likely to achieve alignment (85 per cent in 2018, increasing to 94 per cent in 2023).

High-performing teams are also twice as likely to agree that stakeholders share a common vision for organizational learning. Shared vision is vital for both business impact but perception management. We saw the fate of ByteDance's Talent team in Chapter 1 – a painful reminder of what might happen without alignment.[4]

Dave Buglass captures this well in the foreword of the 2015/16 Learning Performance Benchmark Report, when he said the most significant question for a people professional to ask a business leader is 'How can I help you deliver what is really important to the business?'[5] Common direction isn't just lining up to someone else's goals – it's about relationships.

(B) COLLABORATING TO DEFINE SUCCESS

Alignment isn't a one-way street. As Jonathan Kettleborough highlighted in his book on the subject, alignment is about seeing 'eye to eye'.[6]

High-performing L&D teams state that board members are more likely to have skin in the game through board-level accountability for organizational learning, while business leaders recognize L&D value. These teams are more likely to analyse problems before jumping to solutions. What's more, high performers (both in 2018 and 2023) are three times more likely to agree that every stakeholder shares a common vision for organizational learning.

This collaboration includes agreeing on what success looks like. It's not just about delivering training – it's about targeting business metrics and co-creating outcomes that drive business performance. Top performers excel at fostering this collaborative spirit, and continuously refine it.

(C) REMAINING FLUID

Aligning to business priorities means understanding the overarching strategy day-to-day tactical needs, as well as changing timing and priorities. It's about being nimble and responsive to the business rhythm.

High performers have a strong grasp of business priorities. They're more likely to explore the business problem before recommending a solution, but that's only part of the job. It's not enough to 'talk the talk'; we have to 'walk the walk' and to keep pace. More L&D teams are trying to understand business problems, but if solutions aren't delivered in time to meet needs they're not worth the paper they're written on or the app they're coded into.

Sebastian Tindall at Vitality is a strong example of remaining fluid.[7] In their fast-paced health insurance environment, products and partnerships constantly evolve. When Apple announces a new watch, customers call the next morning expecting support. Sebastian's team had to develop an approach that could respond at the speed of business – moving from traditional multi-week training cycles to just-in-time support. His mantra: 'Don't get people to adhere to what works for L&D. Get L&D to adhere to what works for other people.'[8] We'll explore how Sebastian did this in Chapter 7.

ALIGNING TOGETHER

- What are your organization's top three strategic priorities, and how will your L&D initiatives support them?

- How did you collaborate with stakeholders to define success for your most recent learning initiative?

- What mechanisms help you sense and respond when business priorities shift? Choose one to strengthen in the coming month.

- Who else needs to share your vision for learning and how might you create stronger alignment?

- When did you last challenge your assumptions about what the business needs? What surprised you?

2. Connecting to Individuals

While Aligning Together is about Tuning In to the organization's needs, Connecting to Individuals ensures we pay attention to what matters to the people in our organization.

Nick Shackleton-Jones, creator of the affective context model, emphasizes connecting with individuals' emotions to understand what they truly care about.[9] His approach recognizes that learning is tied to emotional responses, and solutions addressing genuine concerns engage people more effectively.

Sandra Loughlin, the Chief Learning Officer at EPAM Systems, leans into 'Theory One', which she attributes to Harvard professor Dr David Perkins. 'People will learn much of what they have the reasonable opportunity and motivation to learn,' she explains.[10] We'll explore how EPAM applies this idea in Chapter 8.

There is a tension we need to address. Business goals don't always align with individual needs and motivations. Studies on why people leave organizations, what makes them stay and what drives their engagement consistently show this disconnect. Throughout the Learning Performance Benchmark research, understanding individual motivations has consistently been a hallmark of successful organizations.

When pressed for time, we often default to unproven generalizations about age differences or learning styles rather than connecting with our learners. It's no wonder we've been disappointed by the results.

How do we know we're Connecting to Individuals effectively? We recognize it through three key behaviours.

(A) LISTENING ACTIVELY

Design thinkers focusing on human-centred discovery emphasize genuine curiosity and empathy for those we're designing solutions for. Yet the Learning Performance Benchmark consistently shows that less than a third of L&D professionals are proactive in understanding how their people currently learn what they need for their jobs, compared with over 80 per cent of high-performing teams.

LAURA'S INSIGHT: MAPPING THE LEARNING LANDSCAPE

For almost a decade, the Learning Performance Benchmark highlighted L&D's frustration with their learner's lack of engagement with digital learning. Yet Google, YouTube and Facebook had taken the world by storm. I wondered whether learners were reluctant to use digital tools, or just reluctant to use ours.

This kick-started a five-year study exploring how 'learners' learned what they needed for their jobs.[11] Over 50,000 workers took part – directors, apprentices, project managers, nurses, doctors, consultants, baggage handlers, white collar workers and blue collar workers – pretty much every type of worker was represented over the years. We discovered very few differences across sectors. Over 70 per cent engaged in learning because they wanted to work faster and smarter. Many already used mobile devices or social networks to learn from each other, even in some organizations where these were off-limits.

We identified what worked, what didn't and what motivated them. Despite common characteristics, each organization had a unique learning landscape. Understanding these differences helped L&D teams navigate their own terrain more effectively.

Active listening and genuine curiosity reveal what truly matters to the individuals in our organizations, creating the foundation for all other connection efforts.

(B) ACKNOWLEDGING AUTONOMY

The Learning Landscape studies show individuals are motivated to engage with learning with or without L&D's help.[12] They learn to make work easier, improve career prospects and often simply because they like to learn.[13]

In *Drive: The surprising truth about what motivates us*, Daniel Pink identifies autonomy as a key driver of motivation.[14] He argues that the desire to direct our own lives is essential for engagement and performance across various contexts and time.

Acknowledging autonomy means recognizing learning participation as an individual choice. High-performing L&D teams create conditions where autonomy flourishes by ensuring people are aware of and have access to all types of learning opportunities.

Between 2019 and 2023, high-performing teams were twice as likely to offer access to non-job related content. Some extended this to families – a UK telecommunication company offered 'friends and family' access to online libraries in the early 2000s. More recently, Uber offered drivers in their Uber Pro loyalty programme the opportunity for themselves or family members to enrol on Open University courses. A study found many drivers had previously experienced educational barriers or sought career development.[15]

Creating autonomy, even extending to families, connects with individuals while offering a retention benefit to organizations.

(C) SUPPORTING CAREERS

All high-performing L&D teams in 2023 proactively supported career progression using technology (compared with 43 per cent on average across all participants). They also helped people gain business-related qualifications, which were offered by 90 per cent of high performers versus an overall average of 50 per cent.

When Stockland, a leading diversified property group in Australia, outlined ambitious growth plans in 2021 their L&D team needed to do more than just fill immediate capability gaps.[16] Through focus groups, the team discovered a critical insight: while their people were hungry for development and career advancement, they needed improved support structures and more diversified pathways to progress. Despite having motivated employees, development conversations with managers were happening sporadically and career pathways remained unclear for many.

This deep listening led to a powerful response. The L&D team crafted Future Ready Careers – a learning strategy that married individual career aspirations with the organization's strategic capability needs to support the delivery of the enterprise growth strategy. They launched a learning and careers festival and developed practical tools to help employees not just see potential career paths but take actionable steps towards achieving them.

To enable career development we need more than another HR 'skills initiative' – we need to Tune In to the career concerns and aspirations, creating clear links between learning and progression, as we'll explore further in Chapter 8.

CONNECTING TO INDIVIDUALS

- How would you go about identifying the learning landscape in your organization? What's already motivating individuals to learn? How can you tap into that more?
- Identify one learning initiative where you could increase individual autonomy and choice. What changes would make the most difference?

- For a recent learning initiative, how did you connect it to people's career aspirations? How could you determine whether this was meaningful to participants?
- When were you last surprised by learner feedback? What did this reveal about your assumptions and how did you adjust your approach?
- What data could you gather in the next month to test an assumption you might be making about learning preferences based on your own experiences?

3. Grounding in the Real World

Aligning to our business goals and connecting with our learners is essential, but we ignore the environment that we operate in at our peril. 'Context is king' and 'culture eats strategy for breakfast' – we know these phrases, but how often do we consider how we're tuning in to the organizational culture and micro-cultures that surround us?

High-performing L&D teams pay attention to existing cultures, practices, rhythms and routines in their environment – factors they don't control but which influence their success. They operate using the sub-principle of Grounding in the Real World.

How do we recognize Grounding in the Real World? We see it through three key behaviours.

(A) RECOGNIZING CULTURE

One of the most striking findings of the initial Linking Learning to Business study in 2002 was that learning leaders didn't try to change culture or establish a learning culture.[17] Rather, they identified the prevailing culture within their organization and sought to amplify elements that enabled learning and minimize factors that inhibited it – a strong response to complexity. Those with an empowering culture amplified this with technology-based learning, creating a pull strategy with minimal tracking. Those with a pragmatic 'can do' culture reflected that in their approach to e-learning – involving their people, focusing on concrete outcomes and celebrating successes.

As the research developed, we saw that high-performing L&D teams are twice as likely to agree that they have a safe environment to work out loud or an organization that understands the value of learning from mistakes. Importantly, they position themselves to take advantage of that culture to amplify learning.

Recognizing culture involves understanding how your organization actually works rather than how it appears on paper. This means identifying formal and informal networks, recognizing cultural enablers and barriers, using appropriate communication channels, understanding power dynamics and decision-making patterns, and building on what already works well.

(B) UNDERSTANDING YOUR TECHNOLOGY

Tuning In to the existing technology environment is as vital as understanding organizational culture. Yet only 40 per cent of learning professionals know what technology-enabled learning their existing IT systems can support, compared with over 80 per cent of high-performing L&D teams who leverage those systems to increase access and reach.

Understanding your technology goes beyond knowing what tools exist to understanding their actual use and user perception. This includes:

- mapping current technology landscape
- understanding technical limitations and opportunities
- considering accessibility for all users
- evaluating digital readiness across the organization
- understanding user preferences and habits
- assessing technical capabilities and constraints

Understanding technology also means recognizing when the best technology solution is no technology at all, as in the following example from Northern Land Council.[18]

Across 200,000 square kilometres of Australia's Northern Territory, Aboriginal rangers of the Northern Land Council work to conserve their traditional lands and seas. These rangers don't just protect the environment – their work preserves cultural knowledge, passing down ancient wisdom from old to young while creating meaningful employment in remote communities.

In 2024, when refreshing their learning strategy, the L&D team could have followed the crowd toward digital solutions. Instead, they connected deeply to their rangers' reality: spotty internet connectivity and a work culture rich in hands-on, practical experience and oral knowledge sharing. Through conversations with IT, they learned that while network upgrades were planned, the current infrastructure couldn't support reliable digital learning. Rather than force-fitting technology, they embraced what already worked naturally in their rangers' world – on-the-job learning, knowledge sharing between experienced and newer rangers and mentoring. This approach not only aligned with how work actually happened in the field but also honoured traditional Aboriginal ways of passing down knowledge.

(C) WORKING ACROSS SILOS

Josh Bersin talks about Systemic HR™ – a mature HR function that moves beyond traditional silos like learning, talent and recruitment to work in a highly interconnected way.[19] While few HR functions have achieved this integrated state, high-performing L&D teams don't wait for formal structures to change. Instead, they are proactively Tuning In to what matters at every stage of the employee journey, finding ways to collaborate across boundaries.

For decades, the benchmarking data shows high-performing teams exploring how digital learning integrates into onboarding and ensuring succession planning connects to development. They recognize that high-impact L&D work happens at the intersections with other functions.

At Domain, an Australian property technology company, this cross-functional approach transformed their onboarding experience.[20] As they grew from 200 to nearly 800 staff, their L&D team collaborated closely with IT, office managers, hiring managers and buddies to create a personalized journey for new starters. This integration across functions produced consistently high satisfaction scores and became one of the most praised aspects of the employee experience.

A not-for-profit company that took part in the benchmark study took a simpler but equally effective approach.[21] Their L&D team spent a morning with their contact centre, listening to calls, understanding friction points and exploring data on time-consuming topics. This direct connection helped them target short interventions that addressed pressing needs, including engaging help desk staff to provide learning as part of their service. The result was reduced call times and rates for those topics.

When we explore business value through the eyes of other departments, we discover natural learning opportunities and friction points where L&D can make a meaningful difference. Working across silos builds relationships that help us better serve the organization as a whole.

GROUNDING IN THE REAL WORLD

- How well do you understand the specific technologies your learners use daily? Choose one technology to explore.

- Identify two unwritten cultural norms affect how your learning initiatives are received. How might you work with these rather than against them?
- Which organizational silos most constrain the impact of your learning initiatives? What specific relationship could you build to bridge the most important gap?
- Which aspect of your organization's context (culture, systems or workflow) most needs your deeper understanding right now? What steps will you take to build this understanding?
- Describe a situation where data conflicted with your experience. How did you resolve this, and what would you do next time to make a balanced decision?

Tuning In at a glance

Tuning In helps position L&D as a strategic partner rather than a support function. It's a continual check-in to ensure our efforts remain relevant and impactful, even in rapidly changing environments.

The three dimensions of Tuning In work in concert to create comprehensive awareness of your organization's landscape:

- **Aligning Together** connects us to strategic goals and business priorities.
- **Connecting to Individuals** helps us understand what truly motivates people.
- **Grounding in the Real World** ensures our solutions work within the realities of organizational culture and technology.

Practical ideas to improve Tuning In

Tuning In is most powerful when applied in your specific context, addressing the unique barriers and opportunities you face. The following example demonstrates how Tuning In helped one L&D leader to understand their organization before designing learning approaches that would resonate with their distinctive workplace.

BE A CULTURAL ANTHROPOLOGIST

When Kristina Tsiriotakis joined Deciem as their first L&D leader, she noticed a vibrant but undefined culture.[22] Rather than importing L&D approaches from her past experience, she first observed the company's unique character.

'I kept a diary on what the cultural experience was,' Kristina explains. 'I really started to think almost like a historian, or cultural anthropologist.'

With no formal documentation of company strategy or values, she observed daily interactions to uncover what people meant when they said something was 'so Deciem'. Through these observations, Kristina identified patterns of self-direction, autonomy, inclusivity and co-creation that became the foundation for their learning strategy.

'These were all of the words that really started to form and shape the approach that I wanted to take to learning, which was something that was completely choice-based.'

You don't have to benchmark as a high performing learning team to start practicing Tuning In. Table 3.1 outlines a few shifts in both mindset and practice that can help us overcome our barriers to Tuning In.

For aspiring leaders

As someone newer to L&D, your fresh perspective is a powerful asset for Tuning In. You're less constrained by 'how we've always done things' and can notice patterns that long-time employees might miss. Focus on building a foundation of awareness before rushing to prove your value through solutions.

Consider these approaches:

- Be curious and ask questions others might not think to ask.
- Build relationships across the organization while observing different perspectives.
- Develop a systematic approach to capturing insights.
- Start with smaller-scale Tuning In practices before expanding.
- Explore models that provide structured approaches to Tuning In.

Remember, business leaders often respond positively to newcomers who show genuine interest in understanding business context before proposing solutions.

TABLE 3.1 Tuning In to create opportunities

Barriers	Mindset shift	Try this	To improve this
The tyranny of time	From: Tuning In takes too much time away from real work To: Tuning In makes all my work more effective and relevant	• Add 1–2 strategic questions to existing meetings • Observe team dynamics in meetings and detect unspoken concerns and motivations • Create a simple key business metrics dashboard to review monthly in 15 minutes	• Alignment with strategic priorities • Relevant learning solutions that address real needs • Reduced rework from misaligned initiatives
Once and done	From: Tuning In is a task to complete To: Tuning In is an ongoing state of awareness that evolves with the organization	• Create a connection calendar with brief touchpoints before key decision points in your organization's business cycle • Schedule quarterly 'listening tours' with different business units • Implement brief monthly check-ins with key stakeholders	• Continuous awareness of evolving organizational needs • Ability to adapt to shifting priorities • Stronger stakeholder relationships through regular connection
Action bias	From: Activity equals progress To: Understanding precedes effective action	• Gather 3 perspectives before responding to requests • Use the 5-Why technique to uncover root causes before proposing solutions • Keep a decision journal comparing initial instincts with final outcomes	• Solutions that address root causes rather than symptoms • Effective use of resources • Deeper understanding of complex performance challenges

(continued)

TABLE 3.1 (Continued)

Barriers	Mindset shift	Try this	To improve this
Analysis paralysis	From: I need to understand everything before I can act To: I can identify the vital signals from the noise	• Create a 2×2 impact/actionability matrix to filter signals and prioritize information • Instead of asking 'What information do I need?' ask 'What information would definitely change my decision if I had it?' • Consider the cost of delay – define what you lose by waiting for more data. How much data is 'clear enough'?	• Faster decision-making with sufficient information • Clearer prioritization of learning initiatives • Focused attention on what genuinely matters
Permission and pushback	From: I need permission to ask strategic questions To: My curiosity creates value for the business	• Lead with stakeholder goals rather than L&D processes • Prepare 2-minute success stories showing Tuning In's business value • Ask 'What if' questions to explore impact possibilities together	• Credibility as a strategic partner • Influence in business conversations • Opportunities to create value
Our blind spots	From: My expertise tells me what to look for To: What I don't see may be more important than what I do see	• Ask 'What might I be missing?' in team discussions • Seek perspectives outside your professional circle • Log surprising insights to identify assumption patterns	• Fresh perspectives that challenge assumptions • Reduced impact of confirmation bias • Comprehensive understanding of diverse needs

Developing Tuning In takes practice. Initially it may feel unfamiliar, which is where great models can help scaffold these new ideas until they become part of your routine.

MODELS TO SUPPORT TUNING IN

These models provide structured approaches to Tuning In until it becomes more intuitive:

- 7-Step Performance Consulting process: Identifies business needs before jumping to solutions.[23]
- Design Thinking: Emphasizes empathy and user research before solution design, with excellent tools for understanding learner needs and contexts.[24]
- 5Di: Places people's concerns at the centre of learning design, helping discover what truly matters to your audience.[25]
- Culture Map: Offers a framework for understanding cultural contexts that influence how learning lands in organizations.[26]
- PESTLE analysis: Assesses broader environmental factors (political, economic, social, technological, legal and environmental) that shape organizational context.[27]

Remember, these models are tools, not rulebooks. Use them to guide your exploration, not to replace genuine curiosity and observation.

For seasoned L&D leaders

Your experience gives you valuable context and credibility, but it can also create blind spots. The challenge lies in refreshing your perspective and questioning long-held assumptions.

Consider these approaches:

- Deliberately adopt a beginner's mindset in familiar situations.
- Create space for team members to share observations without filtering through your perspective.
- Test assumptions by seeking contradictory evidence.
- Use your credibility to ask deeper, more challenging strategic questions.
- Model Tuning In practices for your team or peers.

Organizations with seasoned L&D leaders who regularly revisit their assumptions report significantly higher business impact than those who rely primarily on past experience.

WHAT WILL YOU TRY?

Take out your Field Notebook and set an intention to try Turning In:

- Which specific Tuning In practice will you implement this week to understand a current business challenge or opportunity?
- What might this practice reveal that you're currently missing? What assumptions could it challenge?
- How will you reflect on what you learned from this practice?

Shifting mindset and practice

L&D professionals often ask: 'How can we move from being order-takers to being strategic business partners?'

Tuning In reframes this question: 'How can we become more attuned to our organization – noticing what's needed through others' eyes, agree on our destination and remain adaptable throughout the journey?'

This shift fundamentally changes how you approach your role. Rather than focusing on position or title, you cultivate awareness and connection to what truly matters in your unique context. The most effective L&D professionals develop a 'navigator's mindset' – observant, curious and attuned to changing environments.

As you practise Tuning In, you'll become more comfortable with uncertainty, more sensitive to subtle signals and more confident in your ability to detect patterns that others might miss.

Moving forward to Responding

Tuning In establishes the foundation for effective L&D practice. Like a navigator who observes their environment before setting course, this continuous awareness helps us detect patterns and signals that inform action.

Jodie Pritchard's experience at Barnardo's demonstrates the power of Tuning In. By spending her first year listening to colleagues, understanding the organization's strategy and identifying pockets of excellence, she created a learning strategy perfectly tailored to Barnardo's unique needs and constraints. Her 'test and learn' approach and recognition that they were launching 'the start of something different' show how Tuning In is never complete but constantly evolving.

However, avoid getting trapped in endless observation. Effective navigation requires making decisions with available information, not waiting for perfect clarity. You need enough awareness to chart a better course, not a perfect one.

The value of Tuning In emerges when it leads to informed action – which brings us to Responding, our focus in Chapter 4.

Notes

1 Author interview with Jodie Pritchard, 18 October 2024.

2 Source of all benchmarking data in this chapter: Learning Performance Benchmark study, see Appendix 1.

3 Author interview with Arun Pradhan, 15 October 2024.

4 A Ng. TikTok owner ByteDance dissolved a global team in its HR department in December, CNBC, 2022. www.cnbc.com/2022/01/31/tiktok-owner-bytedance-laid-off-a-global-hr-team-in-december.html (archived at https://perma.cc/SA4U-WMHF)

5 L Overton. Embracing change, Towards Maturity, 2015. www.learning changemakers.com/articles/the-evolution-of-the-ld-maturity-benchmark (archived at https://perma.cc/GP6V-9YTD)

6 J Kettleborough. *Seeing Eye to Eye: How people professionals can achieve lasting alignment and success within their business*, 2021, AuthorHouse UK, London.

7 S Tindall. Resource-led learning strategy, Sebastian Tindall, Learning Uncut podcast, episode 66, 17 November 2020.

8 Author interview with Sebastian Tindall, 14 August 2024.

9 See Appendix 2 for an introduction to the 5Di and affective context model from Nick Shackleton-Jones.

10 S Loughlin. Learning to adapt: How theory one can make upskilling work for your organization, EPAM, 2020. www.epam.com/insights/blogs/how-theory-one-can-make-upskilling-work-for-your-organization (archived at https://perma.cc/S9TN-UJ3W)

11   The Learning Landscape study was reported in a series of learner voice reports. All are published at: Learning Changemakers. The evolution of the L&D maturity benchmark, 2.2 The learner voice, Learning Changemakers, nd. www.learningchangemakers.com/articles/the-evolution-of-the-ld-maturity-benchmark/#22_the_learner_voice (archived at https://perma.cc/Z4CK-QUL3)

12   Learning Changemakers. The evolution of the L&D maturity benchmark, 2.2 The learner voice, Learning Changemakers, nd. www.learningchangemakers.com/articles/the-evolution-of-the-ld-maturity-benchmark/#22_the_learner_voice (archived at https://perma.cc/DJC5-SWC4)

13   Learning Changemakers. The evolution of the L&D maturity benchmark, 2.2 The learner voice, Learning Changemakers, nd. www.learningchangemakers.com/articles/the-evolution-of-the-ld-maturity-benchmark/#22_the_learner_voice (archived at https://perma.cc/N8JR-UGUJ)

14   D Pink (2011) *Drive: The surprising truth about what motivates us*, Penguin Putnam Inc, New York.

15   L Overton. Closing the opportunity gap: The economic drivers for learning as a benefit, Open University, nd. https://info1.open.ac.uk/PDF-TZ-Closing-the-Opportunity-Gap (archived at https://perma.cc/5MFF-NBJ4)

16   Example based on Michelle Ockers learning strategy project with Stockland. Approved by Stockland.

17   L Overton. Linking learning to business, Learning Changemakers, 2004. www.learningchangemakers.com/research_whitepapers/linking-learning-to-business (archived at https://perma.cc/FRA7-DNGJ)

18   Based on Michelle Ockers' learning strategy project with Northern Land Council (NLC). Approved by NLC.

19   J Bersin. Introducing the Systemic HR™ Initiative, Josh Bersin Company, 2023. joshbersin.com/2023/12/introducing-the-systemic-hr-initiative (archived at https://perma.cc/8VTZ-5KJA)

20   N Barry. Improving the onboarding experience – Nic Barry, Learning Uncut podcast, episode 21, 3 March 2019.

21   Based on Laura Overton's benchmarking project with the organization.

22   K Tsiriotakis. Making learning human – Kristina Tsiriotakis, Learning Uncut podcast, episode 56, 30 June 2020.

23   N Harrison. What is Performance Consulting? Perform Consult, nd. performconsult.co.uk/what-is-performance-consulting (archived at https://perma.cc/2HVU-N3EZ)

24   IdeoU. What is Design Thinking and why is it beneficial? IdeoU, nd. www.ideou.com/blogs/inspiration/what-is-design-thinking (archived at https://perma.cc/P4B2-333G)

25   See Appendix 2 for an introduction to the 5Di from Nick Shackleton-Jones.

26   E Meyer (2014) *The Culture Map: Breaking through the invisible boundaries of global business*, PublicAffairs, New York City.

27   CIPD. PESTLE analysis factsheet, CIPD, 2025. www.cipd.org/en/knowledge/factsheets/pestle-analysis-factsheet (archived at https://perma.cc/GNX2-GHX8)

4

Responding

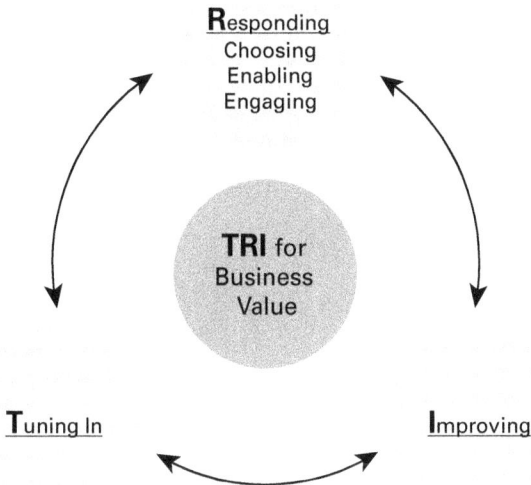

Designing the complete journey: Evidence-informed choices at Sydney Trains

As Director of Capability and Learning at Sydney Trains, Simon Jobson led the development of the Elevate Customer Service programme in 2023 to support the organization's strategic priority of putting 'customer at the centre' for 1.1 million daily passengers.[1]

Simon wanted to create a blended learning approach with spaced repetition rather than traditional single-event training. 'If you think about the Ebbinghaus forgetting curve, you forget 90 per cent after 30 days,' Simon explains. 'What's the point?'

When faced with operational constraints that made his ideal approach impossible, he made intentional choices to create impact within these limitations.

His team conducted 25 co-design workshops with frontline staff to understand what would resonate. They discovered Sydney Trains' strong family culture and used this as an emotional hook. The team also interviewed 120 customers across four stations to gather insights about service expectations, pain points and what created memorable experiences for them.

They designed digital postcards featuring colleagues that participants received before attending workshops, creating excitement and conversation. During sessions, they moved beyond PowerPoint to iPads with interactive content, real customer stories and empathy-mapping exercises.

Influencers were strategically engaged to support participants in applying learning. Lanyard pins, awarded on completion, were crucial as they helped managers and mystery shoppers easily identify trained staff. This provided a conversation starter for senior managers visiting stations, with their interest reinforcing behavioural change. It also allowed mystery shoppers to track participants.

For post-training reinforcement, they implemented a mobile app using spaced retrieval practice, which continued the learning journey through bite-sized questions delivered at optimal intervals.

The results were impressive: a 5 per cent increase in customer service behaviours assessed through mystery shopping and a 96 per cent participant agreement that the programme would help them apply principles daily.

'Focus on the complete learning journey,' Simon advises. 'Don't just focus on "the during". Think about what you're doing before and what you're doing after.'

Responding: What the data reveals[2]

Organizations that excel at the principle of Responding are making intentional, evidence-informed choices that extend beyond just producing programmes. Like Simon, through choice or necessity, they have shifted their focus to enabling the learning needed to deliver business value. They do that by looking beyond the course to explore how learning science and technology can be combined to meet the needs of the organization.

The Learning Performance Benchmark data shows that high-performing learning teams approach learning challenges differently (Figure 4.1). Ninety-four per cent of high performers in 2018 considered courses as only one of many options, reaching 100 per cent in 2023. Meanwhile, only 60 per cent of L&D teams overall regularly look beyond courses as their default solution – an eight percentage point rise, but still lagging far behind.

FIGURE 4.1 How are L&D leaders Responding? Shifts in practice 2018–23

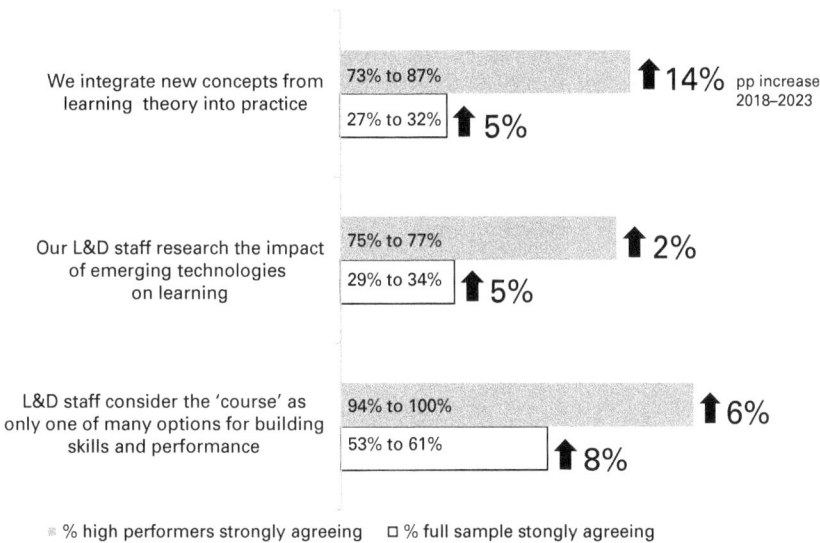

We integrate new concepts from learning theory into practice — 73% to 87% · ↑14% pp increase 2018–2023 · 27% to 32% ↑5%

Our L&D staff research the impact of emerging technologies on learning — 75% to 77% ↑2% · 29% to 34% ↑5%

L&D staff consider the 'course' as only one of many options for building skills and performance — 94% to 100% ↑6% · 53% to 61% ↑8%

■ % high performers strongly agreeing   □ % full sample stongly agreeing

Even more telling is how these teams approach learning science and new technologies. High performers have shown a 14 percentage point increase in integrating learning science concepts, compared to an improvement of just five points for average teams. This scientific foundation shapes how top-performing teams approach learning holistically across their organizations.

Navigation fundamentals 2: Responding

Responding is the intentional application of professional insight to create learning value. Unlike reacting – which rushes to deliver requested solutions – Responding involves making deliberate, evidence-informed choices about how best to enable performance and development.

Like a master navigator makes thousands of small adjustments based on observations, effective L&D professionals respond with purpose and adapting as they go, rather than simply fulfilling orders. They build their capability to make better choices by applying learning science, digital curiosity and a willingness to consider multiple options beyond traditional courses.

This shift from reacting to Responding is critical to transform L&D teams from order-takers to strategic partners. Consider the key differences in Table 4.1.

In practice, Responding positions L&D as those who make wise choices that enable effective learning experiences and engage stakeholders as business allies. It's about applying professional judgement in service of business

TABLE 4.1 Reacting versus Responding

	Reacting	Responding
Input	Requests and orders	Signals and patterns (including initial request)
Motivation	To please	To achieve goals with others
Approach	Speed, time-pressured	Proactive – creating time to think and apply insight
Community	Working for others	Working with others
Output	Repeating past solutions	Considering the best route to impact
Goal	To deliver the service	To achieve the mutually agreed outcome
Role	Producers	Enablers

value rather than learning inputs – focusing on performance impact rather than training delivery.

This principle is at the heart of our professional practice, it differentiates us from others but shows up differently across organizations. High-performing teams don't simply react to training requests – they respond intentionally to the signals and patterns they observe in their own organizations.

But what does intentional Responding look like in practice? And just as importantly, what isn't it?

A navigation reference point, not a procedure

As with Tuning In, Responding isn't a linear process with distinct phases. The principle serves more as a reference point that helps determine direction regardless of where you are in your L&D journey or what conditions you face.

For his first voyage as a non-instrumental navigator, Nainoa Thompson spent weeks preparing his sail plan on land to ensure a successful journey. Once at sea, he explains that a master navigator makes 5,000 observations daily to inform 500 choices about positioning the crew and canoe, at the end of each day they ask, 'Where are we now?'[3] Similarly, effective L&D professionals make countless small decisions based on the insights gathered through Tuning In.

The Sydney Trains example illustrates this principle in action. Rather than simply delivering customer service training, the L&D team responded intentionally – considering learning science, engaging multiple stakeholders and creating a complete learning journey that extended beyond the classroom.

For another organization, Responding might be noticing how people perform a particular task and creating a simple job aid or nudge that helps individuals work smarter.

What Responding isn't

Taking a principle-led approach to Responding differs from common practices. It's not about:

- reacting quickly to every training request
- implementing the latest learning trends without considering context
- standardizing solutions across different situations
- showcasing your technical expertise for its own sake

Instead, Responding involves making intentional choices informed by professional judgement – deliberately applying your expertise to create value, not just deliver services.

Strategically, Responding balances flexibility and scale, addressing immediate needs while anticipating future requirements. The principle underpins our professional relevance at every career stage.

What gets in our way?

When it comes to making intentional, evidence-informed choices rather than reactive decisions, several common barriers hold us back:

- **Pressure to perform:** 'We need this training yesterday. Can you just roll out what we did last time?' In today's high-pressure environment, the demand for immediate solutions often leads us to skip considering multiple options. We reach for familiar approaches rather than taking time to determine what would best serve the current need.

- **Comfort of familiarity:** Our professional identities become tied to familiar approaches. If you've built your reputation on creating e-learning, it's natural to view problems through that lens. The benchmark data reveals that while 100 per cent of high-performing L&D teams consider courses as only one of many potential solutions, on average, L&D teams default to training.

- **Evidence gap:** L&D often operates based on personal experience or industry trends rather than solid evidence. Bridging this gap doesn't require us to become a researcher – just to develop a working knowledge of fundamental learning science and question approaches that contradict them.

- **Technology trap:** Technology offers powerful tools, but can distract from our core purpose. We now have more tools, including generative AI, that help us produce more content, faster – but is that what's needed? Seventy-seven per cent of high-performing teams actively research emerging technologies with purpose (compared to 34 per cent of average teams).

- **Expectations challenge:** People expect learning to look a certain way. They may want a course simply because it's familiar, so if we challenge their request we also challenge their understanding of how learning works. High-performing teams are three times more likely to work with managers to prepare for learner participation, and nearly twice as likely to have managers discuss learning objectives.

Geraldine Voost, a global learning leader from the Netherlands, expressed these challenges well: 'In the past, I have had trainers in my team, and they loved standing in front of a group and teaching. They were very reluctant when I started talking about performance support, social learning, blended learning, and so on because they thought I was taking away what they enjoyed.'[4]

Recognizing what holds us back is the first step toward overcoming barriers.

What does effective Responding actually look like in practice? Once again, success leaves clues.

Success leaves clues: Unpacking the principle of Responding

The principle of Responding can be broken into three key sub-principles that work together to create a comprehensive approach to our core mission: ensuring that individuals, teams and organizations are equipped and ready. Each sub-principle represents a different focus of intentional choice, all essential for creating effective learning interventions.

1. Choosing Well

Just as ancient navigators needed a stable canoe and a clear reference point before adjusting course, we need the stability that comes from balancing learning fundamentals with the tools available to us.

This dimension isn't just about knowledge – it's about building foundations that enable better decisions. In a world being shaped by technology and changing work patterns, we remain stable by understanding the core principles of how our brains operate and adapt and maintaining digital curiosity. Choosing Well isn't about becoming cognitive scientists or technical experts but developing sufficient knowledge and curiosity to make informed decisions that navigate toward better business impact.

Our benchmarking data reveals three key behaviours that characterize this sub-principle.

(A) APPLYING LEARNING SCIENCE

Understanding how people learn is fundamental to effective L&D practice. While experience and intuition matter, evidence-based insights from multiple scientific disciplines improve learning design and implementation.

High-performing teams lead the way in exploring how the science of learning underpins effective practice. Seventy-three per cent of high performers in 2018 agreed that they were integrating new concepts from learning theory into practice (compared to the average of 27 per cent). By 2023, the gap had widened further – 87 per cent actively applying new ideas from learning science versus the average of 32 per cent. They not only recognized the importance of understanding how we learn, but also adopted new ideas nearly three times faster over the five-year period.

Research into learning spans multiple overlapping, intertwined fields, including:

- neuroscience
- cognitive science
- behavioural science
- social science

Those approaching how we learn from a neuroscience lens explore the nervous system and the brain – the physical processes that occur to impact the way we learn. The cognitive science lens explores the mental processes governing how people think and learn, helping us to understand attention, memory, motivation and knowledge construction. Behavioural and social science lenses illuminate learning as both an individual and a social process, highlighting the importance of environment, culture and social interaction in learning. They explore complex workplace learning dynamics.

This evolving field of science will open professional doors of the future for learning leaders. Leaning into the scientific evidence of how memory works, and how behaviour and habits can be helped to grow is our unique differentiator.

Use the checklist in Appendix 3 to be more intentional about how you apply learning science on your next project.

LEARNING SCIENCE: A WORD OF WARNING

- **Question research claims:** The tagline 'learning science shows' can be misleading. Use Stella Collins' framework to question research: examine who conducted the research, their agenda, publication details, timing and methodology.[5]

- **Consider holistic context:** Workplace learning is holistic and interwoven. Applying a single learning theory won't lead to results. As Nick Shackleton-Jones notes: 'Science shows that lemons help XYZ but we won't get results just by putting lemons in our training rooms.'[6]

When we ignore these fields, we risk basing our practice on assumptions or oversimplified models. Approach learning science with curiosity and critical thinking, recognizing our understanding is evolving. As Stella Collins advised, 'What we don't know about the brain is far greater than what we do know about it.'[7]

Apply science with care! Question assumptions, seek evidence and stay humble about the complexity of human learning.

Build competence by engaging with researchers and practitioners like Dr Paul Kirschner,[8] Lauren Waldman,[9] Stella Collins,[10] Julie Dirksen,[11] Patti Shank,[12] Amy Brann,[13] Clark Quinn[14] and Will Thalheimer,[15] who translate research into practice while acknowledging complexity and context.

(B) BEING DIGITALLY CURIOUS

'Curiosity is the aphrodisiac of the digital age.'[16]

The Curious Advantage discusses curiosity sparked by the question 'I wonder if...?' This kind of curiosity adapts us for the digital age, driving passionate inquiry, exploration of new communities and experimentation.

'I wonder if technology can help individuals really learn?' No doubt high-performing teams ask this question. In 2023, 77 per cent agreed that their L&D team members were active in researching the impact of emerging technologies on learning (compared to 34 per cent of the average and just 14 per cent of transactional teams).

Over 20 years of Benchmark research, new tools and technologies appeared and changed our lives (e.g. smartphones and social media), while some never quite took off (virtual worlds spring to mind). The study never found a correlation between specific technologies and business results.

What matters is how technology is applied. High performers were twice as likely as transactional teams to research emerging tools; in 2023, 84 per cent were more likely to be confident incorporating the use of new media in their learning design (compared to 19 per cent of transactional teams). Additionally, 77 per cent agreed their L&D teams had the right skills to exploit learning technologies for business advantage (compared to 12 per cent of transactional teams).

Exploiting technology for business advantage means using tools for more than content and training delivery. While most organizations have remained focused on online content and events, high-performing teams – perhaps guided by learning science – explore ways for technology to help them improve learning in the flow of work and application of new skills back in the workplace.

Generative AI represents the latest frontier. It topped Donald H Taylor's Global Sentiment Survey in 2024 and 2025, offering applications across all three areas in Figure 4.2.[17] AI agents can support coaching, communities, practice and role plays. However, most are currently using it to support content generation, ignorant of the learning science.

The learning team at Ericsson demonstrates digital curiosity through their Learning NEXT community of 450+ members across the business who experiment with new technologies and make informed decisions about future use. They provide evidence that informs critical decisions on whether to build solutions in house, buy them or wait until the technology matures.[18]

This ongoing experimentation prepares L&D to respond proactively, using technology to solve immediate problems and support long-term capability building. As Pauline Rebourgeon, Head of Learning Technology and Innovation at Ericsson, observes, 'The worst thing that could happen with these kinds of experiments is that people might have learned things.'[19]

FIGURE 4.2 Supporting the learning process with technology

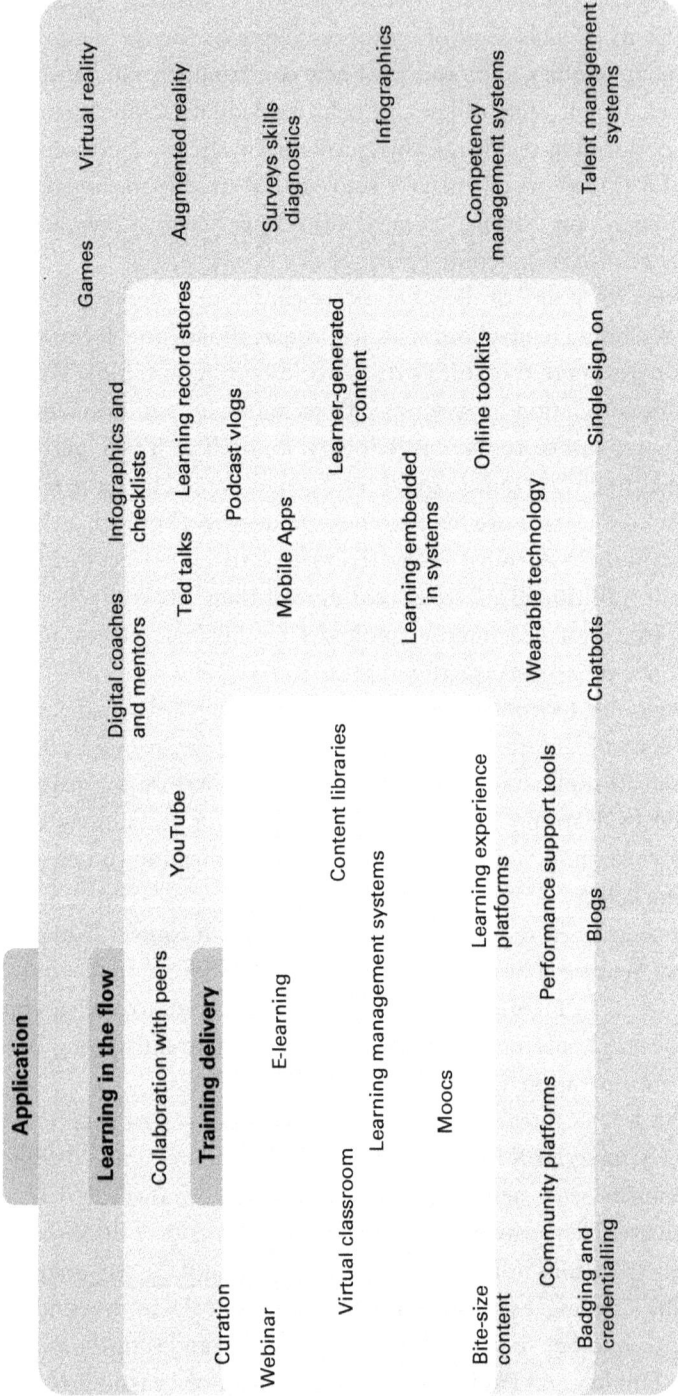

Application

Learning in the flow

Collaboration with peers

Training delivery

Curation

Webinar

E-learning

Virtual classroom

Learning management systems

Moocs

Community platforms

Bite-size content

Badging and credentialling

YouTube

Content libraries

Learning experience platforms

Performance support tools

Blogs

Digital coaches and mentors

Infographics and checklists

Ted talks

Learning record stores

Podcast vlogs

Mobile Apps

Learner-generated content

Learning embedded in systems

Wearable technology

Online toolkits

Chatbots

Single sign on

Games

Virtual reality

Augmented reality

Surveys skills diagnostics

Infographics

Competency management systems

Talent management systems

(C) WIDENING YOUR OPTIONS

The third behaviour highlighted in **Choosing Well** is looking beyond the course. All (yes, 100 per cent of) high-performing L&D teams consider the 'course' as only one of many options for building skills and performance, unlike transactional teams, who focus on building courses.

'To a man with a hammer, everything looks like a nail.'[20] In his 1995 Harvard University speech American businessman and investor Charlie Munger referred to the hard-earned skill of academic mathematicians being applied inappropriately to analyse financial markets. It was clear to Munger that in this instance expertise would not generate needed insights. Similarly, L&D experts face the challenge of being open to widen their options.

Think about it: if you're a coach, will your Tuning In point you to always Responding with coaching? If you excel in e-learning, do you only see opportunities for designing online experiences?

High-performing teams demonstrate one of the hardest behaviours to learn – looking beyond our past expertise of yesterday to what is needed today. Applying learning science and being digitally curious helps maintain an open mind.

CHOOSING WELL

- Track your responses to requests for a week. What percentage were reactions versus intentional responses? What patterns do you notice?

- Think of a recent learning solution you designed. How did you leverage your knowledge of how our brains work to inform your design?

- Identify one digital tool or approach you've been avoiding. What small experiment could you run to expand your comfort with this approach?

- In the past month, how many times have you suggested a non-course solution to a learning request? What barriers prevented you from suggesting more?

- Take a moment to think about your current learning approaches, make a list of five endings to this question: 'I wonder if... ?'

2. Enabling Learning

Choosing Well is the foundation of Responding – the stable canoe from which we can navigate.

But having a well-built vessel isn't enough. We must also know how to move it forward. This brings us to our second sub-principle: Enabling Learning.

Benchmark research identified four approaches that consistently correlate with better results: supporting performance, designing to engage, embedding new behaviours and encouraging connection. These work as an interconnected cycle rather than sequential steps – high performers flow between these approaches as circumstances require.

Through Responding, we make intentional daily choices that help learners, teams and organizations. Many of these choices are small, incremental adjustments – and that's perfectly appropriate. Meaningful improvements often begin with small steps. Change doesn't always need to be dramatic or transformative.

When Responding well, you might realize that our 'go-to' solutions like courses aren't required. Perhaps connecting people will better resolve a challenge. This thoughtful approach – making evidence-informed choices that equip people to perform better – shifts L&D from delivering outputs to enabling outcomes.

High-performing teams aren't lucky – they're intentional in how they support performance, design learning experiences, facilitate transfer and embed behaviours. From 2018 through 2023, the gap between high performers and others has widened as top teams continue making excellent choices in response to evolving challenges and opportunities.

Twenty years of benchmark data has taught us to recognize effective Responding through four key behaviours. We introduce these behaviours below and provide many varied real-world examples of Enabling Learning in Part Three.

(A) SUPPORTING PERFORMANCE

Performance means carrying out tasks and functions effectively. Our research consistently shows that people want to work faster and smarter with less friction in their daily activities.

By Responding with intentional choices based on what people truly need, we can help them achieve this goal. Nick Shackleton-Jones discusses eliminating learning when possible – providing support at the point of need instead of defaulting to knowledge-intensive programmes.[21] This aligns with the 70:20:10 model[22] and the performance support work of Bob Mosher and Dr Conrad Gottfredson.[23]

(B) DESIGNING TO ENGAGE

Learning often falls flat because it isn't designed with engagement in mind. When learning is intentionally designed to engage, learners and their needs remain centre stage.[24] This involves blending different learning approaches – including digital and face-to-face – based on learning science and effective storytelling.

As we saw in Choosing Well, high-performing teams apply learning science in design. Advances in our understanding of how people learn – like the spaced repetition Sydney Trains implemented through their mobile app – provide evidence-based approaches we can incorporate into our designs.

Storytelling creates communication and connection, helping stakeholders understand why learning matters and engaging them with it. Sydney Trains gathered and shared authentic employee stories of memorable customer service moments in their Elevate programme. While technology is a powerful enabler, the human touch remains essential. High performers blend different approaches based on specific situations and needs.

(C) EMBEDDING NEW BEHAVIOURS

Learning transfer typically involves behaviour change, which people often resist. Our role extends beyond the classroom into the workplace – helping people apply what they've learned days, weeks and months later.

Manager involvement is crucial for successful learning transfer. When line managers actively support the process, new behaviours are much more likely to take root. Help managers create opportunities for team members to practise and strengthen new skills on the job.

(D) ENCOURAGING CONNECTION

Our position gives us visibility across the organization at all levels, enabling us to connect people, break down barriers and build collaborative learning communities. This is particularly valuable in today's complex environments where cross-departmental collaboration converts challenges into opportunities.

High-performing L&D teams excel at facilitating connections through mechanisms like action learning sets or communities of practice. People enjoy connecting and sharing knowledge, and these relationships enhance organizational learning.

We met Geraldine Voost earlier in this chapter. With her background including cognitive science and exposure to artificial intelligence at university, she recognized the transformative potential of AI early on. While her excitement wasn't universally shared by her team and colleagues, she understood the importance of learning together and soon won her team over.

Noticing pockets of AI experimentation were happening across the organization after the launch of ChatGPT, Geraldine approached leadership about missed opportunities for shared learning and strategic alignment. She was given one dedicated day per week to track AI trends, identify internal experimenters, create a knowledge platform and establish collective guidelines – effectively building organizational knowledge and a unified approach to AI adoption.

ENABLING LEARNING

- How do you currently identify friction points in people's workflow where performance support would help? How could you improve this process?

- Which of your learning experiences would benefit most from redesigning with emotional engagement in mind?

- How might you improve follow-up mechanisms to support behaviour change after formal learning?

- Where do you see opportunities to connect people across your organization to increase knowledge sharing?

- When have you experimented with a new learning approach despite uncertainty about the outcome?

3. Engaging Influencers

Learning solutions, however well-designed, rarely succeed in isolation. Even the most skilled navigators need a crew. Our third sub-principle, Engaging Influencers, recognizes that sustainable learning requires an ecosystem of support.

The Learning Performance Benchmark shows three key behaviours that consistently correlate with better results.

(A) ACTIVATING YOUR LEARNING ECOSYSTEM

Finding champions who understand the importance of learning, want to learn themselves, support others to learn and champion your cause is invaluable. Champions can come from anywhere – people interested in what you are doing and who care about your intended outcomes, from line managers or project managers to employees who want to make a difference. These engaged people notice what's happening around them and often have significant influence. Who doesn't want to have a band of champions!

Sometimes champions emerge from unlikely places.

Your fiercest critics can become your strongest champions. Maybe they initially objected with comments such as, 'Why should I do things differently? It's working very well this way, thank you very much.' By listening to these naysayers and addressing their concerns, you can convert them from sceptics into powerful advocates.

Sydney Trains strategically cultivated champions through branded pins that participants received upon completing the Elevate programme. These pins were more than recognition symbols – they created visibility for the initiative and enabled managers to identify staff who had completed the training, prompting supportive conversations about applying new customer service behaviours.

Trainers are important allies, occupying a privileged position guiding people through learning in safe, supportive online or face-to-face classroom spaces. They can introduce new ways of working and new technologies, enabling exploration in a safe environment.

Since the first Benchmark study in 2002 we have consistently seen that when trainers gain experience building skills and using new technologies, they become great advocates of tech-enabled learning who share their enthusiasm with others.[25] Their behaviour helps move people from feeling threatened by technology to being open to explore.

(B) EQUIPPING MANAGERS

Managers are vital to effective employee learning yet are often overlooked and unsupported. One of the Benchmark's key findings was the importance of equipping managers to help their teams. It came up repeatedly, but it still doesn't happen. When managers have the resources, skills and confidence to help team members apply their learning it makes all the difference.

There was a 'aha' moment back in 2003 when the results of the first benchmark study came in. We had asked individuals whose opinion mattered most in determining whether they would engage with learning or not. The results were very surprising – L&D was very low on the list at 4 per cent. Senior leaders were marginally more important at 8 per cent. So, who was most important? Line managers, at nearly 60 per cent. This prompted a sea change in how we talked about engaging with learners. We shifted our focus from senior leaders to line managers because line managers have the biggest influence.

High-performing teams equip managers to support learning transfer in the workplace. Managers can take on a quasi-coaching role, helping team members reflect on learning and giving them space to practise – either in casual conversation or more deliberately.

We like the Power Hour concept created by Reuters in 2012.[26] The concept was to set aside an hour each month, run by a manager with their team for a focused conversation and collaboration around a learning topic. You can find out more about it in the L&D Playbook for Enabling Busy Managers.[27]

(C) COMMUNICATING WITH INTENT

We don't want to work in isolation. If we want the learning to speak to the learner (and we really, really do want that) then effective communication is vital.

Effective communication is vital for co-creating learning with a range of stakeholders – individual learners, line managers, teams, subject matter experts and so on. It sounds easy – communicating. We all do it all the time.

Communicating with intent across a wide range of stakeholders takes effort. Generic marketing campaigns telling everybody how great a piece of learning is rarely land. Communication works better as an integral part of the overall learning offer, connecting our responses to what matters to people.

Lots of people can help – workplace champions, trainers and, critically, managers can all amplify your communication when they understand and see the purpose of the learning. These influencers become your best marketers when engaged effectively. Connect with them using language that resonates with their needs and priorities. Communicating with intent isn't about 'us and them' – it's about achieving mutual goals together, smarter and faster.

When you're Tuned In so that you understand what's needed and Responding with the right choices, much of the communication groundwork is already done. You're not trying to gain buy-in for a programme after it's developed – you already have buy-in because stakeholders were involved from the beginning.

ENGAGING INFLUENCERS

- Identify three potential learning champions in your organization that you haven't yet engaged. What will you do to engage each one of them this month?

- What tools or resources do you provide managers to support learning transfer? How might you improve this?

- For your next learning initiative, how will you tailor communication to address needs of different stakeholder groups?

- How do you evaluate whether your stakeholder engagement approach is working effectively?

- Think about a recent time when you encountered resistance from a stakeholder. How did you respond? How might you approach similar situations in the future?

Responding at a glance

When Responding effectively, we are proactively making evidence-informed choices rather than defaulting to familiar solutions. It requires continuous professional judgement to ensure our efforts remain relevant and impactful, even in rapidly changing environments.

The three dimensions of Responding work together as an integrated approach:

- **Choosing Well** grounds our solutions in evidence and learning science.
- **Enabling Learning** designs experience that support performance and engage learners.
- **Engaging Influencers** activates key partners who amplify and sustain learning impact

By mastering these dimensions, L&D professionals ensure their solutions are grounded in evidence, well-designed for impact and properly supported throughout the organization.

Together they shift us from content producers to performance enablers.

Practical ideas to improve Responding

The principle of Responding is most powerful in helping you to land on business value when applied intentionally to your specific context. While copying others rarely works, we can learn from their examples.

EXPERIMENTATION AND LEARNING SCIENCE IN ACTION

Russell Woods, Learning & Organizational Development Partner at Aster Group, was asked to explore what succession planning would look like at this not-for-profit UK social housing association.[28] He soon realized that the real challenge was more about building core skill to strengthen the whole organization. Given that 'Experimenting is one of the things I love about working in L&D', Russell first wanted to discover what skills were important to individuals and managers as they all plan for the future. Through surveys and conversations, he quickly found that critical thinking, questioning, learning agility, strategic thinking and focus topped the list and provided a place to start exploring.

Russell had taken part in Lauren Waldman's Joining Forces with Your Brain programme, which focuses on helping people understand how their brain works so that they can take ownership of how they learn, think and perform.[29] Inspired, he experimented with a Skills Sprint approach that incorporated quick insights, storytelling, spaced practice, reflection prompts and community learning via Microsoft Teams. He strategically used AI to enhance engagement by creating personalized skill stories featuring actual colleagues' roles, generating diverse visual images representing the workforce and developing thoughtful reflection questions for discussion groups.

The first experiment was open to the whole company. He was hoping 20 would join; 73 signed up and immediately engaged not only in the short weekly sprints but also in community discussions, where they freely shared how they were already using their new skills in the workplace.

'We knew that with limited resources, we had to make choices that were grounded in science, harness the tech that we had around us and focus on applying new ideas, not just knowing about them. Our initial experiments demonstrated value, shifting organizational mindsets towards innovative rather than traditional approaches to people development.'

Taking small, intentional steps to shift from reacting to Responding can steadily increase your impact. Consider the practical approaches to overcome common barriers (see Table 4.2) and create new opportunities for yourself and your organization.

TABLE 4.2 Responding to create opportunities

Barrier	Mindset shift	Try this	To improve this
Pressure to perform	From: We need to deliver what's asked for immediately To: We need space to make better choices	• Create a simple decision framework with key stakeholders to guide common requests. • Consider Cathy Moore's Is training really the answer? flowchart • Create a 'minimum viable solution' addressing key needs quickly while building a comprehensive solution • Check whether people have the resources they need at their fingertips	• Business impact through targeted solutions • Solutions that address actual needs • Sustainable performance improvement
Comfort of familiarity	From: This is how we've always done it To: What's the best approach for this specific situation?	• Try a small experiment to test a new approach for a specific need • Generate a 'solution matrix' mapping different approaches to common performance needs • Develop a simple job aid rather than a course for your next knowledge-based request	• Innovation in learning approaches • Solutions tailored to specific contexts • Expanded capability to address diverse performance needs
Evidence gap	From: What's the latest trend? To: What does the evidence suggest?	• Review Tuning In insights to consider which approaches would motivate individuals and fit with organizational culture • Identify one learning approach that you commonly use and review the evidence for/ against its effectiveness • Create a learning science checklist to evaluate proposed solutions against	• Effective learning design • Engagement through science-based approaches • Improved credibility with stakeholders

(continued)

TABLE 4.2 (Continued)

Barrier	Mindset shift	Try this	To improve this
Technology trap	From: How can we use this new technology? To: What problem could this technology help us solve?	• Research emerging technologies with a focus on their learning applications • Try the user experience for a new tool with colleagues • Identify one way to purposefully integrate a digital tool into face-to-face training to enhance practice or application rather than just content delivery • Adopt Ericsson's decision framework (buy/build/wait/stop) for evaluating new learning technologies	• Technology that enhances human learning • Focus on performance outcomes rather than technology • More impactful technology investments
Expectations challenge	From: We need to meet stakeholder expectations To: We need to shape expectations together	• Equip managers with simple tools to support learning transfer • Develop a toolkit with ready-to-use resources for local champions • Create a communication plan to build understanding of your learning approach	• Enhanced stakeholder partnerships • Shared ownership of learning outcomes • Shift from service provider to strategic partner

SOURCE C Moore. Is training really the answer? Ask the flowchart. Cathy Moore, nd. blog.cathy-moore.com/is-training-really-the-answer-ask-the-flowchart; W Thalheimer. The Decisive Dozen, Work-Learning Research, 2013. www.worklearning.com/wp-content/uploads/2017/10/Decisive-Dozen-Research-v1.2.pdf

For aspiring leaders

Newer L&D professionals have an advantage when Responding. Without established habits to break, you can adopt evidence-informed, intentional approaches from the start. Your challenge is establishing effective new ones while building your expertise.

Consider these approaches:

- Use a spaced retrieval practice to learn key learning science concepts.
- Explore multiple options before choosing a learning solution.
- Design for practice, not just content consumption.
- Track your solution choices and rationale.
- Scaffold with models – explore models that provide structure for Responding.

Being international about smaller choices builds the foundation for greater impact as your role grows.

MODELS TO SUPPORT RESPONDING

These models provide structured approaches to Responding until it becomes more intuitive:

- Action Mapping: Focuses on business outcomes and what people need to do differently, eliminating unnecessary content to create targeted, performance-based solutions.[30]
- COM-B model: Analyses the capability, opportunity and motivation needed for behaviour change, helping identify specific barriers and design targeted interventions.[31]
- 5 Moments of Need: Identifies five critical moments when learners need support, enabling performance-focused solutions delivered at the point of need.[32]
- 9 Events of Instruction: Outlines nine instructional events based on cognitive psychology, creating a systematic approach to designing effective learning experiences.[33]
- 12 Levers of Transfer Effectiveness: Provides evidence-informed factors that influence whether learning transfers to workplace performance, improving application and impact.[34]

Remember, these models are tools, not rulebooks. Use them to guide your exploration, not to replace genuine curiosity and observation.

For seasoned L&D leaders

Experienced professionals face a different challenge – breaking free of successful patterns that may no longer serve you well. Responding effectively means holding your knowledge lightly enough to recognize when circumstances call for something new.

Consider these approaches:

- Connect recommendations explicitly to learning science principles when discussing solutions.
- Create space for curiosity and experimentation in your team and with others.
- Involve stakeholders in design, including involving managers from early in the design process (88 per cent of high performers involve managers early compared with 48 per cent on average).
- Notice where learning is happening organically and consider how to amplify it.
- Model Responding practices for your team or peers.

Your leadership position gives you opportunities to model intentional Responding and create conditions where your entire team can make more thoughtful choices.

WHAT WILL YOU TRY?

Take out your Field Notebook and set an intention to shift from reacting to Responding:

- Which specific approach from this chapter will you implement in the coming month?
- What one small change could create more space for intentional choice and experimentation in your next project? Who might you involve to support this shift?
- What might make it difficult to shift from reacting to responding? How might you navigate these constraints?

SHIFTING MINDSET AND PRACTICE

The Responding principle helps us shift from being service providers who fulfil training requests to skilled navigators who make intentional, informed choices about how best to enable performance.

Instead of asking 'How can we efficiently deliver what's being requested?' we ask 'What's the most effective way to address the real need?' The insights gained through Tuning In become more valuable when they shape how you choose to Respond. This principle moves L&D from a reactive posture of taking orders to a proactive role of applying professional judgement – grounded in evidence and context – to meet defined needs.

At its core, Responding reframes L&D's role from producing content to enabling performance, shifting focus from the volume of learning assets to the quality of decisions and business impact.

Moving forward to Improving

As Simon Jobson and his team demonstrated at Sydney Trains, Responding helps create meaningful impact. They made evidence-informed choices that engaged their frontline workforce throughout the learning journey. When faced with operational constraints, they responded with creative alternatives that honoured learning science principles and supported behavioural change.

Yet intentional responses are only part of the journey. Even the most thoughtfully designed solutions need to evolve as conditions change.

No voyage remains on the same course the navigator initially plotted.

The next step is to sustain momentum through continuous refinement, tracking progress, communicating success and adapting to feedback. This is the heart of our next principle, Improving, which we'll explore in Chapter 5.

Notes

1   S Jobson. Sydney Trains elevate customer service – Simon Jobson, Learning Uncut podcast, episode 133, 17 October 2023.
2   Source of all benchmarking data in this chapter: Learning Performance Benchmark study, see Appendix 1.
3   Hōkūleʻa Crew. The way of the navigator, YouTube, 2023. www.youtube.com/watch?v=3TmvlM7B7dk (archived at https://perma.cc/5CRD-KRSH)
4   Laura Overton interview with Geraldine Voost, 25 September 2024.

5   S Collins (2023) *Neuroscience for Learning and Development: How to apply neuroscience and psychology for improved learning and training*, KoganPage, London.

6   N Shackleton-Jones. Practice should never be based on research…, LinkedIn, 2019. www.linkedin.com/pulse/practice-should-never-based-research-nick-shackleton-jones (archived at https://perma.cc/JK62-EMAE)

7   S Collins (2023) *Neuroscience for Learning and Development: How to apply neuroscience and psychology for improved learning and training*, KoganPage, London.

8   Paul A Kirschner. LinkedIn, nd. www.linkedin.com/in/paulkirschner (archived at https://perma.cc/XUZ3-F8XG)

9   Lauren Waldman. LinkedIn, nd. www.linkedin.com/in/lauren-waldman-4666bab (archived at https://perma.cc/7ZAE-M4QY)

10 Stella Collins. LinkedIn, nd. www.linkedin.com/in/stellacollinslearningrevolution (archived at https://perma.cc/8HKV-PFNU)

11 Julie Dirksen. LinkedIn, nd. www.linkedin.com/in/juliedirksen (archived at https://perma.cc/P5T9-X3GE)

12 Patti Shank. LinkedIn, nd. www.linkedin.com/in/pattishank (archived at https://perma.cc/887R-KW6F)

13 Amy Brann. LinkedIn, nd. www.linkedin.com/in/amybrann (archived at https://perma.cc/QJ3T-NZZW)

14 Clark Quinn. LinkedIn, nd. www.linkedin.com/in/quinnovator (archived at https://perma.cc/RU32-ZNQC)

15 Will Thalheimer. LinkedIn, nd. www.linkedin.com/in/willthalheimer (archived at https://perma.cc/H7AM-44SU)

16 P Ashcroft, S Brown and G Jones (2020) *The Curious Advantage*, Laïki Publishing.

17 D H Taylor. Global Sentiment Survey 2025, Donald H Taylor, 2025. donaldhtaylor.co.uk/research_base/global-sentiment-survey-2025 (archived at https://perma.cc/PGY5-TRD9)

18 P Rebourgeon and P Sheppard. L&D innovation with AI – Pauline Rebourgeon and Peter Sheppard, Learning Uncut podcast, episode 152, 27 August 2024.

19 P Rebourgeon and P Sheppard. L&D innovation with AI – Pauline Rebourgeon and Peter Sheppard, Learning Uncut podcast, episode 152, 27 August 2024.

20 C Munger. The psychology of human misjudgment, speech transcript, James Clear, 1995. jamesclear.com/great-speeches/psychology-of-human-misjudgment-by-charlie-munger (archived at https://perma.cc/Q5X7-FLA8)

21 Author interview with Nick Shackleton-Jones, 25 March 2025.

22 J Arets, C Jennings and V Heijnen. What is the 70:20:10 model? 70:20:10 Institute, nd. 702010institute.com/702010-model (archived at https://perma.cc/9RZS-SM33)

23 Refer to Appendix 2 for an overview of the 5 Moments of Need model from Bob Mosher and Dr Conrad Gottfredson.

24 Refer to Appendix 2 for an overview of the 5Di model from Nick Shackleton-Jones which tackles this issue.

25 L Overton. Linking learning to business, Learning Changemakers, 2004. www.learningchangemakers.com/research_whitepapers/linking-learning-to-business (archived at https://perma.cc/UUF7-NHRR)

26 K Thomas. Thompson Reuters finds the recipe that ensues learning is linked to business success, Learning Changemakers, 2012. www.learningchangemakers.com/wp-content/uploads/Thomson_Reuters_Casestudy-final-2012.pdf (archived at https://perma.cc/X7U7-AZ3K)

27 L Overton, M Ockers and S Tipton (Emerging Stronger Alliance). Tool 5: L&D playbook for enabling busy managers, Learning Changemakers, 2024. www.learningchangemakers.com/research_whitepapers/tool-5-ld-playbook-for-enabling-busy-managers (archived at https://perma.cc/GXR2-NMZQ)

28 Laura Overton interview with Russell Woods, 12 February 2025.

29 L Waldman. Joining forces with your brain, Learning Pirate, nd. www.learningpirate.com/joining-forces-with-your-brain (archived at https://perma.cc/4R4G-5RQA)

30 C Moore. Action Mapping: A visual approach to training design, Cathy Moore blog, nd. blog.cathy-moore.com/action-mapping-a-visual-approach-to-training-design (archived at https://perma.cc/7DK8-Q9UA)

31 S Michie, M van Stralen and R West. The COM-B model for behavior change, The Decision Lab, nd. thedecisionlab.com/reference-guide/organizational-behavior/the-com-b-model-for-behavior-change (archived at https://perma.cc/WQ5A-QZKP)

32 See overview at Appendix 2.

33 Instructional Design Australia. Gagne's 9 Events of Instruction quick reference guide, Instructional Design Australia, nd. instructionaldesign.com.au/gagnes-9-events-of-instruction (archived at https://perma.cc/76EE-4N4G)

34 See overview at Appendix 2.

5

Improving

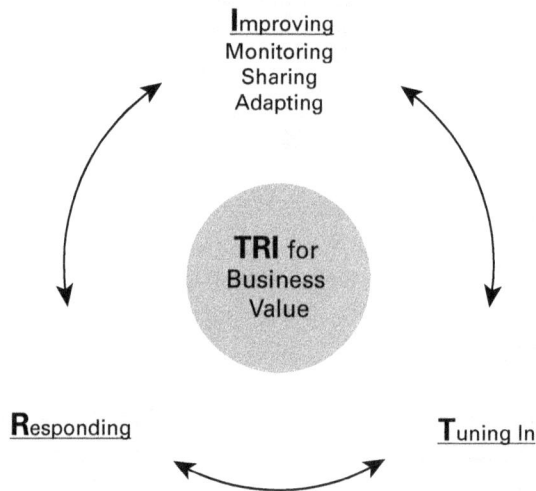

Improving
Monitoring
Sharing
Adapting

TRI for
Business
Value

Responding

Tuning In

From proving to Improving at a global eye-care company

When Marie Daniels joined a global eye-care company to lead the Commercial L&D function across APAC in early 2022, she discovered a function predominately focused on training events, where success was measured by attendance and feedback forms with limited connection to business results.[1]

Rather than trying to prove L&D's value through traditional metrics, Marie began monitoring what mattered to the business. For high-value programmes, she created metrics dashboards that listed potential business indicators already being tracked by the organization. She would review these with senior leaders, asking 'What impact do you want this initiative to have?' Together, they would select the most meaningful metrics to monitor.

In India, Marie and her team tracked three key indicators for a coaching programme: manager ratings of sales competencies, confidence scores and engagement survey results. By connecting these with sales performance, she gained insights into how the programme was influencing business outcomes. The data revealed that participants who fully engaged in the coaching process were showing improved results – several even went on to win top sales awards.

She established twice-yearly calibration sessions where sales managers reviewed real sales calls together, aligning on what 'good' looked like for specific selling skills. These sessions were not just about measurement – they created a feedback loop that continually improved both the learning initiatives and sales performance. When calibration revealed inconsistencies in how skills were being applied, Marie adjusted training approaches to address these gaps, leading to more consistent skills development across teams.

Over a three-year period, business leaders became more engaged, recognizing L&D as a critical partner in achieving their goals. The shift was a result of working closely with business leaders to measure and monitor what mattered to them, sharing progress and continually improving impact.

'The key is to stop looking for the perfect metric and start looking at what already exists. The business tracks so much data. When you collaborate with leaders to connect learning to the metrics they care about, suddenly L&D isn't just an add-on – it's a driver of real impact.'

Improving: What the data reveals[2]

The principle of Improving is where we see high-performing L&D teams dramatically pulling ahead of their peers. Data from the Learning Performance Benchmark reveals striking differences in how top-performing organizations approach data, evaluation and the process of adapting over the five-year period 2018–23 (Figure 5.1).

High-performing teams have fundamentally shifted their focus from proving value to improving it. While on average, less than two in five organizations tap into performance data, high-performing teams are not only Tuning In to metrics that matter to the business, they are four times as likely to be revisiting them to understand their progress.

What's particularly revealing is how these organizations approach continuous improvement. High performers are four times as likely to use

FIGURE 5.1 How are L&D leaders Improving? Shifts in practice 2018–23

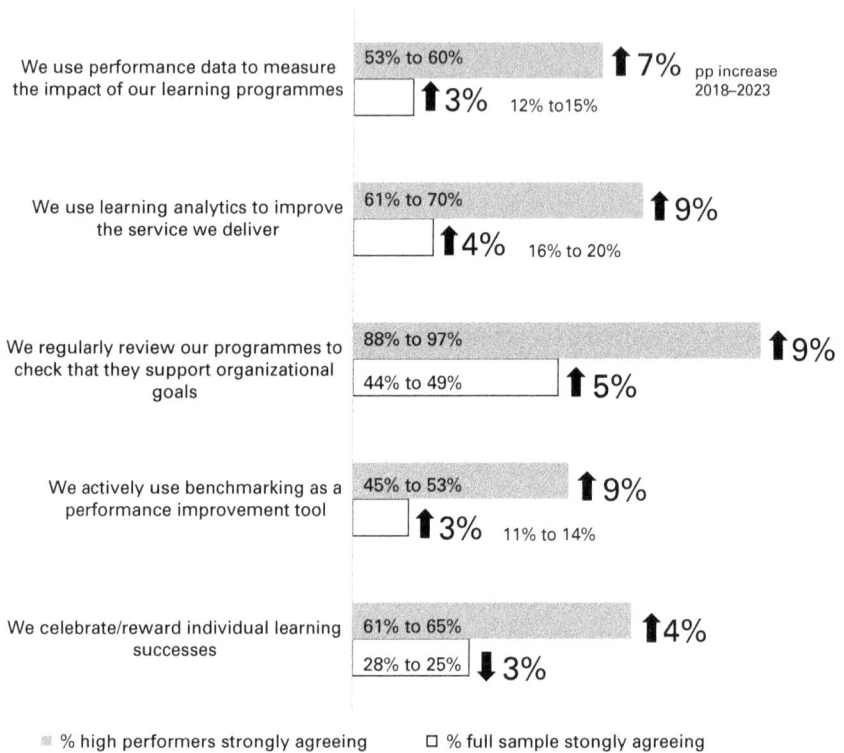

We use performance data to measure
the impact of our learning programmes
- 53% to 60% ↑7% pp increase 2018–2023
- ↑3% 12% to 15%

We use learning analytics to improve
the service we deliver
- 61% to 70% ↑9%
- ↑4% 16% to 20%

We regularly review our programmes to
check that they support organizational
goals
- 88% to 97% ↑9%
- 44% to 49% ↑5%

We actively use benchmarking as a
performance improvement tool
- 45% to 53% ↑9%
- ↑3% 11% to 14%

We celebrate/reward individual learning
successes
- 61% to 65% ↑4%
- 28% to 25% ↓3%

▨ % high performers strongly agreeing   ☐ % full sample stongly agreeing

benchmarking as an improvement tool and conduct regular programme reviews, compared to only a quarter of average organizations.

The patterns in Figure 5.1 extend to tracking application, where high performers are three times more likely to observe how learning is applied in real work settings. They're also significantly more proactive in communicating this impact, with 55 per cent regularly sharing insights with managers compared to just 35 per cent of average teams.

They are twice as likely to calculate meaningful return on investment (ROI) in ways that connect directly to business outcomes. But perhaps most significant is that it appears that success seeds success. In each of the metrics shared above, they are twice as likely to have increased their practice between 2018 and 2023.

These statistics tell a compelling story: high-performing L&D teams don't just excel at measuring – they excel at measuring what matters and using those insights to drive ongoing adaptation rather than simply justifying their existence.

Like Marie Daniels, high performers have shifted from proving value to improving it.

Navigation fundamentals 3: Improving

Improving is the navigation principle that shifts our focus from justifying L&D's value to continuously enhancing it through evidence-guided refinement. It transforms evaluation from a backward-looking proof exercise into a forward-looking adaptation tool that ensures solutions continue to deliver value.

At its core, this principle is about continually refining our responses based on evidence and feedback to land on the business impact that matters to our organization. It is not simply about evaluation. Many of us chase the perfect metric – ROI direct business results – hoping to capture the attention of budget holders.

But there's a problem with conflating Improving with evaluation: these 'perfect' metrics rarely materialize in the real world. Only a small percentage of organizations ever achieve comprehensive ROI measurement, with the majority trapped in discussions about why it can't be done rather than making incremental improvements based on available evidence.

Marie Daniels took a different path at her global eye-care company. Rather than pursuing perfect metrics, she became curious about what 'good' looked like to the business. By Tuning In to what mattered to stakeholders she created connections that led to collaboration. She realized that linking to existing business metrics told a more compelling story than creating L&D-specific measures disconnected from business realities.

Like a navigator who agrees their destination and then constantly adjusts course based on changing conditions, effective L&D leaders create feedback loops that drive ongoing adaptation. In complex environments, success comes not from perfectly executing a predetermined plan, but from continuously sensing, responding and refining their approach.

The practice of Improving

As learning professionals we often get trapped in linear thinking:

- 'How do I get buy-in?'
- 'How do I maintain funding?'
- 'How do I prove ROI?'

These questions assume a predictable world, but improvement isn't a straightforward process. I think we might have mentioned this before but reality is complex, interwoven and messy!

Improving is an ongoing practice which, working together with Tuning In and Responding, helps us anticipate rather than predict. High performers understand this distinction. They don't follow rigid processes but engage in continuous improvement practices, embracing uncertainty and developing the ability to tack and shift course when needed.

This builds anti-fragility – lasting improvement – not just a resilient return to the status quo.[3] When the unexpected happens (and it always will), we simply continue adapting, using evidence as our guide.

Using evidence to read the signs

Evidence guides our navigation. Just as wayfinders read the signs in their natural environment to guide their journey, L&D professionals need to accurately interpret the signals around them to maintain course. Each TRI principle relates to evidence in different ways:

- Tuning In helps us look for signals in our environment.
- Responding supports making evidence-informed choices about how to reach our goals.
- Improving involves gathering evidence to continuously assess our progress.

Think about how Nainoa Thompson approached his voyages. Each morning and evening as the sun rose and set, he asked himself: 'Where am I now?' He continuously adapted his course based on observations of stars, currents, wildlife and clouds. One journey that he expected to take a certain number of days and miles ended up being an entirely different route – yet his navigational skills, combined with continuous adaptation, still got him to his destination.

That's what we all need to be doing, each and every day. Improving is about the daily shifts we make to our sail plan rather than providing proof that our original plan was right.

What Improving isn't

To avoid misconceptions, let's clarify what Improving is not:

- an afterthought at the end of a project
- a beautiful dashboard to impress stakeholders
- equivalent to traditional evaluation (though sharing progress and impact is vital)

Instead, this principle keeps our goal of improving business value at the forefront while using evidence to stay on track.

Sometimes that is easier said than done!

What gets in our way?

Even when we recognize the value of the Improving principle, many of us struggle to put it into practice consistently. Here are common obstacles that get in the way of effective Improving:

- **Evaluation paradox:** We know evaluation matters, yet it remains one of our most neglected practices. Traditional approaches often feel disconnected from daily work – adding administrative burden while rarely delivering actionable insights. High-performing teams integrate lightweight measurement into their workflow.

- **Fear of findings:** When our professional identity is tied to the success of our initiatives, honest assessment feels threatening. Finding that our carefully designed programme missed the mark might trigger defensiveness, yet this discomfort is where real learning happens. Top performers treat unexpected outcomes as valuable data rather than failures.

- **Measurement misalignment:** We often track completion rates and satisfaction scores because they're easily available, even when they reveal little about business impact. If we only talk about cost efficiency or engagement we'll continue to be seen as a cost centre rather than a value creator.

- **Urgency trap:** Delivering the next project always seems more urgent than reflecting on the last one. The 'do more with less' pressure focuses us on output over outcomes. Successful teams protect time for reflection, knowing that small course corrections prevent larger problems.

- **Going solo:** Reviewing data without involving stakeholders or learners limits effectiveness and undermines buy-in. Top performers approach improvement collaboratively, involving business partners, managers and learners in reviewing impact and co-creating refinements.

- **Perfect metric pursuit:** Many of us search endlessly for the definitive metric that will prove our value – but there isn't one. This leads to unrealistic expectations. High performers use available evidence that enables action rather than waiting for perfect information.

Recognizing these barriers helps us become aware of what's holding us back. Effective Improving isn't about complex evaluation models or impressive reports – it's about creating simple, sustainable practices that help us continuously adapt based on what we observe.

Success leaves clues: Unpacking the principle of Improving

The principle of Improving shifts our focus from justifying L&D's value to continuously enhancing it through evidence-guided refinement. Like Polynesian navigators who constantly adjusted their course based on changing conditions, effective L&D professionals create feedback loops that drive ongoing adaptation.

Twenty years of benchmark data has taught us to recognize we are operating through Improving with three key behaviours.

1. Monitoring Progress

Monitoring isn't about proving value after the fact but actively gathering signals that guide ongoing adjustments.

Marie Daniels demonstrated this. Rather than creating separate L&D metrics, she collaborated with business leaders to identify existing indicators that would signal impact. In India, she monitored three key metrics for a coaching programme: manager ratings of sales competencies, confidence scores and engagement survey results. These indicators allowed her to make ongoing adjustments to improve outcomes.

High-performing teams establish feedback loops that provide timely insights, enabling them to adjust course before facing significant headwinds. This sub-principle manifests through two key behaviours.

(A) MEASURING THE RIGHT DATA

The evidence we gather shapes our understanding of value. When monitoring progress effectively, we start by ensuring we're tracking the right data points – those that genuinely indicate whether we're heading toward our destination.

How we perceive L&D's value profoundly impacts what evidence we pursue (Table 5.1). Consider the L&D Value Spectrum introduced in Chapter 1. Many teams get stuck monitoring only learning activity metrics like attendance or completion rates, missing what truly matters further to the right on the spectrum toward business impact.

TABLE 5.1 Indicators of value across the L&D Value Spectrum

Indicator	Value perception	Indicators of value
Leading	Activity	Attendance figures, completion rates, training hours delivered, on-demand resource usage
Lagging	Efficiency	Net savings in time/money/resources, reduced costs per participant, learner-to-facilitator ratio
Leading	Engagement	Net promoter scores, peer recommendations, voluntary participation rates, active contribution levels, social learning interactions, time in programme
Leading	Usefulness	Intention to apply, self-reported application in work, job aids accessed, confidence gains
Lagging	Performance	Speed to adoption/competency, error reduction, quality improvements, productivity gains, business KPI achievement
Lagging	Talent	Promotion readiness, skill levels, capability ratings, internal mobility, key talent retention, succession pipeline strength
Lagging	Culture	Innovation metrics, knowledge sharing behaviours, continuous improvement initiatives, organizational agility indicators, employee engagement

Measuring the right data involves selecting metrics that matter – beyond satisfaction scores as proxies for success. High-performing teams focus on impact, measuring skill development, behaviour change and business KPIs. They analyse data from multiple sources and use it for decision-making that drives continuous improvement.

Business impact data form lagging indicators – we can only access it after we have responded with an intervention. But given that the journey to business impact is a process of continually Tuning In, Responding and Improving, the learning impact data can provide us with leading indicators of success that help us adjust our course before reaching our destination.[4] McKinsey's feedback skills surge (Chapter 8) exemplifies this by tracking key metrics in a comprehensive dashboard that enables leaders to identify improvement opportunities before performance issues arise.

(B) EVALUATING IMPACT TOGETHER

Navigation requires coordination among all the stakeholders – a shared understanding of where we are headed and how we know we are on course. Similarly, Improving highlights that evaluation is almost always a collective endeavour.

When all stakeholders share ownership of both the journey and the destination the results are more sustainable. When Improving is a shared journey, we're much more likely to reach the desired destination.

The Benchmark data demonstrates that high-performing teams take a collaborative approach to evaluation. They routinely collect information on learning comprehension. But they don't stop there. They gather application data directly from learners about how they're using what they've learned. Most importantly, they involve line managers in the evaluation process, collecting their observations on how learning is being applied.

Marie Daniels' twice-yearly calibration sessions exemplify this collaborative approach. Sales managers reviewed real sales calls together, aligning on what 'good' looked like for specific selling skills. These sessions weren't just about measurement – they created a feedback loop that continually improved both the learning initiatives and sales performance.

This multi-perspective approach ensures that evaluation reflects the full reality of impact, not just a single viewpoint, while strengthening relationships that sustain Improvement.

MONITORING PROGRESS

- What business metrics currently exist in your organization that could serve as indicators of your learning initiatives' success? How might you connect to these?

- Which stakeholders might you involve in defining and monitoring progress for your next learning initiative? How will you engage them in this process?

- Think of a recent evaluation that didn't provide actionable insights. What would you change about your approach to make it more useful for decision-making?

- Which aspect of your current measurement approach feels most disconnected from business priorities? What small step could you take to better align it?

2. Sharing Progress

Effective navigation needs clear communication among the crew. Similarly, our ability to share progress in ways that resonate with stakeholders determines whether our initiatives maintain momentum or lose support.

While Tuning In and Responding create the opportunity for us to work together toward shared goals, Sharing Progress maintains that alignment through effective communication and shared celebration. Success lies in establishing common business goals and working toward them together.

High-performing teams excel at communicating progress and impact in ways that build credibility and support. They demonstrate two key behaviours that strengthen both specific initiatives and the overall perception of L&D's value.

(A) USING THE LANGUAGE OF BUSINESS

Successful navigation depends on clear communication – the whole crew must understand the signals that indicate whether we're on course. In L&D, sharing progress in ways that resonate with stakeholders influences whether our initiatives maintain momentum.

In the early 2000s, a large UK DIY chain was rolling out their first store credit card, to be sold by staff in store.[5] The L&D team supported this with online training initiatives. Instead of just tracking completion rates, they worked with their management information team to gather and display completion rates alongside card sales for each store. They shared this visual information regularly without claiming correlation or cause. Store managers could clearly see that locations with the highest completion rates also sold more cards. The L&D team didn't need to make a big thing of the results – the dashboard spoke for itself. It not only celebrated successful stores but motivated others to engage with the training. Good practice is timeless, and this straightforward approach to sharing learning progress alongside business progress remains relevant today.

High-performing learning teams don't just report against agreed targets; they ensure those who need to know about progress stay informed. The Learning Performance Benchmark found that high-performing teams are twice as likely to regularly communicate performance impacts to senior managers and line managers, creating transparency around progress and challenges.

When we communicate in business language – focusing on performance metrics, talent objectives and organizational priorities – we position learning as a driver of business outcomes rather than a separate activity. This shifts perception from L&D as a cost centre to a value creator.

(B) CELEBRATING TOGETHER

Recognition amplifies success. When we celebrate progress – even small wins – we reinforce the behaviours that lead to greater impact and build momentum for continued improvement. These moments strengthen bonds, reinforce habits and motivate continued effort. In L&D, celebration creates visibility of the link between learning initiatives and business outcomes.

A simple dashboard that displays success metrics can be a powerful celebration tool. When stakeholders can see the connection between learning engagement and business results, the case for continued investment becomes self-evident.

The Learning Performance Benchmark shows that high-performing teams excel at communicating how learning benefits the business. They celebrate individual learning successes and use external recognition opportunities, such as awards, to demonstrate achievement internally. These practices don't just recognize past success – they catalyse future improvement by making the impact of learning visible to the entire organization.

Multiplex (Chapter 7) demonstrated this by celebrating successes through industry awards and sharing their story through public platforms. This external recognition complemented their internal communication, creating multiple channels to showcase impact.

Effective celebration connects directly to business outcomes, acknowledging not just learning completion but application and impact. When we highlight how learning contributes to performance improvements, we reinforce the behaviours we want to see while building credibility for future initiatives.

SHARING PROGRESS

- How do you currently communicate progress to different stakeholder groups? What adjustments would make your communication more relevant to each audience?

- What opportunities exist to make the impact of learning more visible in your organization? Identify three places where successes could be shared more effectively.

- Think about your last 'celebration' of learning success. Did it focus on learning activity or business impact? How might you shift the emphasis?
- Which stakeholders currently receive no regular updates about learning impact? What simple, systematic communication approach could you implement to keep them informed?

3. Adapting Course

Conditions change – winds shift, currents alter and sometimes we run into unexpected storms. Adapting Course ensures we remain responsive to changing conditions, using evidence and feedback to refine our approach and maintain progress toward our destination.

While Monitoring Progress generates the insights and Sharing Progress communicates them, Adapting Course puts those insights into action. High-performing teams demonstrate two key behaviours that transform feedback into continuous improvement.

(A) BRINGING THE OUTSIDE IN

No navigator operates in isolation. Traditional wayfinders learned from each, sharing knowledge of stars, currents and islands across generations. Today's L&D professionals need the same external perspective to avoid becoming trapped in organizational echo chambers.

Benchmarking is a powerful way to access this crucial outside view. When AstraZeneca (Chapter 6) embarked on their learning transformation journey, they used external benchmarking data to demonstrate that despite comparatively high learning spend, its quality and impact were below par. This evidence-based approach helped secure buy-in for their transformation initiative by showing clear gaps and opportunities.

Benchmarking can be informal – through conversations, awards, events and case studies – or formal, involving systematic evidence gathering from a wide range of organizations. Both approaches help us make strategic decisions based on evidence rather than assumptions.

The choice of what to benchmark significantly influences how L&D is perceived and valued. Table 5.2 contrasts old-style benchmarks that focus on inputs and activities with new benchmarks that measure business impact and outcomes.

Traditional benchmarking comparisons often focus on the learning value end of the spectrum – cost per learner, pass rates and course completion rates. These metrics, while easy to measure, contribute little to driving business

TABLE 5.2 Benchmarks and consequences

Learning benchmarks	Benchmark consequences
Old benchmarks	
Input indicators:	
• Budget	• L&D perceived as cost centre
• Head count	• Business expectations are to cut costs
• Completion rates	• Busyness/keep up and/or complacency
• Hours spent training	
Industry trends:	
• Who is doing what?	• Following fads
	• L&D caught in the past
New benchmarks	
Business KPIs:	
• Productivity gains	• L&D providing added value
• Agility improvements	• Business expectation is to increase resources
Staff KPIs:	
• Engagement rates	• Prioritized actions that deliver results
• Time to competency	
L&D metrics:	
• Evidence-informed learning effectiveness metrics	• Firm foundations
• Key L&D metrics proven to drive results	• L&D prepared for the future

impact. In contrast, benchmarking at the business value end of the spectrum provides a completely different perspective, focusing our attention on what genuinely matters to the organization and shifting how L&D is valued.

The Learning Performance Benchmark data shows that organizations actively using these new benchmarks as performance improvement tools achieve significantly better results. Those participating in the Benchmark year after year are nearly twice as likely to report benefits in agility, productivity and process improvement.

A word of caution – benchmarking only produces good results when we do it thoroughly and with intent. Blindly copying what others do isn't the same as learning from others and adapting practices to our own context.

(B) EMBRACING IMPROVEMENT

Conditions change in the workplace constantly! The principle of Improving reconnects us to Tuning In – listening to what's happening around us and what people are saying.

While analytics and dashboards provide valuable data, they often lag behind the real-time insights that come from conversation and observation. Inviting those around us to share their thoughts and insights can reveal subtle shifts before they appear in formal metrics. Perhaps someone in sales has noticed a change in customer conversations that hasn't yet impacted the numbers, but warrants consideration.

Improving means creating an environment where feedback flows freely and adaptation becomes second nature.

Coles and Liberate Learning (Chapter 9) demonstrated this approach by starting with a minimum viable product (MVP) and iteratively improving it based on feedback from business subject matter experts and end-users. Their technical team proactively suggested new features that improved the user experience, showing how improvement thrives in environments where feedback is valued and acted upon.

The Learning Performance Benchmark shows that organizations with strong feedback loops adapt more quickly to changing business conditions and deliver more relevant solutions. They don't wait for perfect information before making adjustments – they embrace a pragmatic approach that values progress over perfection, making small course corrections that keep them moving toward their destination.

ADAPTING COURSE

- How might you gather more real-time feedback about how your learning initiatives are working? Consider both formal and informal approaches.

- When was the last time you made a significant adaptation to a learning initiative based on feedback? What barriers prevented earlier adjustment?

- What external benchmarks or comparisons could provide valuable perspective on your current approach? Who might have solved similar challenges?

- What's one practice from another industry or function that you could experiment with in your L&D approach? How might you adapt it to your context?

Improving at a glance

Improving shifts us from proving our value to continuously enhancing it through evidence-guided refinement. When it comes to demonstrating our business value, rather than evaluating learning as an afterthought, the Improving principle embeds ongoing adaptation into our daily practice so that we reach our business goals.

The three dimensions of Improving work together as an integrated approach:

- **Monitoring Progress** creates meaningful feedback loops that provide timely insights about what's working and what isn't.
- **Sharing Progress** communicates learning's impact in ways that build credibility and maintain momentum.
- **Adapting Course** ensures we remain responsive to changing conditions, using evidence to refine our approach.

By applying these dimensions, L&D professionals transform evaluation from a backward-looking proof exercise into a forward-looking navigation tool that keeps us on course toward meaningful impact.

Practical ideas to improve Improving

The principle of Improving is most powerful when applied intentionally to our specific context, addressing the unique barriers and opportunities we face. The following example demonstrates how one L&D leader addressed a business challenge through deliberate application of the Improving principle.

USING AI FOR DATA-DRIVEN IMPROVING

When global consultancy firm Leyton shifted to hybrid work, James Swift, their Talent Director, faced a familiar but critical challenge: client retention was falling and managers could no longer observe critical client interactions that drove engagement.[6]

Rather than guessing at solutions, James identified what excellence looked like by analysing top performers' calls. By Tuning In he identified eight specific behaviours that consistently appeared in successful client interactions and then went on to find out the extent of the challenge ahead. Working with their technology team, James customized their AI system to explore the extent to which these behaviours showed up in client interactions. The initial findings were sobering – critical skills appeared in fewer than 20 per cent of client calls.

James' team used this insight to transform their approach to addressing the challenge, developing tools and guidance and creating a skills framework for targeted coaching and implementing weekly data reviews. The AI continued to monitor the expected behaviours, and when certain behaviours didn't improve he adjusted the coaching, creating focused practice scenarios for those specific skills.

Within eight months, 80 per cent of best-practice behaviours appeared in 80 per cent of client calls and client retention significantly improved.

James shows us that Tuning In to specific observable behaviours linked to business outcomes creates a foundation for meaningful improvement. By establishing clear success criteria and continuously adapting interventions based on evidence, he demonstrated how the Improving principle transforms performance challenges into measurable progress.

Improving transforms our L&D practice from seeking perfect measurement to taking pragmatic action based on available evidence. The approaches below offer practical ways to overcome common barriers, shifting our focus from proving worth to continuously enhancing impact.

TABLE 5.3 Using the Improving principle to create opportunities

Barriers	Mindset shift	Try this	To improve this
Evaluation paradox	From: We need to prove our value To: We're continuously enhancing our contribution	• Integrate simple check-ins into existing processes rather than creating separate evaluation activities • Create one-page dashboards that track 3–5 key indicators aligned with business priorities • Conduct 'progress pulse' mini-surveys (up to 3 questions) after key milestones	• Strategic alignment with business priorities • Faster decision-making based on timely insights • Reduced administrative burden while increasing valuable feedback

(continued)

TABLE 5.3 (Continued)

Barriers	Mindset shift	Try this	To improve this
Fear of findings	From: Feedback threatens our value To: Feedback strengthens our impact	• Begin team meetings by sharing one thing that didn't work as expected and what you learned • Use 'What? So what? Now what?' framework to make feedback constructive and action-oriented • Develop a simple recognition system that celebrates both individual application and team progress toward learning goals	• Psychological safety that encourages honest assessment • Growth mindset that embraces learning from outcomes • Willingness to experiment and innovate
Going solo	From: L&D owns improvement alone To: We improve through collective wisdom	• Create improvement pairs with key stakeholders to review data together • Run a 'data story circle' where stakeholders interpret data from their perspective before drawing conclusions together • Involve diverse functional experts to bring fresh perspectives to your improvement approach	• Shared responsibility for improvement across functions • Richer insights through multiple perspectives and expertise • Stronger partnerships with business stakeholders
Perfect metric pursuit	From: We need perfect data before acting To: Actionable insights trump perfect information	• Apply the 80/20 rule: identify the 20% of metrics that deliver 80% of insights • Set time limits on data analysis before moving to action • Ask 'What's the least amount of data we need to make a better decision?'	• Action orientation that prevents analysis paralysis • Resource optimization by focusing on high-value measurement activities • Practical approach, evidence-based decisions that balance rigor with timeliness

(continued)

TABLE 5.3 (Continued)

Barriers	Mindset shift	Try this	To improve this
Measurement misalignment	From: Measure what's convenient To: Measure what creates value	• Map your current metrics against business priorities to identify gaps • Interview stakeholders about what metrics actually influence their decisions • Connect learning data to existing business KPIs rather than creating separate measures	• Direct connection between learning initiatives and business outcomes • Credibility through metrics that matter to senior leaders • Relevant insights that drive business value
Urgency trap	From: No time for improvement To: Improvement is how we work	• Block small, regular time slots for improvement rather than waiting for large chunks • Create improvement rituals that become habitual (e.g. 15-minute Friday reflections) • Make improvement visible by tracking small wins on a shared board	• Sustainable improvement practices integrated with daily work • Cultural shift that values reflection as productive work • Incremental progress that accumulates over time

For aspiring leaders

You don't need a senior title to begin Improving today. In fact, your fresh perspective and curiosity to ask 'Is this working?' can be your greatest asset in helping to unlock business value. Start small, document what you learn, and you'll build both confidence and credibility.

Consider these approaches:

• Have brief follow-up conversations with participants to discover how they're applying what they learned.

• Collaborate with data-minded colleagues to strengthen your measurement approach.

- Gather perspectives from participants, their managers and performance data to see the complete picture.
- Recognize and share instances of successful learning application to build momentum.
- Explore models that provide structured approaches to Improving

Improving doesn't require perfect metrics or complex analytics. Start with curiosity and the willingness to adapt based on what you learn.

MODELS TO SUPPORT IMPROVING

These models provide structured approaches to Improving until it becomes more intuitive:

- Kirkpatrick-Katzell Four Levels: Provides a progressive framework for measuring reaction, learning, behaviour and results to guide evaluation efforts across different dimensions of impact.[7]
- Learning-Transfer Evaluation Model (LTEM): Offers eight tiers from attendance to effects of transfer that create guideposts for continuous improvement based on learning science principles.[8]
- Success Case Method (Robert Brinkerhoff): Focuses on identifying and analysing successful learning applications to understand what drives real-world impact in your specific context.[9]
- Plan, Do, Check, Act (PDCA): Delivers a systematic cycle of planning, execution, verification and refinement for the continuous improvement of learning initiatives.[10]
- Action Learning: Combines working on real organizational challenges with reflective questioning to create dual outcomes of addressing immediate issues while developing people.[11]

Use these models to guide your exploration, combining elements that work for Improving in your context rather than implementing any single approach in isolation.

For seasoned L&D leaders

Giving yourself and your team the gift of time to breathe, reflect and adjust isn't a luxury, it's a necessity. Creating space for Improving provides permission to learn and safeguards your team's strategic relevance as business needs evolve.

Consider these approaches:

- Identify which metrics actually drive decisions and eliminate those that merely create unused reports.
- Integrate improvement into existing business processes rather than creating separate evaluation activities.
- Share your own course corrections openly to create safety for honest improvement conversations.
- Equip managers with simple tools to support learning transfer and communicate results to their teams.
- Protect time for reflection by building it into project timelines and team responsibilities.

Your leadership influence offers the opportunity to shift organizational perception of evaluation from a burdensome requirement to a valuable navigation tool that keeps learning aligned with business needs.

WHAT WILL YOU TRY?

Take out your Field Notebook and reflect on how you might strengthen the Improving principle in your practice:

- Which specific approach from this chapter resonates most strongly with your current challenges? How might you implement it in the next two weeks?
- What current measurement practice is taking significant time but providing limited value? How might you refocus that energy toward more meaningful improvement?
- Which barriers to Improving do you encounter most frequently? What one adjustment could help you overcome your most significant barrier?

These reflections will help you begin shifting from evaluation as a periodic event to improvement as an ongoing practice, ensuring your learning initiatives remain relevant and impactful.

Shifting mindset and practice

The Improving principle shifts the question for L&D professionals from 'How can we prove our value?' to 'How can we continuously enhance our impact?'

This fundamentally changes not just what we measure but why we measure it. Rather than collecting evidence to defend our existence, we gather signals that guide the adaptation of our journey. Instead of treating evaluation as a final judgement that happens after the work is done, we embed feedback loops throughout the entire learning process.

At its core, Improving reframes L&D's relationship with evidence – from using data defensively to wielding it as a powerful tool for continuous adaptation in service of business value.

Moving forward to TRI principles in action

The Improving principle transforms evaluation from a justification exercise into a powerful navigation tool. Marie Daniels demonstrated this shift by tracking what mattered to the business rather than just L&D activity. Through her calibration sessions and continuous refinement based on real-world evidence, she kept learning initiatives on course toward meaningful business impact even as conditions changed. Her approach reminds us that improvement isn't about proving our worth but about continuously enhancing our value.

As we move forward, we'll examine how all three TRI principles work together in practice through comprehensive real-world examples. To round out Part Two, we'll explore AstraZeneca's learning transformation, which offers a powerful demonstration of the TRI principles working together. Their journey illustrates how Tuning In to business priorities, Responding with evidence-informed choices, and continuously Improving created a learning ecosystem that delivered measurable impact during a period of strategic change.

Part Three will then take us deeper into how different organizations have applied these principles to address specific challenges in various contexts. These stories will help us envision how we can adapt these principles to navigate our own unique terrain, whether we're dealing with immediate performance needs, preparing for uncertain futures or building stronger partnerships.

By seeing these principles in action across diverse organizations we'll gain practical insights that can guide our own navigation, helping us chart a course that creates lasting value in our own context.

Notes

1 Michelle Ockers interview with Marie Daniels, 4 March 2025.

2 Source of all benchmarking data in this chapter: Learning Performance Benchmark study, see Appendix 1.

3 D Hillson. Beyond resilience: Towards antifragility? *Continuity and Resilience Review*, 2023, 5 (2), 210–26.

4 B Marr. What's the difference between lagging and leading indicator? Forbes, 2020. www.forbes.com/sites/bernardmarr/2020/10/23/whats-the-difference-between-lagging-and-leading-indicator (archived at https://perma.cc/N5B2-BDB9)

5 Example from the experience of Laura Overton who worked on this project.

6 J Swift. James Swift: Human centric organizational performance, Diary of a CLO podcast, 8 January 2025.

7 Known in popular shorthand as the 'Kirkpatrick' model. Kirkpatrick Partners. The Kirkpatrick model, Kirkpatrick Partners (nd). www.kirkpatrickpartners.com/the-kirkpatrick-model (archived at https://perma.cc/2SN3-QGXW)

8 W Thalheimer. The NEW LTEM was published on 31 October 2024, Work–Learning Research, 2024. www.worklearning.com/ltem (archived at https://perma.cc/5RVS-28V9)

9 R O Brinkerhoff (2018) *The Success Case Method: Find out quickly what's working and what's not*, Berrett-Koehler, San Francisco.

10 Lean Enterprise Institute. Plan, Do, Check, Act (PDCA), Lean Enterprise Institute, nd. www.lean.org/lexicon-terms/pdca (archived at https://perma.cc/K6XS-PGGZ)

11 Action Learning Institute. What is Action Learning? Action Learning Institute, nd. actionlearning.edu.au/what-is-action-learning (archived at https://perma.cc/6RZZ-G4AP)

6

Integrating TRI

AstraZeneca's learning transformation

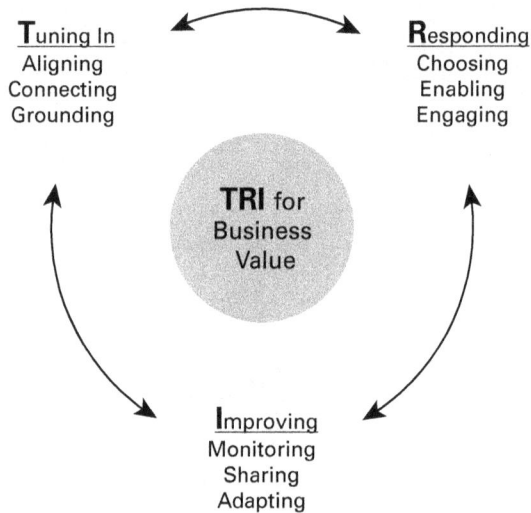

Tuning In — Responding

Tuning In
Aligning
Connecting
Grounding

Responding
Choosing
Enabling
Engaging

TRI for
Business
Value

Improving
Monitoring
Sharing
Adapting

In Chapters 3–5 we explored each TRI principle individually, examining how Tuning In creates awareness, Responding enables intentional action and Improving drives continuous adaptation.

At this pivotal point in your journey, we turn to a comprehensive example from AstraZeneca that demonstrates how these principles work as an integrated system. This bridge between understanding individual principles and applying them in specific contexts helps solidify your understanding of TRI as a holistic approach to navigation.

As you read about AstraZeneca's learning transformation, your unique perspective will shape what you notice. Whether you are an aspiring or seasoned L&D leader, bring experience from multinational corporations or small businesses, specialize in digital learning or leadership development or come from L&D, HR or another field entirely, your lens matters. Your industry background, professional expertise, organizational culture experiences and personal learning journey all influence how you interpret their transformation.

There's no 'right' way to see this example; the richness comes from your individual insights. If you are reading this book alongside colleagues, discuss this example with them to share different perspectives and deepen your collective understanding.

WHAT DO YOU SEE?

Use these questions to reflect on the AstraZeneca example in your Field Notebook:

- Which elements of Tuning In, Responding and Improving do you recognize in AstraZeneca's approach?
- How did their organizational context (for example, size, industry, global presence) influence how they applied the TRI principles?
- Which specific approaches resonated with you, and why might they have been effective in AstraZeneca's environment?
- How might similar approaches need to be adapted to work in your context?

AstraZeneca: Transforming learning to create business value

The catalyst for change

In 2019 AstraZeneca,[1] a global science-led pharmaceutical company with over 85,000 employees across more than 100 countries, embarked on a learning transformation to support their new business strategy. The business strategy focused on Growth Through Innovation and included a pillar to be a Great Place to Work. Under this pillar AstraZeneca sought to engage, equip and support its workforce to meet evolving business needs and support its employees to reach their full potential. The Talent and Development team shaped a unified and strategic approach to learning which was integrated with other initiatives to being a Great Place to Work.

Confronting learning transformation

AstraZeneca's learning infrastructure was fragmented, with 75 different technology platforms and content siloed by business units, mostly limited to English. This disjointed approach hindered access to high-quality learning resources and created inefficiencies that did not align with the company's vision of agility and innovation.

It was clear to Marc Howells, VP Talent & Development, that a simplified, modular and connected learning strategy and ecosystem was critical to attract, retain and develop the agile workforce needed to achieve AstraZeneca's business goals. However, a business case and value proposition had to be established to gain traction in the organization.

Garnering executive support: The art of strategic persuasion

To gain buy-in, Howells focused on business value, linking learning transformation to the Great Place to Work strategy pillar. This pillar focused on three key elements: shifting leadership behaviours for better cross-functional collaboration; upskilling and reskilling employees to meet future needs; and developing a diverse leadership pipeline to sustain the company's long-term strategy.

Howells used benchmarking data to demonstrate that despite comparatively high spend, its quality and impact were sub-optimal.[2] This data-driven approach showed that an overhaul was needed to improve the business value of learning and learner experience. By linking learning transformation to business objectives and value creation, Howells successfully secured the funding for the initiative.

Democratizing learning: A vision for inclusive growth

At the heart of AstraZeneca's vision was to make learning a daily habit accessible to all employees, regardless of location, language or department. They expanded learning resources into 14 languages, covering over 85 per cent of the workforce's primary languages. They also removed silos restricting access to resources by business unit, enabling cross-functional development.

This democratization of learning fostered collaboration and a growth mindset across the organization, where employees feel empowered to be proactive about their development and equipped with future-ready skills to support long-term business objectives. By making learning a part of everyday work, AstraZeneca aimed to drive both individual and organizational growth through innovation.

Leveraging technology as an enabler

Technology was pivotal to achieving AstraZeneca's vision. They reduced 75 disjointed systems to 12 core platforms, anchored by a modern learning experience platform designed to be as intuitive as a consumer app. This platform offered resources ranging from technical skills to leadership development, with personalized learning recommendations based on employee preferences and career goals.

The integration of AI-powered adaptive learning technologies provided personalized learning suggestions and connected employees with communities of practice, fostering collaboration across the company. This shift helped AstraZeneca build a culture of learning that was not only accessible but also scalable to meet the needs of a rapidly changing industry and push the boundaries of medical science.

Executing the vision

AstraZeneca adopted a measured approach, focusing on strong governance and stakeholder engagement to ensure a successful rollout. An enterprise learning board composed of senior business leaders ensured alignment with the company's strategic goals, while an advisory board of learning subject matter experts helped shape the new learning ecosystem.

Leadership development was a key focus, with 21 business specific academies created to support role-specific development. The company also launched targeted learning programmes in fast-growing markets, ensuring that talent from these regions could take on global roles, contributing to a more diverse and future-ready leadership team.

Making learning a daily habit

Central to AstraZeneca's learning culture was the idea of making learning a daily habit. The company conducted a behavioural change trial with 300 employees, encouraging them to journal their daily learning moments. Initially met with resistance, the practice gained traction, and by the end of the trial over 80 per cent of participants had adopted the habit of reflection.

Building on this experimental insight, AstraZeneca integrated behavioural nudges into its learning technologies, encouraging employees to engage in continuous, bite-sized micro learning. The content was diversified, offering a range of formats to increase accessibility and motivation, further embedding learning into the everyday fabric of work to support ongoing growth.

Navigating challenges and gaining buy-in

Implementing the learning transformation was not without its challenges. Convincing business leaders to transition from established systems required careful stakeholder engagement. Howells and his team focused on understanding each business unit's priorities and identified quick wins to build credibility. These early successes were critical in gaining wider support and maintaining momentum.

The governance model ensured continuous alignment with evolving business needs. This approach also helped build advocacy for the transformation across the organization, ensuring that learning remained a priority even as business goals shifted.

Measuring progress and success

AstraZeneca established a robust system for tracking the impact of its learning transformation. The company monitored 26 key metrics on a quarterly basis, focusing on leadership confidence, effectiveness of upskilling initiatives and alignment with business goals. Employee engagement surveys measured perceptions of skill development and the quality of discussions with line managers, while turnover rates were tracked to assess the impact of learning investments on retention.

The impact was directly tied to the Great Place to Work pillar – engaging, equipping and supporting its workforce to contribute to Growth Through Innovation. Employees engaged in learning are twice as likely to stay with the company and 20 per cent more likely to be promoted, supporting the goal of building a diverse leadership pipeline. Leadership effectiveness also improved, with 89 per cent of employees reporting quality discussions with their managers.

Additionally, the overall cost of learning decreased by 25 per cent whilst increasing the offering by 600 per cent annually supporting 12,000 employees to experience a facilitated cohort-based offering. This expanded access to learning resources and experiences enhances AstraZeneca's ability to upskill its workforce which is critical to meeting future business needs.

Conclusion

AstraZeneca's learning transformation created a scalable, flexible and intuitive learning ecosystem and fostered a lifelong learning culture that contributed to the organization's business strategy. By embedding learning into the organization's culture, AstraZeneca not only enhanced employee engagement and leadership effectiveness but also equipped its workforce with the future-ready skills necessary for sustained growth and innovation. This strategic alignment of learning with business objectives positioned AstraZeneca for long-term success and to create value for people, society and the planet in an increasingly competitive and complex industry.

> We needed to build a coalition of the willing that understood that where we were going would benefit everybody. It would improve the experience, help us be ready for the future and ultimately build an agile and adaptable workforce.
> *Marc Howells, Former VP Talent and Development, AstraZeneca*[3]

TRI principles in action at AstraZeneca

Here are some of our key observations of how AstraZeneca's learning transformation demonstrates the TRI principles in action, noting that they may be different to what stood out to you.

Tuning In

- **Aligning Together:** Connected learning directly to the Great Place to Work strategic pillar with board-level accountability.
- **Connecting to Individuals:** Expanded learning resources into 14 languages, recognizing diverse needs across their global workforce.
- **Grounding in the Real World:** Acknowledged fragmented technology limited and built solutions compatible with existing culture and systems.

Responding

- **Choosing Well:** Used benchmarking data to inform decisions and created 21 business-specific academies with varied learning approaches.
- **Enabling Learning:** Implemented intuitive platform, conducted behavioural change trials and embedded learning into daily work.
- **Engaging Influencers:** Established both a senior leadership board and expert advisory panel to ensure alignment and advocacy.

Improving

- **Monitoring Progress:** Tracked 26 business-relevant metrics quarterly.
- **Sharing Progress:** Communicated impact in business terms that resonated with stakeholders.
- **Adapting Course:** Continuously refined their ecosystem based on feedback and performance data.

The power of AstraZeneca's transformation came from integrating all three principles into a cohesive approach that maintained alignment with business goals while enabling continuous adaptation.

BOLD mindset: A preview

While we'll explore the BOLD mindset more fully in Part Four, we can already see elements of it emerging in Marc Howell's actions:

- **Business-First** thinking was evident in the consistent connection of learning transformation to strategic business pillars rather than positioning it as a separate L&D initiative.

- **Open Minded** approaches appeared as a willingness to challenge the existing learning infrastructure and experiment with new techniques like the learning journal trial.
- **Leading and Learning** showed in the balance of immediate implementation with continuous refinement, maintaining both direction and adaptability.
- **Deliberate** action was clear in their measured rollout, thoughtful governance structure and systematic measurement approach.

These glimpses suggest how a BOLD mindset supports effective application of the TRI principles – a connection we'll explore more deeply in Part Four.

From understanding to application: The path ahead

In Part Three we'll explore how the TRI principles apply in specific contexts – from supporting current performance to preparing for future challenges and building strategic partnerships. These targeted examples will provide practical insights that will spark ideas for applying the principles in your own unique environment.

Notes

1 Example based on Learning Transformation at AstraZeneca. Marc Howells, Learning Uncut podcast, episode 128, 8 August 2023, and author interview with Marc Howells, 14 October 2024.

2 Benchmarking was undertaken using the best High-Impact Learning Organization (HILO) model as outlined by J Bersin. The new best-practices of a high-impact learning organization, Josh Bersin Company, 2012. joshbersin. com/2012/09/the-new-best-practices-of-a-high-impact-learning-organization (archived at https://perma.cc/BW4Z-F8UC)

3 Author interview with Marc Howells, 14 October 2024.

PART THREE

Charting your course

7

Navigating safe waters

Equipped for today

Back in 2009, Adam Harwood was working as a Senior L&D consultant at Thomas Cook, a well-known travel company.[1] His team was running week-long classroom training courses for new holiday reps before they headed to their resorts. The feedback was fantastic. 'This is amazing,' Adam thought. 'Everyone's loving it.'

But the feedback changed. When those reps started working in their resorts, the managers began raising concerns. 'Hold on a minute,' they said. 'That person's not very good at what they're doing – they're not performing. You didn't train them right. Your course should have been longer or better.'

This feedback hit Adam hard. He thought the training had gone well, but it wasn't translating into on-the-job performance. That's when Adam realized something critical: it's about much more than classroom training. 'L&D isn't just about turning up, saying some stuff and hoping people perform,' he explained. 'There's so much more to it than that.'

This was a turning point for Adam, and it's shaped how he has approached L&D ever since. His experience makes us ask ourselves: how can we better equip people to perform well in their current roles? Since Adam's 'Aha!' moment things have only become more complex. The old way of doing things – mostly by delivering content – isn't cutting it anymore.

In this chapter we'll dive into how the TRI principles – Tuning In, Responding and Improving – can help us support people to do their best work right now. We'll examine today's L&D landscape, its challenges and see how two teams have tackled these challenges in ways consistent with the TRI principles. The goal? Practical insights to help you navigate your own organizational terrain more effectively to help people to perform well today.

The familiar waters of today

For us in L&D navigating today's waters means meeting day-to-day organizational needs. It's ensuring new starters ramp up quickly. It's making sure compliance training gets done. It's helping everyone develop skills to perform their current job well.

Our approach to today's challenges is often shaped by past successes. We easily get stuck in a loop. Old methods don't just constrain us – they shape other people's expectations. This makes it harder to evolve our practice.

This pattern begins with onboarding – the first impression new starters get of learning in our organization. It continues with compliance training that people repeat, often yearly.

It's like driving the same route daily. Autopilot kicks in. As RedThread Research put it in their 2021 learning content study, 'L&D functions have historically spent most of their time and energy enabling employees to consume content. Creating and delivering training courses is a core L&D competency.'[2] They went on to state that their research emphasizes 'that there's much, much more to employee development than courses alone – and L&D needs to expand its repertoire of learning methods accordingly'.

The study identified six key learning behaviours: plan, discover, consume, experiment, connect and perform. Yet most organizations over-rely on just one: content consumption. The ATD's 2023 *State of the Industry* report backs this up.[3] In particular, content-heavy approaches still dominate onboarding and compliance.

We create content because it's what we've always done, despite having better options. Many of us feel trapped in this content creation cycle. We worry that without tangible outputs our value will be questioned.

This over-reliance on content means missed opportunities for deeper learning and better performance. We need a better way.

Yet these familiar waters offer opportunities to experiment. We can involve employees in co-designing solutions or test methods to support skill development during work. These small experiments in low-stakes environments prepare us for the more complex challenges that lie beyond the horizon which we will explore in Chapter 8.

The overwhelm of equipping people for today

The volume and repetitiveness of tasks for today's needs can feel relentless. Compliance. Onboarding. Product rollouts. But getting these basics right matters in ways that might not have crossed your mind.

It creates space for more strategic initiatives that drive adaptability. Effective essentials free up time. They conserve energy. They preserve budget. They release critical resources to respond to shifting business needs.

Beyond content overload, other challenges await us. You've likely encountered them yourself:

- **Information overload:** Stakeholders constantly push for 'all the detail' – especially in compliance programmes. More isn't better.

- **Ticking boxes:** Few things are as professionally unsatisfying as designing learning that meets legal requirements but fails to engage learners in any meaningful way.

- **Scaling personalization:** It's a tough balance to deliver training that meets individual needs at scale, creating a nagging sense of never quite hitting the mark.

- **Learning that sticks:** Moving beyond 'one and done' training to build lasting skills and behaviour change.

- **Balancing priorities:** Creating effective learning while minimizing disruption to operations is a tough balance.

- **Maximizing limited resources:** The art of stretching budgets and capacity while maintaining quality is a stress many of us are familiar with.

- **Measuring real impact:** Going beyond completion rates to measure performance improvement can feel like mastering a foreign language.

- **Fostering connection:** Creating genuine human interaction in increasingly remote environments has become simultaneously more essential and more elusive.

These challenges lead to low engagement with learning, frustrating follow-up on mandatory training completion and outdated materials. They can leave us feeling stretched thin and questioning our impact. When stakeholders keep pushing for more content despite evidence it isn't working, the frustration intensifies. The gap between what we know works and what we're able to implement can be disheartening.

Recent shifts compound these challenges. Remote work limits interactions. Digital tools evolve rapidly, making content obsolete quickly. Compliance grows more complex with new regulations in data protection, privacy and cybersecurity. Corporate ethics and social responsibility training expands. Global workforces demand culturally inclusive experiences that comply with local laws.

Sound familiar? You're not alone. But there's a better way forward.

TRI stepping back to get control

The TRI principles offer a deliberate approach to meet today's needs more effectively.

- **Tuning In** helps you to identify what really matters. It helps to align organizational priorities with individual motivations.
- **Responding** enables purposeful action. It guides you to use evidence to design learning that fits work environments and supports performance.
- **Improving** makes efforts more sustainable by monitoring progress and adapting solutions for greater impact.

Together, these principles provide a way to regain control. They ensure we're not just working efficiently but providing learning that makes a real difference.

But what does this look like in practice? Let's explore two real-world examples where L&D teams worked in ways that align with the TRI principles. These examples are intended to help you navigate your own challenges. They show how forward-thinking professionals move beyond the comfortable patterns, embracing new approaches and finding what truly works in their organization.

Breaking established patterns requires courage. It means letting go of the familiar. The professionals in our examples took calculated risks. They proposed new approaches that challenged organizational norms and faced the discomfort that of trying something new. As we will explore in Part Four, they adopted BOLD thinking habits.

As you read these examples, consider how the TRI principles are demonstrated. How did these teams navigate their unique challenges? What approaches might you apply in your context? After reflecting, compare your observations with our analysis to extract further insight.

EXPLORATION QUESTIONS

Tuning In

- How did the L&D team align their initiatives with the strategic organizational goals?
- What methods did they use to understand individual needs and motivations?
- How did they ensure their solution was grounded in workplace realities, culture and systems to ensure they were relevant and practical?

Responding

- How did they use insights and apply learning science when designing their approach?

- What strategies did they use to support and enable individuals and teams to apply what they learned?

- How did they involve and equip managers, peers or other stakeholders to support the initiative?

Improving

- What methods did they use to track the effectiveness and impact of their solution?

- How did they communicate progress to stakeholders and celebrate success?

- What steps did they take to refine their approach?

Multiplex: Re-shaping compliance training in the construction industry

Multiplex,[4] a leading global construction company, saw the need to tackle cultural issues in the industry to attract and retain diverse talent, particularly women. The construction industry is known for its tough working conditions. While there is growing openness to change, pockets of resistance remain, making it difficult to create an inclusive environment. Driven by their purpose to 'construct a better future', Multiplex developed the Appropriate Workplace Behaviour (AWB) programme to build a more welcoming, inclusive and respectful workplace. Their efforts aligned with the culture standard set by the Australian Construction Association, where Multiplex plays a key role.

Changing individual behaviours and organizational culture

The AWB programme was designed to help employees recognize what is appropriate and inappropriate behaviour, including subtle, 'blurry' behaviours that, whilst not illegal, can be damaging. A key goal was to empower employees to become 'upstanders' instead of bystanders, giving them the confidence to speak up when they see inappropriate behaviour. The programme also aimed to help employees manage their own behaviour, ensuring they stay 'above the line'.

The company aimed to change not only individual behaviours, but the entire organizational culture to attract and retain a diverse workforce. AWB was pivotal in promoting an inclusion mindset across all levels, making diversity and inclusion a shared responsibility. It is also a core part of their broader approach to creating a supportive and respectful environment where everyone feels valued and safe. It lays the foundations for other initiatives, including a comprehensive bias and inclusion programme, an enhanced parental leave policy, employee networks and a new process to actively manage female talent.

Creating a meaningful, memorable learning experience

Multiplex wanted to create a learning experience that was meaningful and memorable, moving away from a simple 'tick-the-box' approach to truly support behavioural change in their workplace context. They designed for a workforce spread across different locations, mainly on construction sites, including long-term industry workers who might resist change. The programme had to create a sense of psychological safety, especially in workshops, to allow open discussions on sensitive topics. They used a fresh, modern, visually appealing approach to connect with their large Millennial workforce group.

The programme was a blended learning experience, starting with an interactive online course that introduced key behaviour frameworks. This online course was especially useful for reaching Multiplex's workforce spread across multiple locations. Participants watched engaging videos showing real-life scenarios filmed on construction sites with Multiplex employees from all levels of the business. After watching, they answered questions to identify upstanders and bystanders or to classify behaviours as above, below or on the blurred line.

The importance of a safe space

After completing the course, participants joined a 90-minute live virtual workshop to apply what they learned. These small-group sessions, usually with about 12 participants and two facilitators, were designed to create a safe space for open discussions. Participants shared real-life experiences in breakout groups, often revealing personal and powerful stories about workplace behaviour issues they had faced. Having two facilitators allowed for better support in these smaller breakout groups.

Co-creating ongoing support

To maintain behaviour change, Multiplex provided ongoing support and follow-up activities to ensure that the principles introduced during training were reinforced and integrated into daily work. These follow-up actions were created with input from participants, who anonymously shared their thoughts on a digital whiteboard about the challenges of being an upstander, their commitments to change and ideas for implementing appropriate workplace behaviour. More than 3,000 Post-it notes were collected from these sessions and used to develop an action plan for an ongoing campaign to embed behaviours. This includes a participant hand-out with key messages and access to relevant policies and procedures on workplace behaviour, and posters across all construction sites and offices.

Impact and next steps

Multiplex evaluated the AWB programme through participant feedback, unsolicited feedback, rates of reporting inappropriate behaviour and data from sources like employee experience surveys and exit interviews. After completing the workshops, nearly all participants reported feeling confident in recognizing and addressing inappropriate behaviours. The rise in reporting of inappropriate behaviour suggested that employees felt more empowered to speak up. Anecdotal evidence shows that the language from the key frameworks introduced in the programme is being used and behaviours are changing. Multiplex continues to make positive strides in diversity supported by a broad range of initiatives.

The online course has been embedded in new starter induction and is being piloted with their contractor workforce to identify adaptations required for this audience. Multiplex also plans to extend the course to their subcontractor workforce, generating a broader industry impact. Lessons from the AWB programme have been integrated into the design of other programmes, emphasizing the importance of creating real and engaging learning experiences, particularly for compliance training.

> If you're going to put every single person in your organization through a learning experience, that's a massive opportunity. You can get a huge ripple effect of change if you do it really well. So, invest the time, invest the money and invest the creativity. *Annaleigh McKay, Director of Learning and Culture, Global, Multiplex*[5]

> WHAT DID YOU SEE?
>
> Reflect on the Multiplex example:
>
> - How did Multiplex address the common L&D challenges outlined earlier in the chapter?
> - Which TRI principles were most clearly demonstrated?
> - How did the construction industry context shape their application of these principles?
> - What might you have done differently if you were leading this initiative?
> - What one idea from this example could you adapt for your own context?

Multiplex: Principles in action

Tuning In

ALIGNING TOGETHER

- Linked programme to organizational purpose of constructing a better future.
- Established clear link between workplace behaviour and strategic goal of attracting diverse talent.
- Connected initiative to industry culture standards.

CONNECTING TO INDIVIDUALS

- Created safe spaces in workshops for open discussions on sensitive topics.
- Collected over 3,000 anonymous Post-it notes from participants about challenges and commitments.
- Considered the diverse backgrounds of employees from long-term industry workers to Millennial workforce.

GROUNDING IN THE REAL WORLD

- Filmed real-life scenarios on actual construction sites with employees for relevance and authenticity.
- Ensured the programme was accessible across all work locations.
- Recognized cultural aspects of the construction industry that needed addressing.

Responding

CHOOSING WELL

- Designed for meaningfulness, moving away from 'tick-the-box' compliance.
- Created fresh, modern, visually appealing approach for Millennial workforce.
- Applied self-determination theory to empower participants.

ENABLING LEARNING

- Developed a blended approach with interactive online course followed by workshops.
- Provided actionable frameworks to help employees identify and address inappropriate behaviours.
- Placed posters across construction sites and offices to reinforce behaviours.

ENGAGING INFLUENCERS

- Involved employees from all levels of business in videos, demonstrating organizational commitment.
- Used participant input to shape ongoing campaign to embed behaviours.
- Created participant handouts with key messages to support application.

Improving

MONITORING PROGRESS

- Evaluated through participant feedback and rates of reporting inappropriate behaviour.
- Used data from employee experience surveys and exit interviews to assess impact on organization culture.

SHARING PROGRESS

- Entered and won industry awards (Best Diversity and Inclusion programme at Australian Institute of Training and Development Excellence Awards).
- Communicated results through public platforms.

ADAPTING COURSE

- Incorporated course in new starter induction.
- Piloted programme with contractor workforce to identify audience-specific adaptations.
- Applied lessons learned to the design of other programmes, emphasizing engagement.

This programme strongly demonstrates the TRI principles, particularly **Grounding in the Real World** through authentic site scenarios and real employee involvement, and **Connecting to Individuals** by fostering psychologically safe workshop spaces. They effectively **Enabled Learning** through their blended design and practical behavioural frameworks, while demonstrating **Adapting Course** (literally!) by modifying the programme for different audiences and applying lessons to other initiatives. This example shows how a well-considered compliance approach can drive meaningful cultural change.

While Multiplex took on the challenge of deep cultural change in a traditionally resistant industry, in our next example Vitality faced a different challenge – keeping their workforce up to date in a fast-paced customer-focused environment.

Vitality: Supporting frontline performance in real-time

Vitality, a UK-based health and life insurer, uses a business model that incentivizes healthier lifestyle choices, delivering benefits to members, society and the business itself.[6] At the heart of this model is the Vitality programme, a behaviour change initiative embedded across their products. By partnering with various organizations Vitality offers rewards such as discounted Apple Watches or weekly coffees to members who meet weekly activity goals. This means that many members interact with the insurer each week.

Adopting a business-first approach

Vitality's customer service teams, 1,200 frontline workers in the UK and South Africa, operate in a complex and fast-paced environment, handling customer enquiries and issues related to health and life insurance. The roles require staying up to date with frequent product and services changes and continually integrating new information into their daily tasks while maintaining a customer-centric approach. This adaptability is critical to deliver high-quality service to their members in a high innovation organization.

The L&D team, led by Sebastian Tindall, faced an increasing workload due to the growing number of changes – from 14 projects per year in 2017 to over 170 by 2022. Recognizing the need for a more agile, efficient approach, Tindall shifted the team's focus to a business-first mindset, adapting L&D practices to align with rapidly changing business needs.

Training as a last resort

Classroom training had been the preferred method as it provided a comprehensive understanding of Vitality's products and services. However, as the frequency of updates and changes to products increased it became less viable. The workload to develop and deliver classroom changes became too high for the size of the L&D team. The sheer volume of changes also made it impractical to take employees away from their roles for classroom training. With a maximum of 140 minutes of training time allocated per frontline worker each month, classroom training simply couldn't keep up. The team needed a new approach to equip their workforce to perform effectively and best support their members, without relying solely on formal training, one that could provide just-in-time support and adapt quickly to frequent changes.

In response, the L&D team shifted to a resource-led approach, providing performance support resources that could be easily accessed and used by employees wherever feasible. They used a systematic approach to prioritize their work based on the size and complexity of each project. This approach focuses on collaboration and using the expertise of the people doing the job. Who knows better where to allocate resources or how to adapt systems to ease the load on frontline teams? Who can help create intuitive processes that don't rely on memory? These questions shaped how the team began operating. Training became only one option and was often replaced wherever possible with embedding knowledge into the process.

In 2022, Vitality introduced digital adoption platforms (DAPs), providing real-time process guidance for employees. This technology, especially beneficial for new starters and complex tasks, allows for quick updates as processes change, ensuring employees always have current information. The system also provides data on employee interactions, helping to refine training materials and resources.

Collaborating with the frontline workforce

The team grew from three people to 16 by 2020. Nine of the new hires came from frontline Vitality roles, bringing insight, credibility and relevance to the team's work. They also engaged frontline workers early in the learning design process, conducting structured sessions to identify critical tasks and key challenges in their daily workflow. This gained essential insights about their work and day to day tasks. This collaboration ensured that resources were aligned with work processes and were easily accessible when needed.

To decide whether classroom training was necessary the team developed a custom scoring tool to assess the complexity of any new processes. This tool engages end-users to evaluate task difficulty, facilitating informed discussions with business owners about process design and training needs. If a process requires extensive training they explore how to simplify it, improving customer outcomes and easing the burden on employees. The principle is simple: intuitive processes always trump complex ones. At Vitality, high training volume is a warning sign that a process has potentially become too complex, indicating a need for simplification. This is a vital balance to strike. The L&D team advises business projects on how to avoid the need to train people, which in turn has improved organizational agility.

Building stakeholder trust by focusing on performance

The shift to a resource-led, performance-focused approach at Vitality began with explaining the need and value of doing so. Tindall used a data-driven, performance-focused communication approach to achieve this. He participated in business forums, using organizational data to show how L&D could drive performance improvements. This shifted the focus from training requests to measurable business outcomes, positioning L&D as a proactive partner in addressing challenges.

Tindall also adopted the view that as a learning and development professional, it's your responsibility to apply your specialist knowledge to solve business problems in the best way you know. For his team, this meant shifting to a resource-led approach, using performance data to continually refine and ensure that resources were timely and relevant. By demonstrating how L&D could improve business outcomes through practical, resource-led solutions, the team further strengthened stakeholder confidence.

Creating business value

The results have been significant. By 2024, the Learning and Performance team supported over 300 projects annually, with the proportion of changes implemented solely with workflow-embedded support increasing from 2 per cent to 37 per cent. Induction training time has fallen by over 25 per cent and time to competency is 28 per cent lower.

While the day-to-day work of the L&D team still includes some class-room training, it has expanded to include process analysis and creating performance support resources. The team had to develop new skills in data analysis, user experience design and digital adoption. This new approach required a significant mindset shift, pushing the team to constantly seek ways to add value beyond traditional training metrics to organizational performance.

L&D team insights

Along the way, Vitality's L&D team has gained some key insights. They real-ized that simple, effective performance support is more important than making things look good. Embedding support directly into work systems with digital tools has proven valuable. They've seen the power of proactive performance consulting rather than reactive training delivery. Developing skills in data analysis and using business performance data has become essen-tial. By focusing on performance support in the flow of work, leveraging technology and staying aligned with business needs, they've created a more agile and effective approach to learning in a fast-changing environment.

> The aim of L&D isn't the volume of training input provided; in fact it's quite the opposite. It's about efficacy and finding the optimum amount of training to deliver the desired performance. If the input required is zero, your profit and loss and balance sheet will look a lot more attractive at year end. You will also have cultivated a culture of agility and innovation. Think about the last five L&D projects you delivered – now imagine you couldn't use any of the tools you used in those projects, yet you were still required to deliver at least the same performance impact. How would you do it? That's the mindset that we try to take every day. *Sebastian Tindall, Director of Strategic Enablement, Vitality*

WHAT DID YOU SEE?

Reflect on the Vitality example:

- What business factors made it necessary for Vitality to shift their approach?
- Which TRI principles were most critical to the success of their resource-led approach?

- What would you do differently if challenged to deliver the same (or better) value on your last five L&D projects with different tools, as Sebastian asks?
- What key insight or idea from Vitality's approach could you adapt and apply in your context?

Vitality: Principles in action

Tuning In

ALIGNING TOGETHER

- Adopted a business-first mindset to address growing volume of changes.
- Prioritized work based on size and complexity of projects using a systematic approach.
- Linked performance support directly to customer service quality and operational agility.

CONNECTING TO INDIVIDUALS

- Engaged frontline workers early in the learning design process.
- Conducted structured sessions to identify critical tasks and key workflow challenges.
- Recruited L&D team members from frontline roles to bring credibility and contextual insight.

GROUNDING IN THE REAL WORLD

- Recognized the constraint of limited training time allocation.
- Identified operational realities of customer-facing environments.
- Collaborated with business teams to simplify processes rather than train for complexity.

Responding

CHOOSING WELL

- Developed custom scoring tool to assess whether training was essential.
- Evaluated multiple approaches rather than defaulting to classroom training.
- Selected digital tools that supported just-in-time workflow support.

ENABLING LEARNING

- Implemented digital adoption platforms to provide real-time process guidance.
- Embedded knowledge directly into work processes.
- Designed resources to be easily accessed at point of need.

ENGAGING INFLUENCERS

- Positioned L&D as a proactive business partner, gaining stakeholder support.
- Advised business projects on process simplification before implementation.

Improving

MONITORING PROGRESS

- Tracked real business metrics.
- Tracked utilization of resources and digital tools.

SHARING PROGRESS

- Used business data to demonstrate L&D's contribution to core operational goals.
- Communicated in business terms.

ADAPTING COURSE

- Evolved their approach systematically over time.
- Refined their resource-led approach based on user feedback.
- Developed new team skills in data analysis, user experience design and digital adoption.

The Vitality case study shows strong use of the TRI principles. Their L&D team excelled at **Grounding in the Real World** by recognizing operational constraints and **Connecting to Individuals** by involving frontline staff in design. Their shift from traditional training to resource-led, workflow-embedded support demonstrates both **Choosing Well** and **Enabling Learning**. They used clear metrics for **Monitoring Progress** and a mature approach to **Adapting Course** by continuously refining support resources while evolving their approach over the longer term. The Vitality example highlights how aligning with business needs and designing for real-world performance can elevate L&D's impact in fast-paced settings.

Tailoring TRI to different contexts today

The Multiplex and Vitality examples demonstrate how TRI principles can help improve performance when tailored to unique situations. Let's compare key elements of the approaches to see why each succeeded in their context.

Tuning In

- Multiplex created safe spaces for dialogue about sensitive workplace behaviours – crucial in an industry with potential cultural resistance. Their programme used familiar construction site scenarios to ensure relevance and resonance with long-time workers.
- Vitality aligned L&D to support rapid operational updates, embedding learning directly into workflows. Early engagement with frontline workers ensured solutions were practical and relevant in their fast-paced environment.

Responding

- Multiplex tackled behavioural change with a blended approach combining interactive online modules with facilitated workshops. This ensured both accessibility and the critical face-to-face discussions needed for cultural change.
- Vitality adopted a resource-led strategy with digital adoption platforms providing real-time guidance at point of need. Their custom scoring tool helped determine when training was truly necessary versus when processes could be simplified instead.

Improving

- Multiplex gathered workshop feedback to shape a year-long behaviour reinforcement campaign with posters and resources across construction sites, recognizing that cultural change requires sustained effort.
- Vitality used real-time data from digital platforms to enable rapid iterations, allowing their support resources to evolve quickly alongside changing customer service requirements.

Both organizations demonstrate that applying TRI principles offers practical ways to improve performance, with each tailoring their approach to their unique organizational needs and constraints.

TRI streamlining and scaling to equip people for today

You might wonder if TRI is simply another framework layered onto what you already do. In reality, TRI isn't new complexity – it's a lens that brings clarity to what high-performing L&D professionals have always done intuitively. We've surfaced these principles from their work. In Part Two, we uncovered these success patterns; now we're applying that same lens to today's specific challenges. The principles remain constant, but how they manifest evolves with each context. Table 7.1 shows how these enduring principles can help us tackle today's common L&D challenges.

TABLE 7.1 Using TRI to tackle challenges

Challenge	What selected principles help us to do	Example
Information overload	• *Aligning Together*: Ensure content focuses on what drives value • *Connecting to Individuals*: Identify what people really need to know	Multiplex focused on specific observable behaviours rather than overwhelming participants with comprehensive workplace conduct content
Scaling personalization	• *Grounding in the Real World*: Ensure relevance across different contexts • *Enabling Learning*: Offer diverse approaches to support individual needs	Vitality's digital adoption platforms provided contextual guidance tailored to individual roles, delivering just-in-time support for 1,200 frontline workers
Creating sustained learning	• *Enabling Learning*: Design beyond one-off events • *Engaging Influencers*: Activate managers to sustain learning over time	Multiplex created an ongoing reinforcement campaign developed from participant suggestions to embed learning
Balancing priorities	• *Aligning Together*: Ensure learning initiatives address critical business needs • *Grounding in the Real World*: Design learning that integrates into workflow	Vitality's resource-led approach respected limited training time and identified processes needing simplification rather than training

(continued)

TABLE 7.1 (Continued)

Challenge	What selected principles help us to do	Example
Maximizing limited resources	• *Choosing Well*: Use evidence to select appropriate solutions • *Adapting Course*: Ensure resources flow to what actually works	Vitality used a custom scoring tool to assess training needs and continuously refined their performance support resources based on usage data and feedback
Measuring real impact	• *Monitoring Progress*: Establish meaningful feedback beyond completion metrics • *Sharing Progress*: Communicate value in business terms	Vitality tracked business metrics, shifting focus from learning outputs to performance outcomes
Fostering connection	• *Grounding in the Real World*: Create contextually appropriate spaces • *Enabling Learning*: Design opportunities for sharing experience and knowledge	Multiplex's workshops created safe spaces for sharing personal experiences, demonstrating how compliance training can foster genuine connection

Get your bearings: Equipping people for today

The ongoing day-to-day work of L&D can feel relentless, but the TRI principles make it more effective and sustainable. Reflect on your context and identify steps to streamline and scale how you equip people for today.

WHAT HAVE YOU OBSERVED?

Take out your Field Notebook. Reflect on how you equip people to perform today:

• What parts of your work feel most overwhelming or unsustainable?

- Where do you see the biggest gaps between what's needed and what you're currently able to deliver?
- How well are your solutions aligned to business goals and integrated into work?
- How are you measuring progress and using insights to refine your approach?
- What ideas or inspiration do you have for things that might work in your context?

For aspiring L&D leaders

- **Review alignment:** Pick one learning solution and map it against a specific business goal. Share your findings with your manager to check alignment and identify gaps.
- **Assess compliance burden:** Calculate the total time your workforce spends completing one compliance module annually. Consider whether this investment delivers value.
- **Get practical feedback:** Ask people who use one of your learning solutions: 'What part helped you the most?' and 'What part feels unnecessary?' Use answers to identify improvements.
- **Start small:** Test a simpler approach using one of the experiments in Table 7.2.

TABLE 7.2 Experiments to simplify learning

Experiment	Reduce content	Create a resource
Idea	Reduce unnecessary content	Provide a just-in-time job aid
Action	Take one learning module and remove anything nonessential. Test it with a small group and compare to the original	Interview potential users about what they need support with. Create a simple checklist or FAQs. Test for one week
Measurement	Track reduced completion time and gather feedback on relevance and usefulness	Collect feedback on usefulness, time saved and suggested improvements

For seasoned L&D leaders

- **Close performance gaps with targeted support:** Analyse a performance gap with business leaders to understand its root causes and where learning would help. Design a solution that delivers just enough learning and engages managers.
- **Align across HR:** Connect regularly with HR colleagues to identify overlaps, gaps or inconsistencies in the employee experience.
- **Make continuous improvement a habit:** Implement a process to gather feedback, measure effectiveness and identify improvements.
- **Go deeper:** Explore enhancing solutions with one of the experiments in Table 7.3.

TABLE 7.3 Experiments for enhancing solutions

Experiment	Streamline compliance	Create a persona	Equip managers
Idea	Streamline an existing compliance solution	Create an employee persona	Equip managers to support skill development
Action	Review regulations with stakeholders to clarify actual requirements Assess current learning solutions and explore streamlined options	Develop a persona using real interview or survey data Validate with group members Review solutions against the persona	Brainstorm with managers to generate tools that would help them support skill practice Test with one team
Measurement	Compare requirements to original assumptions Gather user feedback on proposed updates	Collect feedback on persona and response to updates	Gather manager feedback on the tool and team progress in skill development

Distance covered

Equipping people to perform today is the ongoing, everyday work of L&D. The TRI principles help you focus, simplify and refine your approach to this essential work. The old days of relying on training and content are over. It's about using a wider range of approaches to sustainably create impactful outcomes that reduce overwhelm and deliver real value.

The TRI principles are practical tools, grounded in evidence, that tackle common challenges from information overload to balancing productivity with effective learning. The Multiplex and Vitality examples show how they can be flexibly applied in different contexts. We invite you to apply them to your everyday work in a way that suits your organization.

Addressing immediate challenges with sustainable solutions not only reduces noise but also creates capacity for deeper strategic work. This frees you to focus on initiatives that prepare your workforce to be ready to adapt to continuous changing.

In Chapter 8, we'll explore how to apply the TRI principles to navigate what lies over the ever-closer horizon. By building on what you've practised today you'll be ready to help your organization adapt to tomorrow's challenges.

Notes

1   A Harwood. Emerging stronger: Taking bold action – Adam Harwood, Learning Uncut Emergent Series podcast, 21 December 2021.

2   RedThread Research. *Learning Methods Study 2021. Final report: Learning methods – what to use, how to choose, and when to cut them loose*, RedThread, 2021.

3   Association for Talent Development. 2023 *State of the Industry Talent Development Benchmarks and Trends*, ASTD DBA Association for Talent Development, 2023. This report stated that 96 per cent of respondent organizations offer onboarding content, with 41 per cent offering the majority of their learning content in onboarding; and 95 per cent offer mandatory and compliance training, with 42 per cent providing the majority of their content in this area.

4   A McKay and K Moon. Appropriate workplace behaviour in construction – Annaleigh McKay and Karina Moon, Learning Uncut podcast, episode 139, 30 January 2024.

5   A McKay and K Moon. Appropriate workplace behaviour in construction – Annaleigh McKay and Karina Moon, Learning Uncut podcast, episode 139, 30 January 2024.

6   S Tindall. Resource-led learning strategy – Sebastian Tindall, Learning Uncut podcast, episode 66, 17 November 2020; S Tindall. Digital adoption platforms: Embedding learning in the workflow – Sebastian Tindall, Learning Uncut podcast, episode 106, 16 August 2022; and author interview with Sebastian Tindall, 13 August 2024.

8

Beyond the horizon

Ready for tomorrow

Trish Uhl, an AI Product Manager and Learning Executive, knows a thing or two about adaptation.[1] Her working life has provided a front-row seat to the disruptive power of technology. As a teenager in the 1980s Trish worked in a McDonald's store on the Jersey Shore. Back then, success on the grill or in the drive-thru required a blend of human skill, precision timing and teamwork. It wasn't just about flipping burgers or frying eggs – it required cooking knowledge and mastery. Trish even competed in regional contests, pitting the quality of her work and speed against others.

Shortly after moving on from McDonald's, Trish witnessed a profound transformation in those same kitchens. Tasks she once executed with precision and expertise had been automated, controlled by systems that diminished the need for cooking experience. The McDonald's of her formative years – where manual dexterity and culinary skill were valued and rewarded – had evolved into an environment where machines guaranteed uniformity and operational efficiency. This technological shift fundamentally altered the type of talent McDonald's sought to employ, prioritizing technical system operators over the food preparation specialists Trish had once trained to become.

'What struck me was how the expertise had migrated from people to machines,' Trish observed. 'The culinary skill – knowing when eggs were perfectly cooked or burgers properly seared – wasn't something workers needed to develop anymore. Those decisions were now embedded in automated systems. The human role had fundamentally shifted from being a skilled food preparer to becoming an overseer of technology that now contained all that accumulated wisdom.'

Trish's story isn't just about the evolution of one organization. It mirrors the seismic shifts happening across many industries.

You're likely no stranger to this accelerating pace of change and the way it is shrinking the time between disruption and the need to act. You see it reshaping the skills your organization needs. You witness how it shifts workforce expectations about their careers.

Success is no longer about merely responding to change – it's about sensing and being ready to adapt to what's coming next. And that's where you come in. As an L&D professional, you have a critical role to play in helping your organization to navigate this uncharted territory.

In this chapter, we explore how L&D can enable organizations to thrive amidst continuous changing. Building on the TRI principles – Tuning In, Responding, Improving – introduced previously, we'll examine how the principles help address the accelerating forces driving disruption and the barriers that often impede adaptation. Through two contrasting approaches – McKinsey's targeted skills surge and EPAM's systemic skills-based practices – you'll discover how to apply the TRI principles to build both emerging skills and long-term adaptability. These examples show that while skills are essential, creating an environment where continuous learning becomes part of how work gets done is what truly prepares organizations for an uncertain future.

Readiness for an accelerating horizon

The pace of change feels relentless. The horizon constantly accelerates towards us. Long-term planning is increasingly difficult. We are under pressure to adapt faster.

It can feel like we're in a constant state of playing catch-up. We may be under pressure to develop skills that weren't on anyone's radar six months ago. Perhaps we face the frustration of seeing carefully designed programmes become outdated before they're fully implemented. The goalposts aren't just moving – they're being redesigned entirely, leaving many of us questioning whether traditional approaches to learning can ever keep pace.

What if there were a different approach that allows us to keep up?

True readiness extends beyond acquiring specific skills. It's about building capability. The capability to continuously sense. To respond. To thrive amid ongoing transformation.

The most adaptable organizations create what Nigel Paine describes as a 'learning culture' – an environment where continuous development becomes part of everyday work rather than a separate activity.[2] In such environments people feel safe to experiment, share knowledge and learn from mistakes as they navigate new challenges.

This approach doesn't diminish the importance of skills but creates conditions where they can be developed and applied more effectively in response to change. Rather than constantly playing catch-up with skills gaps, we help our organizations build environments where workforces continuously adapt.

Understanding shifts on the horizon

We're witnessing four powerful forces driving the need for ongoing adaptation:

- **Technological breakthroughs** are fundamentally transforming work. As Trish Uhl observed at McDonald's, expertise that once resided in people now lives in systems, changing what workers need to know. With innovations like generative AI, traditional L&D approaches simply can't keep pace – we need a new approach to help workers engage with emerging technologies in their everyday work.

- **Sustainability imperatives** are no longer optional extras. According to the World Economic Forum (WEF), climate action ranks as the second biggest driver of business transformation. Environmental awareness isn't just for specialists anymore – it's becoming necessary across all functions.[3]

- **Changing skills requirements** are accelerating at an unprecedented rate. The evidence from the WEF is clear: 44 per cent of workers' core skills will change in the next five years. You've likely experienced the struggle to find qualified talent first-hand. While organizations are prioritizing reskilling, current approaches aren't quick enough to meet the need.

- **Workforce expectations** have already evolved. Employees increasingly demand flexible work, meaningful roles and stronger growth opportunities. Interestingly, people aren't resistant to change itself – PwC found 77 per cent feel ready to adapt.[4] The challenge? Over half feel overwhelmed by concurrent changes, and nearly half don't understand the reasons behind them. Clearly, communication matters as much as the change itself.

When you look at these forces reshaping work, where do you feel most prepared to support your organization – and where do you worry you might be out of your depth?

SKILLS ON THE RISE[5]

The WEF *Future of Jobs Report 2025* lists the 10 skills most quickly growing in importance:

1   AI and big data

2   networks and cybersecurity

3   technological literacy

4   creative thinking

5   resilience, flexibility and agility

6   curiosity and lifelong learning

7   leadership and social influence

8   talent management

9   analytical thinking

10   environmental stewardship.

This mix reveals an important truth: technical skills like AI are essential, but human capabilities – creativity, analytical thinking, curiosity, and resilience – form the foundation of adaptability. These human elements help people navigate complexity and change, giving them the agency to adapt, regardless of which technical skills are hot.

What's holding organizations back from adapting?

In Chapter 1, we introduced the urgent need for organizations to become more adaptable in the face of continuous changing. Some common barriers we've seen constrain adaptability include:

- **Cultural resistance:** Deep-rooted habits that make it feel like we're pushing water uphill.
- **Siloed thinking:** Finding ourselves caught between departments with different languages or disconnected goals.
- **Defining and anticipating future skills:** The tricky challenge of predicting which skills to prioritize as roles shift.
- **Short-term thinking and misaligned priorities:** The tension between delivering quick wins and building longer-term capability.
- **Lack of empowerment:** Seeing people with valuable insights hold back because taking initiative seems too risky.

Which of these do you recognize in your own organization?

I see, in my organization, how much faster we have to upskill our colleagues than ever before. Learning alone isn't going to do it. I fundamentally need to change the way I lead as a chief learning and development officer and [how] my organization operates to meet the rapidly changing pace of surging skills as required for our business. *Heather Stefanski, Chief Learning Officer, McKinsey & Company*[6]

TRI enabling continuous adapting

The challenges facing organizations today demand more than isolated upskilling efforts. They require a dual focus:

- addressing immediate skills gaps
- building capacity for continuous adapting

The TRI principles provide a practical framework for both.

Tuning In leads us to go beyond identifying skills gaps. It helps us to sense both external and internal shifts. It guides us to understand strategic priorities as well as cultural barriers and readiness for change.

Responding enables us to translate insights to action. It's about designing learning that builds specific capabilities *and* develops adaptive capacity. This means creating experiences embedded in real work and supporting peer and cross-functional learning. Crucially, it means equipping people to self-direct development.

Improving supports us to embed continuous adaptation into everyday work through feedback, reflection and shared learning. It shifts the ownership of learning. It becomes everyone's responsibility, a shared habit across the organization.

Sometimes, building adaptability takes more than steady progress – it calls for a surge. At sea a surge is driven by natural forces like tides or shifting winds. In organizations we can create our own: focused, intentional efforts to generate momentum and accelerate change toward a clear goal. Unlike natural surges, skills surges are deliberately planned.

The McKinsey example on the next page shows how a well-executed skills surge can spark broader change. In contrast, the EPAM example explores a more sustained approach – embedding adaptability through organizational-wide skills-based talent management and operating practices.

As you explore these examples consider how their different scope and focus align with their organizational contexts and how the TRI principles could be adapted to your own context.

EXPLORATION QUESTIONS

Tuning In

- How did the organization connect their skill-building initiatives to strategic priorities?
- How did they understand and activate workforce motivations to ensure that skill development resonated with individuals?
- How did they integrate skill-building approaches into existing workflows, systems and culture?

Responding

- How did the organization use evidence from learning science and elsewhere to guide their approach to building adaptability?
- How did they design solutions that developed both specific skills and learning agility?
- How were key stakeholders involved in supporting and sustaining skill development?

Improving

- What methods did they use to track the effectiveness of skill-building efforts and their impact on adaptability?
- How did they communicate wins, challenges and progress to maintain engagement and demonstrate value?
- How did they refine their approaches based on feedback and changing needs?

McKinsey: Receive to Grow – fuelling continuous adapting

Feedback fuels adaptability

Feedback enables people to continually notice and adapt their actions based on real-world activities and outcomes. For McKinsey & Company, a global management consulting firm where accelerated growth is the norm, the ability to give and receive feedback fuels this process.

Before the pandemic, much of this feedback happened through informal, in-person interactions – casual conversations after client meetings or walking back to team rooms. The shift to remote and hybrid work disrupted these natural learning moments, creating a need to rethink how feedback was supported across their global workforce. This challenge also aligned with their strategic priority of supporting accelerated employee development and reinforcing a culture of continuous improvement.

Digging deeper

Data from multiple sources including engagement surveys, performance evaluations and leadership observations indicated that feedback practices needed strengthening. McKinsey conducted extensive research and deep needs analysis, combining insights from their data, conversations with a representative sample of colleagues (i.e. workforce members) and academic literature. Their research went beyond identifying what people were struggling with, to understand why they found feedback challenging. Key insights emerged about emotional reactions to feedback, particularly around distress intolerance and discomfort associated with asking for feedback. While the organization had various approaches for developing feedback skills, they weren't explicitly addressing how to receive feedback – a crucial gap in building learning agility.

Designed for work

The Receive to Grow pilot was a four-week email campaign developed to address the gap. It delivered practical weekly challenges focused on building specific feedback-receiving skills. Drawing on behavioural science, the goal was to keep the challenges simple. One example is to view feedback as data and sort it into categories (e.g. makes sense/feels off) to process and reflect upon.

Each challenge was presented through visually engaging emails that served both as the assignment and performance support. The design emphasized simplicity – from the techniques and challenges to providing everything that people needed each week in a single email.

McKinsey's approach emphasized the crucial role of local leadership rather than central delivery. Rather than distributing communications centrally, they empowered respected leaders to invite their teams to participate. These leaders sent the weekly emails and actively championed the initiative, leveraging their established relationships and credibility to drive engagement. This approach tapped into the firm's entrepreneurial culture, where partners and leaders are trusted to set goals and drive change within their areas. Participants could opt into the programme through various channels, with the invitation from a respected leader serving as a powerful motivator for participation.

Surging systematically

Receive to Grow was one component of a broader initiative that McKinsey called a feedback 'skills surge'. This skills surge began organically with a group of people across different People and Culture teams who all cared about feedback, meeting monthly to share their work. Under the stewardship of their chief learning officer, these informal collaborations grew into a coordinated effort spanning learning, professional development, talent and analytics functions. Over time they developed a systematic approach to improving feedback skills across the organization.

Their skills surge integrated efforts across multiple functions to embed feedback skills into the organization's culture and processes. The team created new accountability mechanisms in evaluation systems and developed new feedback tools. They included a focus on feedback in the firm's annual Values Day and established regular communications through various internal channels. A comprehensive feedback dashboard was developed to monitor progress across the organization.

Dashboards drive improvement

The initial Receive to Grow pilot achieved an 88 per cent participation rate and generated 250 feedback conversations that would not have occurred otherwise. Participants reported increased confidence in giving and receiving feedback, with many describing significant changes in their approach to challenging conversations. In addition to improvements in programme outcomes, McKinsey has seen improvements in performance outcomes, such as a 7 per cent increase in colleagues who felt that end-of-project feedback was helpful and actionable.

McKinsey evaluated the Receive to Grow programme through multiple complementary approaches. They tracked programme health metrics including engagement rates and completion data, while weekly participant check-ins monitored practice completion and experience. They use organizational metrics such as feedback conversation frequency and quality to monitor feedback skills on an ongoing basis. A comprehensive dashboard tracks attitudes, environment and outcomes across the organization, enabling leaders to set their own goals and determine what actions to take locally based on the data rather than having targets dictated centrally.

Building momentum

Building on the pilot's success, McKinsey expanded the Receive to Grow programme globally. Rather than simply replicating the pilot, they wove key elements of the programme into other learning interventions and initiatives to embed key practices. The experience has shaped their understanding of how cross-functional collaboration can accelerate skill development, providing a model for building other skills needed for organizational adaptability.

McKinsey's experience demonstrates how a skills surge approach can rapidly build capabilities that enable adaptation. By focusing on a foundational skill, feedback and deploying a coordinated, systemic cross-functional response, they created an effective model for helping their workforce to continuously develop and adapt.

> Our approach to surging skills brings cross-functional teams together to tackle a challenge across the full talent lifecycle. This isn't just about learning programmes – it's about addressing a development challenge from every angle. *Lisa Christensen, Director, Design and Innovation – Talent Development, McKinsey*[7]

WHAT DID YOU SEE?

Before moving on, pause to consider what you saw in the McKinsey example:

- Why did McKinsey target improvement in feedback skills?
- How did they apply behavioural science to drive change?
- What role did cross-functional collaboration play in scaling the skills surge?
- How did their measurement approach support continuous improvement?
- What foundational skill in your organization might benefit from a similar systematic approach to increase adaptability?

McKinsey: Principles in action

Tuning In

ALIGNING TOGETHER

- Identified that feedback capability needed strengthening to support accelerated employee development in remote/hybrid work setting.
- Formed cross-functional team from various People and Culture functions to address feedback as a shared priority.
- Linked initiative to organizational culture of continuous improvement.

CONNECTING TO INDIVIDUALS

- Identified specific emotional barriers, including discomfort asking for feedback.
- Conducted deep needs analysis to understand why people found feedback challenging.
- Offered opt-in participation to respect individual autonomy.

GROUNDING IN THE REAL WORLD

- Recognized how remote work disrupted natural feedback opportunities.
- Aligned initiative with entrepreneurial culture where partners and leaders drive change.
- Designed programme to work within existing communication channels and workflows.

Responding

CHOOSING WELL

- Applied behavioural science principles to create weekly challenges.
- Developed an email format that served as both assignment and performance support.
- Designed practical techniques like categorizing feedback as data for reflection.

ENABLING LEARNING

- Created four-week structure with focused weekly challenges on specific skills.
- Designed for simplicity to reduce barriers to access and practice.
- Embedded skill development into daily work through actionable tasks.

ENGAGING INFLUENCERS

- Empowered respected leaders to send invitations rather than distributing centrally.
- Created accountability mechanisms in performance evaluation systems to reinforce behaviours.
- Established regular communications through various internal channels to maintain visibility.

Improving

MONITORING PROGRESS

- Developed comprehensive dashboard tracking attitudes, environment and outcomes.
- Established weekly check-ins to gather participant experiences and adjustment needs.
- Tracked both programme health metrics and organizational feedback indicators.

SHARING PROGRESS

- Framed results in business terms.
- Equipped leaders with data to make local decisions based on team needs.
- Shared insights across People and Culture teams to inform wider initiatives.

ADAPTING COURSE

- Integrated key elements into other learning interventions rather than simply replicating the pilot.
- Used the experience to develop a broader skills surge approach for other critical capabilities.
- Used pilot results to inform global rollout.

The McKinsey case study demonstrates exceptional application of the TRI principles, particularly in **Connecting to Individuals** by deeply understanding emotional barriers to feedback, **Engaging Influencers** by empowering local leaders rather than central distribution, and **Monitoring Progress** through their comprehensive measurement approach. Their systematic cross-functional, culture-conscious approach to building feedback capability shows how a targeted skills surge can enhance adaptability.

While McKinsey's skills surge demonstrates a targeted rapid approach to address specific skill gaps, EPAM takes a broader, systemic view of skill-building, embedding it deeply into their operational fabric. Where McKinsey exemplifies a skills surge model, EPAM's strategy reflects a long-term commitment to reimagining workforce planning and development through a skills-first lens.

EPAM: Skills and learning culture

How do you ensure that more than 50,000 tech professionals across more than 55 countries have exactly the right skills for each client project? For EPAM Systems Inc (EPAM), a global technology consulting and software engineering company, the answer started with their engineers, not human resources (HR). As a professional services firm, their success depends on having skilled people ready to solve complex client problems. In a competitive market clients expect expert advice and proven solutions – making the ability to demonstrate credible skills essential for winning and retaining business. EPAM has developed a systematic approach to achieve this at scale.

The business imperative

This focus on skills runs deep in EPAM's history. More than 30 years ago, before they even had an HR team, their software engineers built a skills system to solve a pressing business problem: matching people with the right skills to client projects. What started as a tactical solution has evolved into something far more powerful. Today, this system doesn't just match people to projects – it drives hiring decisions, shapes learning programmes and guides career development.

EPAM's goal is simple: having the right people with the right skills to power business strategy. This focus on skills keeps them agile, ready to adapt as client needs and technologies change.

Building the skills engine

At the heart of EPAM's approach is their skills 'ontology' – a structured collection of skills mapped to tasks, showing how they connect to each other, to roles and to business objectives. By linking skills directly to tasks, EPAM ensures a direct alignment between individual skills and what the business needs. This task-based foundation keeps skills grounded in real-world work and makes it easier to adapt as business strategy evolves.

EPAM tracks skills in two ways: first, by using AI technology to predict skills based on work, education and professional activities (including LinkedIn profiles and internal data); and second, through direct observation of how people perform tasks.

This skills data drives decisions throughout someone's career at EPAM – from hiring to project matching, performance reviews to learning plans. Skills directly influence job retention and promotion decisions, giving employees clear targets for growth. EPAM also uses this data to show people potential career paths based on their current skillset.

Empowering individuals

EPAM believes people will learn when they're motivated and have the opportunity to do so. Directly linking skill development to job retention and career progression creates a strong incentive for employees to engage in continuous learning. They've built capability academies that blend formal training with practical experience, and their STRIVE framework integrates informal learning into daily work. This comprehensive approach encompasses: social learning with colleagues, teaching others to reinforce knowledge, reflection on experiences, investigation of new ideas, vocational activities, and experiential learning through real work.

Learning resources aren't confined solely to a learning management system – they're also embedded in the tools people use every day, making it easier to learn while working. Rather than pushing training onto employees, EPAM has created a 'pull economy' for learning. By making skills requirements transparent and linking them directly to career progression, employees actively seek out learning opportunities. They can see exactly what skills they need to advance and have ready access to the resources to develop them.

Engaging managers

Both people and project managers play a vital role in validating skills. EPAM embeds this responsibility directly into their roles. They're supported by structured assessment tools and technology prompts that fit naturally into their workflow, making it easier to provide feedback during regular work activities.

To keep this manageable, EPAM uses algorithms to select which skills need validation, focusing feedback on the most relevant or recently developed capabilities. This targeted approach ensures skill validation remains meaningful without overwhelming managers. The system prompts managers at the right time to validate specific skills, streamlining the process while building accurate skills profiles over time.

Staying future ready

The ability to anticipate and respond to market changes depends on how well an organization manages its skills. At EPAM, skills frameworks aren't static HR documents, but living systems owned and continuously updated by business experts. For instance, their Cloud Center of Excellence team identifies emerging trends and determines tomorrow's critical skills. This business-led, expert-driven approach helps EPAM stay ahead of industry changes.

EPAM's experience with generative AI demonstrates how well this works. Because their skills frameworks are maintained by business experts, EPAM spotted the potential impact of generative AI before it became mainstream. They quickly began testing its use in real work situations, identified the skills their people would need and developed targeted learning programmes. When generative AI hit the mainstream, EPAM was ready – they had already begun educating employees, experimenting with AI-enabled software development and redefining roles to include these new skills.

This proactive approach extends beyond new technologies. By continuously updating their skills frameworks and mapping skills to roles and business objectives EPAM ensures their workforce is developing the skills needed for tomorrow, not just today.

Improvement and adaptation

EPAM measures success through practical metrics like project staffing efficiency and how quickly people become productive with new technologies. These metrics guide continuous refinement of their approach, showing where adjustments are needed to better serve both business and employee needs.

They continually refine their approach based on feedback and data. They've learned that different parts of the organization need different levels of detail in their skills data. Client-facing roles, for instance, require more detailed skills tracking than internal support functions. This insight has led to a more nuanced approach to skills data collection across roles.

They're now pushing the boundaries further, using AI to capture skills data from daily work, enabling real-time feedback and personalized coaching. These innovations aim to reduce the time it takes for people to become productive with new skills while ensuring precise alignment with emerging client demands and technologies.

By combining deep skills expertise with innovative technology and a constant drive for improvement, EPAM built more than just a skills framework – they created an engine for organizational agility. Their approach ensures their workforce stays skilled and ready for future challenges, while maintaining the credibility and expertise their clients expect.

In order to be agile as a business in a dynamic context, individuals have to keep learning and growing their skills. The business needs to articulate the delta between current and required skills and then incentivize skill-building. *Sandra Loughlin, Chief Learning Scientist, EPAM Systems*[8]

WHAT DID YOU SEE?

Before moving on, pause to consider what you saw in the EPAM example:

- How does EPAM detect shifts in required skills and translate these insights into action?
- What role do different stakeholders (e.g. managers, subject matter experts, employees) play in their skills approach?
- How does EPAM's approach motivate employees to drive their own development?
- What steps could you take to improve organizational readiness to adopt a skills-based approach?

EPAM: Principles in action

Tuning In

ALIGNING TOGETHER

- Originated skills approach from business need to match people to client projects.
- Involved business experts in continuously updating the skills frameworks to stay ahead of market needs.
- Tied skills ontology directly to business goals through task-based mapping.
- Used skills data to drive decisions across the talent lifecycle, ensuring alignment with business objectives.

CONNECTING TO INDIVIDUALS

- Provided transparent skills data to empower individuals to drive their own career development.
- Created strong incentives by linking skills development directly to career progression.
- Designed multiple learning paths based on individual skills profiles and interests.

GROUNDING IN THE REAL WORLD

- Mapped skills directly to tasks, grounding them in actual work.

- Integrated skill assessment and building into operational workflows.

- Tailored skills data collection to different depths across roles.

Responding

CHOOSING WELL

- Applied data-driven insights to predict and validate skills required for future roles.

- Ensured the application of learning science through qualified learning leadership.

- Implemented their STRIVE framework incorporating multiple approaches to learning.

ENABLING LEARNING

- Embedded resources into daily work tools, simplifying access during workflow.

- Created capability academies blending formal training with practical experience.

- Designed learning experiences around real work tasks and challenges.

ENGAGING INFLUENCERS

- Equipped managers with tools and prompts to validate skills and provide feedback.

- Reduced assessment burden on managers using algorithms to select priority skills for validation.

- Made skills framework ownership the responsibility of business experts rather than HR.

Improving

MONITORING PROGRESS

- Analysed skills data to track development and refine learning programmes.

- Measured operational efficiencies.

- Tracked how quickly people became productive with new technologies.

SHARING PROGRESS

- Visualized skills data to help individuals see their progress and opportunities.
- Used skills data to demonstrate readiness for new client challenges.

ADAPTING COURSE

- Continuously updated skills ontology based on industry trends and client demands.
- Refined approach over 30 years, now exploring AI to capture skills data from daily work.
- Adjusted level of detail in skills tracking based on what they learned about different role requirements.

EPAM's approach demonstrates strong application of the TRI principles, especially **Aligning Together** and **Grounding in the Real World,** with a skills ontology that links individual capabilities to business needs and real work tasks. Their approach to **Enabling Learning** embeds development into daily workflow through the STRIVE framework and accessible resources. In terms of Improving, they excel at **Adapting Course** with continuous refinement of their skills frameworks led by business experts. What sets this example apart is its business-first, engineer-led approach and 30-year evolution – creating a deeply integrated skills system that anticipates change like generative AI and prepares the workforce before these changes become mainstream.

TRI building adaptability

A reminder that the TRI principles offer more than just relabelling familiar practices. In Part Two, we identified patterns that the Learning Performance Benchmark show consistently lead to business value – regardless of era or technology.

The examples from McKinsey and EPAM show two contrasting strategies for enabling adaptability. What is common is that both demonstrate that adaptability isn't just about building specific skills – it's about creating an environment where skills can grow, be applied and evolve making learning culture a strategic asset.

These examples also illustrate that the TRI principles in action take different forms in different contexts, allowing you to navigate the specific conditions you face. Table 8.1 demonstrates how these enduring principles address contemporary barriers to adaptability.

Both organizations demonstrate that applying TRI principles creates the conditions for adaptability to become an organizational capability, whether through a focused skills surge or systematic approach. These principles offer practical strategies to develop the capacity to continuously sense, respond to and thrive amid ongoing change.

TABLE 8.1 Using TRI to overcome roadblocks to adaptability

Challenge	What the principles help us to do (selection of 2 principles per challenge)	Example
Cultural resistance	• *Connecting to Individuals*: Surface beliefs and mindsets that constrain adaptability • *Enabling Learning*: Translate insights into experiences that address emotional barriers	McKinsey's weekly challenges tackled 'distress intolerance' around feedback, addressing emotional barriers that prevented learning agility
Siloed thinking	• *Aligning Together*: Create shared goals across functions • *Engaging Influencers*: Build bridges between functions	McKinsey brought diverse teams together around feedback improvement, creating cross-functional collaboration with unified metrics and goals
Future skills anticipation	• *Grounding in the Real World*: Establish sensing mechanisms for emerging skills needs • *Adapting Course*: Continuously refine skills frameworks based on emerging trends	EPAM's business-led skills frameworks enabled them to spot generative AI's potential impact before it became mainstream, allowing proactive skills development
Short-term thinking and misaligned priorities	• *Aligning Together*: Connect learning initiatives to immediate business needs while building longer-term adaptability • *Enabling Learning*: Design solutions that deliver both immediate and future value	McKinsey addressed urgent hybrid work challenges with feedback skills surge while simultaneously building lasting capability for continuous improvement

(continued)

TABLE 8.1 (Continued)

Challenge	What the principles help us to do (selection of 2 principles per challenge)	Example
Lack of empowerment	• *Connecting to Individuals*: Understand what prevents people from taking ownership • *Choosing Well:* Equip people for self-directed development	EPAM provided transparent skills data and clear career paths that motivated employees to drive their own learning and development

Get your bearings: Enabling continuous adapting

In a world where the horizon is accelerating toward us, building adaptability is essential. The TRI principles offer practical ways to help your workforce develop the agility needed to navigate continuous changing.

WHAT HAVE YOU OBSERVED?

Take out your Field Notebook. Reflect on how you are helping your workforce to be ready for the future:

- Which shifts (technological, sustainability, skills requirements, workforce expectations) are most impacting your organization, and how?

- How do barriers like organizational culture or short-term thinking appear in your context?

- Where have you seen pockets of adaptability in your organization? What enabled those?

- How effectively are you balancing addressing immediate skills gaps with building long-term adaptive capacity?

For aspiring L&D leaders

- **Map existing signals:** Identify where early warnings about emerging skills already exist in your strategy documents, customer feedback and industry trends.

- **Explore with stakeholders:** Speak with a business leader about skills their team will need to thrive in the next 12–18 months.

- **Assess learning culture:** Identify a team that adapts well to change and speak with them about how they share knowledge and make changes.

- **Start small:** Pick one of the ideas in Table 8.2 to test a more adaptive approach.

TABLE 8.2 Experiments to improve adaptability

Experiment	Skills sensing	Learning from experimentation
Idea	Create a simple ongoing system to identify emerging skills needs	Foster small-scale experimentation to build comfort with change
Action	Hold monthly 15-minute team meetings where everyone shares a skill that's becoming more important Capture on a shared digital board	Frame an upcoming change as an experiment Create a template to document a skill that's becoming more important, results and learnings Make adjustments based on insights
Measurement	Track how identified skills evolve, whether early signals become mainstream needs, and how this improves response time	Monitor willingness to experiment, speed of learning cycles and changes in ability to adapt to uncertainty

For seasoned L&D leaders

- **Connect skills to business strategy:** Establish regular touchpoints with your strategy team to ensure you're anticipating future skill needs.

- **Grow a sensing network:** Identify forward-thinking colleagues across your organization who can help spot emerging trends and skills.

- **Build a skills intelligence dashboard:** Create a simple visual tracker that combines data on emerging industry trends, internal capability gaps and strategic priorities.

- **Go deeper:** Pick one of the ideas in Table 8.3 to strengthen your adaptive ecosystem.

TABLE 8.3 Experiments for strengthening your adaptive ecosystem

Experiment	Skills surge	AI-powered skills analysis	Learning moments
Idea	Test a focused, cross-functional effort to rapidly build a critical skill	Use AI to identify emerging skills patterns and maintain frameworks	Embed learning moments into team routines
Action	Identify one high-priority skill gap Coordinate a 4–6 week concentrated effort across multiple functions to quickly build and reinforce application of this skill	Experiment with using AI tools to analyse job descriptions, industry reports and internal documents to identify emerging skills patterns Compare AI insights with expert opinions	Introduce a 5-minute segment in existing meetings where team members share work challenges, solutions and insights Coach managers to facilitate these effectively
Measurement	Track skill acquisition speed, application rates, and business impact Compare to traditional approaches	Evaluate accuracy of AI-identified skills trends against human analysis Assess time saved in skills framework maintenance	Monitor frequency of learning discussions and how insights influence team decisions and practices

Distance covered

In this chapter, we've explored how we can apply TRI principles to help our workforce and organization be ready to adapt for the future on an ongoing basis. **Tuning In** helps us to sense shifts in business needs and workforce expectations. **Responding** enables us to adopt evidence-informed approaches that develop both skills and adaptive capability. **Improving** reminds us to continuously refine our efforts through meaningful feedback.

McKinsey and EPAM demonstrated different approaches to enabling adaptation. McKinsey's skills surge showed how working systemically in a focused way can drive broader change. EPAM's systemic approach revealed how embedding skills development into organizational DNA creates environments where workforces continuously adapt rather than merely react to change.

Both examples illustrate that true readiness extends beyond acquiring specific skills. As we saw with Trish Uhl's McDonald's experience, the seismic shifts being driven by the accelerating rate of technological change fundamentally changes how we must approach development. The TRI principles help create conditions where skills can be developed and applied effectively in response to change, moving organizations from constantly playing catch-up with skills gaps to building cultures where continuous adaptation is the norm.

In Chapter 9, we'll explore how to apply TRI principles when working with external partners, expanding your capacity to foster adaptability for both current performance and future challenges.

Notes

1 Author interview with Trish Uhl, 3 September 2024.

2 N Paine (2019) *Workplace Learning: How to build a culture of continuous employee development*, Kogan Page, London.

3 World Economic Forum. *The Future of Jobs Report 2025*, WEF, 2025. https://www.weforum.org/publications/the-future-of-jobs-report-2025 (archived at https://perma.cc/GTY5-3LEE)

4 PwC. PwC's 27th Annual Global CEO Survey: Thriving in an age of continuous reinvention, PwC, 2024. www.pwc.com/gx/en/ceo-survey/2024/download/27th-ceo-survey.pdf (archived at https://perma.cc/3QQK-FJNS)

5 Organizations surveyed for the WEF's *The Future of Jobs Report 2025* about skills that are increasing or decreasing in importance. Figure 3.4 'Skills on the rise' presents this data organized by the net difference.

6 C Coffee. Understanding the ever-evolving skill-scape, Chief Learning Officer, 2024. www.chieflearningofficer.com/2024/03/20/understanding-the-ever-evolving-skill-scape (archived at https://perma.cc/LD39-WLGF)

7 Author interview with Lisa Christensen, 20 December 2024.

8 Author interview with Sandra Loughlin, 8 November 2024.

9

Journeying together

As an internal learning consultant at an energy company, Barbara Thompson was working on a development programme for graduates spread around the globe.[1] When she engaged six different external partners to work on the project – including a technical development company, a pure design agency and a translation service – her manager was concerned. 'You don't need to do this to yourself,' they said. They encouraged her to merge some activities and reduce the number of external partners.

However, for Barbara, working with external partners wasn't about efficiency. She wanted 'to work with the best people who can do the best job'. She chose multiple partners because she believed that each brought valuable unique expertise and insights from working with different clients. When combined, she knew their collective expertise would elevate graduate learning experience.

Over time, Barbara has learned to handle the complexity of these partnerships by being intentional. She sees suppliers as part of her value chain: 'This isn't about lobbing something over the fence. It's about collaborating to get the best possible outcome.' She has developed herself, too, learning to speak the language of different stakeholders in ways that are relevant to them.

Barbara sets clear expectations with suppliers: open communication, mutual respect, and a focus on leaving the organization stronger. Success requires more than creating an effective programme – it means that the client organization is left in a better place. Barbara stands by her philosophy of working with multiple partners to tap into 'collective talent' and multiple perspectives to 'get the best out of everything'.

The landscape of today

Today's workplace is continuously changing. L&D faces growing complexity and increasing demands. We need to help the workforce and organization to be equipped to perform today and ready to adapt tomorrow. It's no wonder many of us feel overwhelmed.

The good news? We don't have to navigate this terrain alone. External partnerships can provide vital support, helping bridge L&D capacity and capability gaps and increase our value.

Think of it as assembling a fleet instead of sailing solo. Partners bring specialized expertise, tools and resources that enable us to tackle bigger challenges together. When everyone plays to their strengths, the fleet can weather storms while maintaining course toward shared goals.

Look at Barbara's approach. She deliberately chose multiple partners for their different strengths, creating a collaborative fleet to deliver an exceptional outcome. Her choice shows partnerships can help tackle complex challenges and seize new opportunities.

Both workplace learning and the partnerships that support it continue to evolve – creating a diverse and dynamic ecosystem. Some suppliers specialize in one area, while others blend multiple capabilities. Effective collaboration transforms these relationships into something powerful. This isn't about transactions; it's about combining our distinct strengths to solve problems neither could tackle alone.

From suppliers comes fresh perspective gained across multiple organizations. From L&D teams comes deep knowledge of specific organizational needs and culture. United, we explore new approaches that push traditional boundaries.

Barbara's choice to work with six different partners illustrates this potential. Each partner contributed unique capabilities, creating something more impactful than any single partnership could achieve. This kind of collaboration shows how modern partnerships can deliver solutions that work for both immediate challenges and long-term aspirations.

In this chapter, we are talking to both those in the supplier 'fleet vessels' and the L&D customer 'flagship' about working together effectively. We'll explore how to overcome potential tensions and use the TRI principles – Tuning In, Responding and Improving – to harness your collective wisdom. Through two real-world examples we'll look at what each party brings to the relationship (the 'offer') and what they need from each other (the 'ask'). These principles are just as crucial for external partnerships as they are for internal collaboration.

WHO MIGHT YOU PARTNER WITH?

Here's who you might find working with an L&D team:

- content library creators and aggregators

- learning solution providers

- external course providers and marketplaces

- ed-tech providers

- strategic consultants

- higher education institutions

- assessment and evaluation providers

- professional associations

It's a journey, not a race

Our mindset shapes what's possible. A win/lose mentality immediately limits the potential of partnerships. When one party tries to benefit at the other's expense, both ultimately lose. True success comes when partners commit to winning together, working toward shared goals.

Even with the right mindset, a subtle trap awaits: the 'conspiracy of convenience'. This emerges when we prioritize quick wins over digging deeper. It happens when an L&D team requests a specific course and receives exactly that – no questions asked about whether it's the right solution. Both sides gain temporary satisfaction while missing opportunities for greater impact.

True partnership means breaking free from this transactional pattern. It's not just about win/win – it's about winning bigger together. This means choosing collaboration over competition, combining strengths and aligning on long-term goals to get the wind in your sails.

Even when we focus on shared goals and creating business value, common tensions can challenge our partnerships:

- **Quick wins vs lasting impact:** L&D teams need fast solutions for urgent demands, while suppliers have sales targets to meet. Time pressure often leads us to make compromises that limit impact.

- **Made-to-order vs open exploration:** Just as L&D teams feel frustrated when stakeholders request pre-defined solutions, suppliers often feel the same when L&D teams approach them with a solution already in mind.

- **Procurement processes vs partnership spirit:** While procurement processes aim to protect both sides, they can hinder collaboration. As we heard from one L&D leader: 'We don't want to feel pressured to choose them in the future, so we are sometimes hesitant to deepen the relationship that could be seen as favouritism in a fair tender process.'[2]

- **Role clarity vs blurred lines:** Lack of clarity about roles can leave us struggling to bring our best to a partnership.

- **Expectations vs reality:** In the drive to win business, suppliers might promise more than they can deliver. When reality falls short, trust suffers.

- **Context vs fit:** From the supplier perspective: 'The majority of L&D people don't understand what their company's business is about. To help them, we need to involve business people as early as possible.'[3] Finding the right fit requires bridging the gap together.

- **Innovation vs risk:** Enthusiasm for trying something may collide with risk aversion, placing us in the uncomfortable position of either playing it safe or advocating for approaches that might not work – with our credibility on the line either way.

Trust stands at the heart of transforming transactional relationships into true partnerships. Without it, meaningful collaboration is impossible.

For L&D teams, trust wavers when suppliers overpromise or when everything reduces to cost. For suppliers, trust erodes when clients withhold critical information or when short-term demands overshadow strategic goals.

Barbara Thompson's approach shows what's possible when trust becomes foundational. By setting clear expectations, encouraging open communication and focusing on shared success, she harnessed collective expertise that a single supplier could never provide.

So how can we overcome these tensions and build partnerships based on trust and shared goals? The TRI principles offer practical guidance.

TRI journeying together from tensions to trust

Strong partnerships don't happen by accident. We create them through shared priorities, thoughtful collaboration and the ability to adapt together. The TRI principles offer practical ways to navigate partnership complexities:

- **Tuning In** helps partners align on shared goals and uncover what truly matters.

- **Responding** enables solution design that balances immediate needs with long-term impact.
- **Improving** keeps partnerships evolving through feedback and iteration.

The real-world examples that follow bring these principles to life. They're not rigid templates – they're stories of partnerships that worked through challenges, managed tensions and achieved shared success. Each shows different ways of balancing competing priorities, sharing responsibility and building trust while working toward common goals.

As you read these examples, consider the tensions in your own partnerships. Think about how the TRI principles might help address similar challenges or spark new ways of working together.

EXPLORATION QUESTIONS

Tuning In

- How did the partners find common ground and align their goals, even with different initial perspectives?
- How did they understand individual needs and motivation to develop relevant solutions?
- How did they adapt to organizational realities like cultural norms, systems and existing processes?

Responding

- How did both sides combine their expertise and experience to develop insights and create practical solutions?
- What steps did they take to design solutions that would improve performance and embed new behaviours?
- How did they equip key stakeholders to build support for learners?

Improving

- How did they gather meaningful data and track progress toward their goals?
- How did they communicate impact to maintain momentum and show the value of the partnership?
- How did they use feedback to refine their approach together?

Coles and Liberate Learning: Partnering to innovate

When Siva Kulasingam joined Coles Group in 2017 as Digital Learning Manager, he quickly realized they had a problem.[4] With 115,000 team members across 2,000 locations – many in grocery, liquor and fuel outlets – their outdated learning management system (LMS) couldn't keep up with the fast-paced retail environment. To maintain performance and engagement, Coles needed to overhaul how they developed, delivered and measured learning.

Listening to the reality of the retail environment

Before jumping to solutions, Siva took the time to listen to team members, line managers and business leaders across Coles. The feedback was clear: the existing LMS and learning approach wasn't working. Their LMS was designed for office workers who sit at computers to complete their training modules. It wasn't working well for Coles' retail staff who spend their days serving customers and managing store operations. On top of this, technical problems and slow internet connections made online learning difficult. As a result, staff viewed training as just another box to tick rather than something valuable for their work.

Building a partnership based on trust

Armed with these insights, Siva knew Coles needed a different approach – and a partner to help make it happen. He was looking for a new mobile-friendly platform that could work in low-bandwidth environments and provide detailed tracking. When he couldn't find a suitable solution on the market, he turned to someone he trusted: Rodney Beach from Liberate Learning. With a working relationship spanning 15 years, Siva and Rod had built a partnership based on mutual trust and a shared commitment to pushing boundaries.

Rod understood the risks to his organization. Building a custom solution could disrupt 40 per cent of Liberate's core business by streamlining content development. But for Rod, staying ahead of the curve was essential: 'If we didn't do it, someone else would.'

Sharing risk to break new ground

Siva and Rod established an arrangement that shared both the risks and rewards. Coles funded half the initial investment, while Liberate retained ownership of the tool and Coles owned the content. They agreed on commercial terms that balanced the risks for Coles as an early adopter.

Starting small, they developed a 'minimum viable product' (MVP) to meet immediate needs like mobile access and shorter, more digestible learning modules. Business subject matter experts and end-users tested the platform, providing feedback that helped refine and add features.

This collaborative approach allowed the platform to evolve over time. Liberate's technical team proactively suggested new features that further improved the user experience. 'They came to me with ideas I hadn't even thought of,' Siva recalls, highlighting how trust and openness continued to drive the project forward.

Transforming learning with an integrated technology ecosystem and support for real work

The new platform made it easier for Coles to develop, deliver and manage a blended approach to learning supported with a wider variety of learning materials – including quick, easy to access microlearning to practical on-the-job activities. This new approach allowed the workers to learn in short bursts using their mobile phones during quieter moments of their shift and supported them to learn on-the-job.

Coles integrated the new mobile platform with Learning Hub, their learning experience platform (LXP) which was implemented in a separate initiative. Line managers had access to dashboards and on-the-job observation checklists on Learning Hub which made it possible for them to track and support their team's progress with all learning, including that completed on the mobile platform.

This integrated technology ecosystem helped ensure that learning became a core part of daily work, with managers actively helping team members apply their new skills on the job.

Moving the needle on results that matter

The new tracking tools gave Coles unprecedented insights into learning effectiveness. In just three years, the results were clear. The technology was easier to use, with technical support tickets dropping by more than half in the first year. Engagement was up with learning completions skyrocketing from 800,000 to 8 million annually.

More importantly, these improvements translated into real business outcomes. Staff turnover dropped by 10.5 per cent for team members with three–six months of service, and by 2.4 per cent for those in their first three months. Safety training, completed over a million times, helped reduce injuries by 15.7 per cent (measured by Total Recordable Injury Frequency Rate).

The availability of detailed data also enabled Siva's team to have more meaningful conversations with the business. They could challenge assumptions and pinpoint where performance issues were not caused by gaps in knowledge or skills, addressing business concerns with greater confidence and clarity.

Continuing the journey

Today, Coles and Liberate continue to innovate together, exploring new possibilities with AI and automation. For Rod, the key to a successful partnership remains simple: 'Don't focus on short-term gains. Look after your partner, and they'll look after you.' Siva adds, 'Be honest about where your strengths are and where they aren't and be ready to learn.'

Their journey shows how trust, openness and a shared vision can transform learning and deliver real business impact. As they look to the future, Siva and Rod continue to push boundaries, knowing that innovation often requires taking calculated risks and challenging industry norms.

> We're all jumping on the ship, and we're going to be sailing that way, because Siva said the land was that way. You know, Siva imagined there was land that way. So, if you're loading a ship full of people, you want the best navigators. And, as far as I'm concerned, we have the best navigators. I was happy to sit in the ship and try to reach land, because Siva said there was land over there. *Rod Beach, founder, Liberate Learning*

WHAT DID YOU SEE?

Reflect on the Coles/Liberate partnership:

- How did they handle the common partnership tensions we discussed?
- What role did shared goals and trust play in their ability to innovate together?
- How did understanding the retail environment shape their solution?
- What one idea from this partnership could you apply in your context?

Coles/Liberate Learning: Principles in action

Tuning In

ALIGNING TOGETHER

- Established a shared vision backed by commercial terms that balanced risks for both parties.
- Used business data to identify the need for a new digital learning approach.
- Combined expertise from both organizations to explore new territory.

CONNECTING TO INDIVIDUALS

- Gathered feedback from staff at all levels about their learning challenges.
- Recognized that retail staff needed a different approach from office workers.
- Built flexibility into the learning modules to accommodate retail working patterns.

GROUNDING IN THE REAL WORLD

- Addressed the reality of low bandwidth in retail environments.
- Designed for staff in stores with limited time for training.
- Created solution for a distributed workforce across 2,000 locations.

Responding

CHOOSING WELL

- Decided to build a custom solution when existing market offerings were inadequate.
- Developed a MVP to test concepts before full implementation.
- Applied evidence about mobile learning to their context.

ENABLING LEARNING

- Created microlearning modules for access during quiet moments in shifts.
- Integrated learning with practical on-the-job activities.
- Provided easier access to learning materials via mobile devices.

ENGAGING INFLUENCERS

- Involved business subject matter experts in testing and refining the platform.
- Equipped line managers with dashboards to track and support teams progress.
- Positioned managers to help team members apply new skills during work.

Improving

MONITORING PROGRESS

- Implemented tracking tools to gain insights into learning effectiveness.
- Measured business impact through staff turnover and safety metrics.

SHARING PROGRESS

- Used detailed data to have more meaningful conversations with the business.
- Provided dashboards for management visibility of real-time progress.
- Communicated measurable business impact to demonstrate partnership value.

ADAPTING COURSE

- Refined the platform based on feedback from end-users and technical teams.
- Evolved from MVP to a comprehensive solution.
- Continued innovation with exploring AI and automation.

This partnership shows how TRI principles can help manage tensions and create real impact. They started by **Tuning In** – using data and staff feedback to identify frustrations and build a shared vision that balanced immediate needs with innovation. In **Responding,** they created accessible microlearning and integrated with on-the-job practice, enabling learning grounded in the retail realities. **Improving** was key – using feedback and business metrics to continuously enhance their solution.

By focusing on shared goals, mutual accountability and calculated risk-taking, Coles and Liberate demonstrated how trust and transparency can overcome potential tensions and lead to sustained success.

Next, we'll look at a very different context: the partnership between North Yorkshire Police and the Open University. As you read, notice how a shared vision, flexibility and trust helped them balance academic rigor with the practical demands of modern policing.

Open University and North Yorkshire Police: Forging a new path in policing

North Yorkshire Police (NYP) and the Open University (OU) joined forces to introduce the Police Constable Degree Apprenticeship (PCDA), a programme designed to elevate standards in policing education.[5] The PCDA was established as part of the Police Education Qualification Framework (PEQF), a national initiative aimed at professionalizing policing by equipping new recruits with both academic knowledge and practical skills. This marked a shift towards evidence-based policing and the introduction of degree-level qualifications as a standard for new officers, addressing the growing complexities of modern law enforcement.

Setting the stage: Why the PCDA was needed

The PCDA emerged from a recognition that traditional police training was no longer enough to meet the demands of the 21st-century policing landscape. In 2010 the Police Leadership and Training Review highlighted gaps in skills, knowledge and ethical standards within police forces.[6] In response, the College of Policing introduced the PEQF, mandating new pathways into the profession, including the PCDA, to integrate on-the-job training with academic learning. NYP partnered with the OU to ensure that its recruits would not only meet these new national standards but also serve the public effectively during their training.

Aligning visions: The foundation of a collaborative partnership

The partnership between NYP and the OU was grounded in a mutual recognition of each organization's strengths. The OU brought deep experience in helping working adults learn through flexible study, while NYP understood what officers needed on the ground. Together, they sought to balance the academic rigour required by the PEQF with the day-to-day realities of policing.

Early conversations focused on practical concerns. How would officers balance study with police work? When should they learn different topics? Through collaborative workshops, they mapped out a programme that made sense for working officers. They scaffolded the learning across the full three years, building from foundational to more complex subjects, and ensured that officers had enough operational experience to put the learning in context.

Blending theory with practice: The learning journey

Figure 9.1 shows how NYP and OU created an integrated three-year programme that builds from foundation skills to full operational competence. Student officers start with classroom training to become 'safe and lawful' before moving to supervised patrols. Throughout the programme, they apply academic learning directly to real policing situations, with written assignments drawing on their operational experiences.

Supporting the journey: A unified approach

The programme's success relies on a strong student support network. NYP's student development officers (SDOs) – experienced officers with coaching training – guide new recruits in developing practical skills on the job. The OU's practice tutors (PTs), who must have recent operational policing experience, help officers connect academic concepts with daily police work.

Protected learning time is crucial. NYP provides a dedicated study day each week, while both organizations work together to develop tailored individual support plans when needed.

This collaborative approach helps maintain both academic progress and operational development.

Navigating challenges together

The partnership faced its first major test when Covid-19 hit just as the programme was launching. Rather than delay, they adapted quickly to deliver training remotely while maintaining quality. Strong communication between NYP and the OU helped address this challenge swiftly.

The strength of the partnership is particularly evident in how they have tackled scepticism within the police force and external environment about formal police education. Together OU and NYP have built a strong evidence base for the value of the PCDA, tracking graduate success including operational effectiveness and promotions. They are now working on ways to showcase how student research projects contribute to force priorities and improvements to continue addressing cultural resistance.

Continuous improvement and real-world impact

NYP and the OU remained committed to measuring impact and continuously improving the programme. Regular feedback is gathered from student

FIGURE 9.1 PCDA student journey

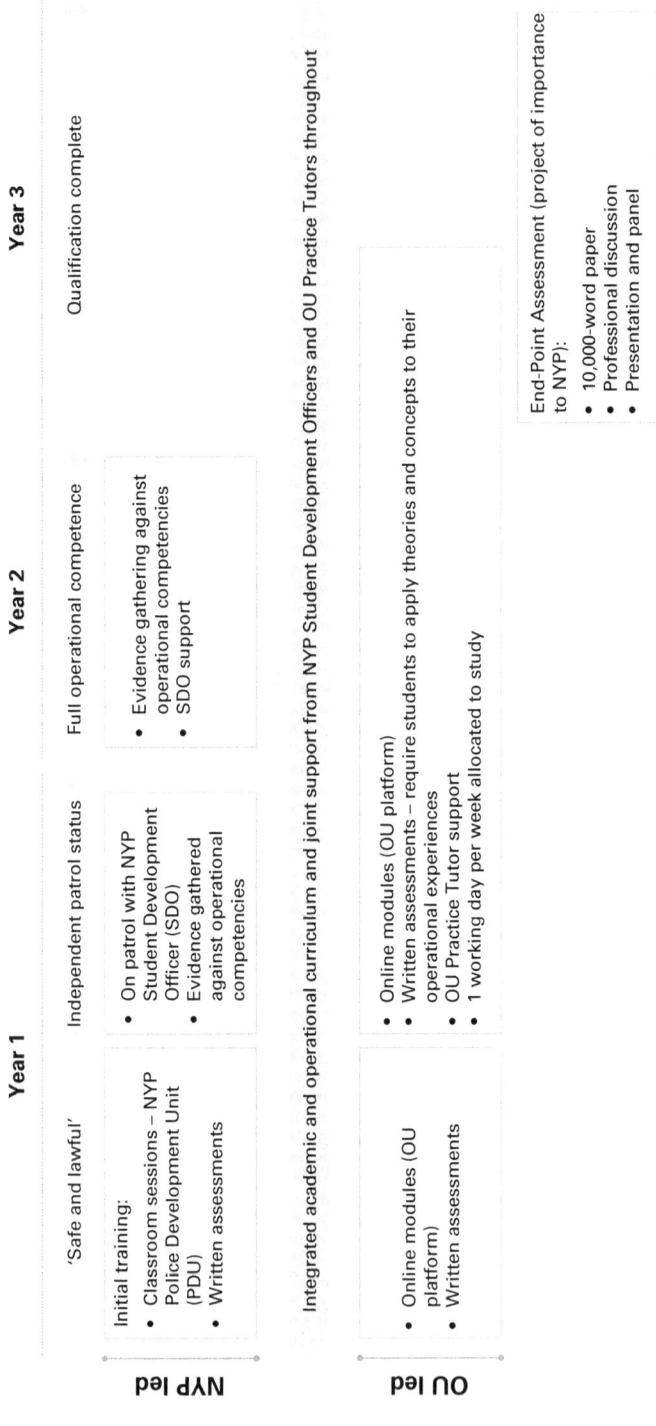

Year 1		Year 2	Year 3
'Safe and lawful'	Independent patrol status	Full operational competence	Qualification complete

NYP led

Initial training:
- Classroom sessions – NYP Police Development Unit (PDU)
- Written assessments

- On patrol with NYP Student Development Officer (SDO)
- Evidence gathered against operational competencies

- Evidence gathering against operational competencies
- SDO support

Integrated academic and operational curriculum and joint support from NYP Student Development Officers and OU Practice Tutors throughout

OU led

- Online modules (OU platform)
- Written assessments

- Online modules (OU platform)
- Written assessments – require students to apply theories and concepts to their operational experiences
- OU Practice Tutor support
- 1 working day per week allocated to study

End-Point Assessment (project of importance to NYP):
- 10,000-word paper
- Professional discussion
- Presentation and panel

officers, SDOs and PTs, providing insights into what was working and what needed refinement. One key improvement was clarifying the role of the PTs which ensured that the they became an integral part of the apprentices' support network.

The programme has shown promising results in its first years. Apprentices are gaining not only the practical skills required for frontline policing but also a deeper understanding of modern policing challenges like digital crime, societal complexity and criminology. The flexible structure of the programme allows them to apply their academic knowledge immediately in the field, making them highly effective officers from the outset.

The power of journeying together in policing education

The partnership between North Yorkshire Police and the Open University exemplifies the power of aligning on a shared vision to drive meaningful change. Strong partnerships are not just about delivering solutions but about journeying together towards greater impact. By embracing mutual trust, a commitment to evidence-based learning and leveraging each partner's strengths, NYP and OU have created a model that enhances both individual and organizational capability, setting a new standard for policing education.

> In those early workshops we brought our expertise, they brought theirs, and together we said: 'You do that really well, we do this really well and we'll work out the bit in the middle.' We built the programme on mutual respect and a clear understanding of each other's strengths. *Dr Jennifer Norman, Head of Policing, The Open University*[7]

WHAT DID YOU SEE?

Reflect on the NYP/OU partnership:

- How did they bridge the gap between academic learning and practical policing?

- What strategies helped overcome resistance to formal education in policing?

- How did they design their programme to work for learners new to higher education?

- What elements of their approach might help with your partnership challenges?

OU/NYP partnership: Principles in action

Tuning In

ALIGNING TOGETHER

- Grounded partnership in national policing education framework requirements.
- Used collaborative workshops to map programme success criteria.
- Connected academic standards with practical policing needs.

CONNECTING TO INDIVIDUALS

- Designed curriculum to progressively build confidence for recruits with diverse educational backgrounds.
- Supported long-term professionalization of policing career paths.
- Created personalized support plans for officers when needed.

GROUNDING IN THE REAL WORLD

- Acknowledged systemic scepticism within police culture about formal education.
- Balanced study requirements with operational police duties.
- Provided protected weekly study time within operational constraints.

Responding

CHOOSING WELL

- Leveraged OU's flexible approach to theory application in practice.
- Created scaffolded curriculum building from basic to complex topics.
- Developed blended learning beyond traditional classroom training.

ENABLING LEARNING

- Connected assignments directly to officers' operational experiences.
- Combined classroom theory with supervised practical application.
- Established a clear progression structure from foundation to operational competence.

ENGAGING INFLUENCERS

- Incorporated experienced officers as development guides for recruits.
- Required tutors to have recent policing experience to ensure relevance.
- Involved police leadership in supporting protected learning time.

Improving

MONITORING PROGRESS

- Gathered regular feedback from students, officers and tutors.
- Tracked operational effectiveness as a core success metric.
- Used evidence of programme impact to address cultural resistance.

SHARING PROGRESS

- Shared success stories of programme graduates in operational roles.
- Demonstrated how student research projects benefited force priorities.
- Used programme outcomes to strengthen partnership credibility.

ADAPTING YOUR COURSE

- Adapted quickly to remote delivery during the Covid-19 pandemic.
- Refined tutor roles based on implementation feedback.
- Built evidence base of programme value to address ongoing cultural resistance.

The OU/NYP partnership demonstrates the TRI principles exceptionally well in their context, particularly in how they balanced academic requirements with policing realities. Their strength in **Tuning In** laid strong foundations through collaborative workshops and recognition of cultural barriers. The **Responding** principle came to life in their integrated learning approach connecting theory directly to police work. While they showed strength in **Improving** through regular feedback and adaptation, particularly during the Covid-19 pandemic, they also built an evidence base that continues to address cultural resistance.

By combining their distinct strengths and maintaining open communication, OU and NYP created a programme that not only met national standards but equipped new officers with the confidence and skills needed for modern policing.

TRI journeying from partnership tensions to success

The real-world examples demonstrate through the lens of the TRI principles how common partnership tensions can be overcome to create value. Both partnerships faced challenges – from technical constraints to cultural resistance – yet they succeeded because the partnerships were fuelled by strong collaboration and mutual trust.

Successful partnerships don't happen by chance. They require understanding what each party brings to the table, navigating tensions and committing to shared action. We can use the TRI principles to guide us in this collective endeavour.

Table 9.1 provides a practical guide for addressing common partnership tensions. It highlights what each party can offer, real-world examples and specific actions both can take together. Use it to spark conversations about enhancing your own partnerships.

TABLE 9.1 Applying TRI principles to build stronger partnerships

Tension and selected principles to address	What each partner offers	Partnership example	Shared action examples
Quick wins vs lasting impact *Aligning Together* *Monitoring Progress*	L&D: Share priorities transparently, connecting immediate needs to strategic goals Supplier: Propose evidence-based approaches that balance quick wins with lasting impact	Coles/Liberate developed a MVP for immediate needs while building toward comprehensive solution, tracking business metrics to demonstrate growing impact	Create a shared roadmap showing both immediate deliverables and future possibilities Schedule quarterly strategic reviews to align priorities and evaluate progress
Made-to-order vs open exploration *Tuning In* *Choosing Well*	L&D: Facilitate access to end-users and stakeholders to explore root causes Supplier: Bring frameworks for exploring business challenges beyond predefined solutions	OU/NYP conducted collaborative workshops to design a curriculum that balanced academic requirements with practical policing needs, rather than using an off-the-shelf solution	Conduct discovery sessions to identify underlying business challenges Prototype and test different approaches before committing to solutions

(continued)

TABLE 9.1 (Continued)

Tension and selected principles to address	What each partner offers	Partnership example	Shared action examples
Procurement process vs partnership spirit *Aligning Together* *Sharing Progress*	L&D: Help navigate internal procurement while advocating for value beyond cost Supplier: Provide clear metrics satisfying procurement requirements and demonstrating impact	Coles/Liberate established a risk-sharing commercial arrangement with clear success metrics focused on business outcomes like reduced turnover and safety improvements	Include procurement early in strategic partnership discussions Create a value scorecard that tracks both quantitative and qualitative benefits
Role clarity vs blurred lines *Aligning Together* *Grounding in the Real World*	L&D: Define clear expectations, decision rights and governance requirements from the start Supplier: Clarify when you're advising vs delivering as the partnership develops	OU/NYP defined complementary roles between SDO and PT, refining these based on implementation feedback	Create a matrix defining roles, responsibilities and decision-making authority Review and update role clarity quarterly
Expectations vs reality *Grounding in the Real World* *Adapting Course*	L&D: Share realistic constraints and success criteria Supplier: Provide honest assessment of solution capabilities and limitations	Coles/Liberate openly discussed technical possibilities and constraints of mobile learning in retail environments, using feedback to continually evolve the platform	Build a risk register that both parties maintain and review Set staged deliverables with clear success criteria

(continued)

TABLE 9.1 (Continued)

Tension and selected principles to address	What each partner offers	Partnership example	Shared action examples
Context vs fit *Grounding in the Real World* *Enabling Learning*	L&D: Share insights about organizational culture and systems Supplier: Translate organizational complexity into actionable recommendations	NYP shared insights about police culture while OU designed assignments directly tied to operational experiences, creating learning that worked in a culturally resistant environment	Create a shared glossary Map the ecosystem of stakeholders and influences together
Innovation vs risk *Choosing Well* *Adapting Course*	L&D: Identify opportunities for low-risk experimentation and testing Suppliers: Share evidence of successful innovations from other contexts and propose staged approaches	Coles/Liberate managed innovation risk through staged implementation, with the technical team proactively suggesting improvements while maintaining system stability	Run small pilots with clear success criteria Create an innovation framework that balances risk and reward

Get your bearings: Building higher-value partnerships

We face complex partnership dynamics, but TRI principles help us see how to navigate tensions. Reflect on your context and identify steps to strengthen your partnerships.

WHAT HAVE YOU OBSERVED?

Take out your Field Notebook. Reflect on your partnerships:

- What patterns do you notice in how you work with partners? What works well and what needs improvement?

- Which tensions from this chapter feel most familiar in your partnerships?
- How well do you and your partners align on goals? Where are the gaps?
- How do your partners' perspectives challenge or complement your own approach?

For aspiring leaders

- **Map your partners:** List key partners and their unique contributions. Share your map with a partner to validate.
- **Practise Tuning In:** Have a conversation with one partner focused on understanding their view of shared challenges.
- **Define success together:** With one partner, discuss what success looks like for both parties. Document shared goals and metrics.
- **Start small:** Pick one of the ideas in Table 9.2 to test with a partner.

TABLE 9.2 Small experiments to build stronger partnerships

Experiment	Test a small improvement	Reset your communication
Idea	Choose one area where your partner's expertise could help solve a specific challenge	Try a different way of communicating for one project phase
Action	Work together to design and test a focused improvement Keep it simple!	Experiment with a new communication approach (e.g. quick weekly check-ins, shared project board, or brief daily updates)
Measurement	Track whether the improvement delivers results or generates insights for future collaboration	Monitor feedback from both teams about clarity and effectiveness of communication

For seasoned L&D leaders

- **Review your partnerships:** Assess where partnerships work well and where alignment or trust-building could make the biggest difference.
- **Make improving a habit:** Set up regular partnership check-ins to evaluate health and progress toward shared goals.

- **Create a partnership framework:** Develop a simple framework defining your partnership approach, including roles, communication and success measures.
- **Grow a partnership:** Pick one of the ideas in Table 9.3 to explore growing a strategic partnership.

TABLE 9.3 Experiments for strategic partnership growth

Experiment	Align on impact	Share expertise	Learn together
Idea	Get everyone clear on what business impact looks like	Find new ways to tap into your partner's expertise	Use project milestones as learning opportunities
Action	Run a workshop with your partner and key internal stakeholders to define and agree on success metrics for an upcoming project	Review a current project to spot where partner expertise could add more value Agree on specific adjustments to roles and workflows	After key milestones, conduct a joint retrospective to reflect on what worked and what you could do better
Measurement	Collect participant feedback on clarity of goals and confidence in agreed metrics	Monitor whether changes lead to faster progress or better outcomes	Assess quality of insights generated and number of improvements implemented

Distance covered

In this chapter, we've explored how we can build stronger partnerships through TRI principles. **Tuning In** allows us to create space for aligning goals and exploring possibilities together. **Responding** guides us to design solutions collaboratively based on real needs and evidence. **Improving** helps us evolve our partnerships through feedback and iteration.

The examples from Coles/Liberate Learning and Open University/North Yorkshire Police showed these principles in action. They highlighted practical ways to handle common tensions and build momentum. A key message emerged: success comes from moving beyond transactions to focus on 'winning bigger together' – creating greater value through trust, collaboration and shared goals.

Knowing how to improve business value in a continually changing work-place is different from taking action in our own environment where the hurdles and hierarchies are real. In Part Four we'll explore the secret ingre-dient to successful navigation – **you**. We'll turn our focus inwards to how we can tune in to ourselves, set course and adjust our own inner game to take bold action.

Notes

1 B Thompson and S Desai. Smarter working partnerships for L&D – Barbara Thompson and Shai Desai, Learning Uncut Emergent Series podcast, 16 September 2020.

2 Unpublished research, data gathered through survey. L Overton. Exploring customer and supplier relationships in L&D – new research, Learning Changemakers, 2024. www.learningchangemakers.com/exploring-customer-and-supplier-relationships-in-ld-new-research (archived at https://perma.cc/7T2M-RE7B)

3 Unpublished research, data gathered through survey. L Overton. Exploring customer and supplier relationships in L&D – new research, Learning Changemakers, 2024. www.learningchangemakers.com/exploring-customer-and-supplier-relationships-in-ld-new-research (archived at https://perma.cc/93TC-F54C)

4 S Kulasingam and R Beach. Partnering for learning innovation – Siva Kulasingam and Rodney Beach, Learning Uncut podcast, episode 93, 1 February 2022; and author interview with Siva Kulasingam and Rodney Beach, 17 October 2024.

5 Author interview with Dr Jennifer Norman and Jo Lambert, 15 October 2024.

6 P Neyroud QPM. *Review of Police Leadership and Training*, UK Government, 2010. www.gov.uk/government/publications/police-leadership-and-training-report-review (archived at https://perma.cc/G86L-L63C)

7 Author interview with Dr Jennifer Norman and Jo Lambert, 15 October 2024.

PART FOUR

Ready

The BOLD navigator

10

Mindset matters

A moment of clarity

'I realized I'd been operating from my own biases,' confesses Cameron Hedrick in a candid interview with Laura and Michelle.[1] 'I assumed people who didn't embrace our solutions were the problem, not the solutions themselves. My thinking was the barrier, not their behaviour.'

This moment of clarity didn't come early in Cameron's career. It arrived after years of success – intermingled with a few failures – as a senior leader at Citibank, one of America's leading financial institutions. As Head of Learning and Culture, Cameron oversaw learning and culture strategy impacting thousands of employees globally. But his journey reveals how even the most accomplished learning leaders can be limited by their own thinking patterns.

Like many professionals drawn to learning and development, Cameron began his career focused on providing both solutions and expertise. 'I was arrogant,' he admits with refreshing candour. 'When data contradicted my gut instincts, I just knew better.' This approach worked – until it didn't. Several 'epic fails' later, Cameron found himself questioning assumptions that had seemed unshakeable.

'You're not an HR person first,' he now insists. 'You're a businessperson who specializes in human capital. You're a revenue driver who specializes in humans, just like a CMO focuses on marketing and a CFO on finance.' This business-first mindset transformed how he approached learning initiatives – starting with commercial outcomes and working backward instead of leading with learning solutions.

Yet Cameron's most profound shift wasn't about business acumen. It was about developing a relationship with his own thinking. The turning point came when he began systematically studying cognitive biases – 50 different types that he reviews monthly – and recognized how they were shaping his perceptions and decisions without his awareness. 'This happens 50 times a day. I'll go, "Oh, this could be confirmation bias, this could be sunk cost fallacy."' To provide a balanced perspective, he deliberately surrounds himself with people who think differently, particularly those more concrete and detail-oriented than his highly abstract style.

Perhaps most remarkably, Cameron models this self-awareness with his team, openly discussing his limitations and encouraging others to challenge his thinking. This vulnerability creates psychological safety that enables experimentation and adaptability – qualities essential in today's rapidly changing environment.

Like Nainoa Thompson preparing for his first voyage as navigator of the *Hōkūle'a*, Cameron Hedrick found himself facing not just external challenges but inner doubts. Both discovered that successful navigation – whether across ocean waters or organizational landscapes – begins with navigating our own thinking.

What if our greatest barrier to impact isn't organizational resistance or limited resources, but how we think about ourselves and our work? What becomes possible when as L&D professionals we develop and hone our self-awareness to recognize and reshape our own thinking patterns?

As we'll explore in the pages ahead, our mindset, dispositions and perspectives may be the most powerful – yet overlooked – instrument in our L&D leader's navigation toolkit.

When we become our own barrier to success

Why do we know so much and yet do so little with what we know?

A broad statement, we know. We are fully aware that learning professionals love to learn – from books, podcasts, communities and, if we are lucky, professional qualifications. But it doesn't take a genius to spot that we are inundated with information. And it is not just in our own profession – our feeds are full of ideas, stories and data about how to improve our climate, productivity, health, income, flexibility, relationships and mental health. Browsing great content and acting on it are often worlds apart. We are more informed through easy access to information – content that is considered and evidence-informed, as well as content that has been curated to create clicks. Our evolving social media platforms and ability to search have opened more access to this content flood. Our ability to get AI to trawl through the tsunami of information can personalize our knowledge diet more efficiently.

And yet knowledge doesn't equate to action.

As L&D leaders, if we are to fulfil the role of ensuring individuals, teams and organizations are equipped and ready, we know that we need to help others shift from just knowing about stuff to actually doing it.

And this applies to us as well.

Navigating through the fog

In Part Two of this book, we recognized that information overload – the tools, techniques and models – have equal potential to either spur us into action or overwhelm us. Like a navigator facing dense fog, we can lose our bearings when surrounded by too much information with no clear reference points. Coupled with the fact that we are operating in a continually changing work environment, full of people who influence each other in countless, unpredictable ways, it's no wonder, as we saw in Chapter 2, that many of us report that we are overwhelmed and underequipped. In Part Three of the book we tried cutting through the noise that is overwhelming us to recover and relate to some of the core principles that underpin effective practices. The TRI principles aren't designed to oversimplify the complex world that we operate in; they are there to help us proactively navigate through the complexity in order for us to land on better business value.

We all know that TRI is not rocket science! Intuitively, the continual flow and connection between Tuning In, Responding effectively and Improving make sense. Retrospectively, we see them at work in our most useful models. From an evidence perspective, we hope that you are now convinced that over the last 20 years, there has been a consistent correlation indicating that these principles help us contribute better business value in our workplaces.

And yet…

Why do we know so much and yet do so little with what we know?

From blame to navigation

Yes, it could be because of others – no time, no permission, no support, no recognition. The CIPD's *Learning at Work 2023* report isolated barriers to achieving our goals into three areas:

- a lack of priority from the business – no time or engagement were at the top of the list
- a lack of capacity within the team to respond – not enough capability, resources or time

- a lack of insight – shared data that allows us to work out what is working and what is not[2]

In various forms, these barriers have been consistently reported across studies over the last 20 years.[3]

But there is a danger of L&D developing 'navigation by blame' – an approach that attributes our inability to move forward entirely to external conditions. We risk limiting our development when we focus solely on external barriers.

The way we ask our questions in our industry research sometimes reinforces that blame culture. Consider how our L&D trend research consistently frames barriers through questions that look outward rather than inward. Top barriers over the years always include some reference to learner reluctance or management resistance.[4]

When it comes to learner engagement, marketing matters, lack of awareness doesn't equal reluctance. But the great programmes that languish on our learning management system and rarely see the light of day will not score high on 'engagement' if our audience can't find them or see the relevance of them when they do.

We know that managers play a critical role in releasing individuals, encouraging reflection and learning transfer.[5] Blaming managers for inhibiting our success helps us pass the buck but to what extent are we equipping them to build relevant learning into their rhythm and routine as we discussed in Chapter 4? Who is really to blame if managers are resistant to encouraging learning – them or us?

High-performing teams face the same challenges over the years, albeit to a lesser degree, but they are proactively finding more ways to navigate through them. Over the years they have typically been twice as likely to provide access to learning that is relevant to the individual's job and twice as likely to be communicating that to all stakeholders involved. They are more likely to expect managers to play an active role in supporting team learning. Perhaps more importantly, they are three times more likely to be equipping managers with resources to help their teams get the most from learning.[6]

The most effective learning leaders don't necessarily face fewer barriers – they just choose to navigate them differently.

Shifting from We to Me… and back to Me again

In earlier chapters, we explored how ultimately we build better business value by co-creating it with others.

The TRI principles are navigation essentials to help L&D help others become equipped and ready. They help us pinpoint how **we work with others** in the organization to:

- clarify priorities, context and action needed
- enable learning transfer effectively
- ensure that we remain on course for impact

Working with others is at the heart of Tuning In, Responding and continually Improving – over the last 20 years they determine if we land on business value. They demand that we **shift from Me to We.**

On paper it is so simple. Common sense? Yes. Common practice? No. Why? Because of them!

To explore this negative cycle more fully, we are turning our attention back onto '**Me**'.

Each of us has unique perspectives, unique skills, unique experiences, a unique role to play now and unique potential for helping others become equipped and ready in the future. These inform and strengthen the mental models that we use to interpret incoming information, make decisions and take action.

In a dynamic and continually changing world of work there may be little within our control, but developing self-awareness of how we uniquely filter the world can help us recognize and sometimes reset the internal navigation instruments that determine our responses to the opportunities and challenges that whirl around us.

Understanding our internal navigation instruments

L&D practitioners are no strangers to the brain.

Over the years we have become more aware of how the brain works and how it influences the way that we learn. In Chapter 4 we saw how high-performing learning teams prioritize decisions based on good learning science. As a profession, we have access to relatable science to help us understand memory, cognition, perception and behaviour, which in theory influences our Responding (Table 10.1). Thanks to learning science translators (introduced in Chapter 4) there really is no excuse not to design learning more effectively.

TABLE 10.1 Learning science insights used in L&D practice

Learning science concept	Description	L&D apply these insights to improve learning by:
Schema theory[1]	Mental frameworks that organize knowledge and guide information processing	• Creating learning paths that build on existing knowledge • Developing frameworks that help organize information into patterns • Providing scaffolding that connects new concepts to prior knowledge • Introducing signposts to prepare individuals for what's coming next
Cognitive load[2]	How working memory limitations affect learning and performance	• Chunking complex information into manageable units • Designing materials that reduce extraneous cognitive load • Using dual coding (visual and verbal) to enhance processing • Sequencing content from simple to complex elements
Retrieval practice[3]	How actively recalling and applying information strengthens memory	• Developing spaced practice schedules with retrieval prompts • Using concept mapping for knowledge consolidation • Designing curriculum with deliberate connections between modules • Creating formative assessments focused on recall and application
Metacognition[4]	Awareness and regulation of one's thinking processes	• Designing reflection activities to enhance awareness of personal learning processes • Teaching learning strategies alongside content • Including prompts that encourage monitoring comprehension • Building in moments to analyse problem-solving processes

(continued)

TABLE 10.1 (Continued)

Learning science concept	Description	L&D apply these insights to improve learning by:
Cognitive bias[5]	Systematic pattern of deviation from rational thinking that affects how we perceive, remember and make decisions	• Include activities that slow down thinking to help learners question assumptions • Encourage multiple viewpoints through group work to surface different perspectives • Integrate activities that help learners notice and reflect on their own thinking patterns. • Provide feedback loops to help learners become aware of how their beliefs or decisions may be biased and adjust accordingly
Social constructivism[6]	How knowledge is constructed through social interaction	• Designing collaborative learning experiences • Creating communities of practice for knowledge sharing • Facilitating meaningful peer discussions and feedback • Using social learning approaches for complex topics

TABLE NOTES

1.   P A Kirschner and C Hendrick (2024) *How Learning Happens: Seminal works in educational psychology and what they mean in practice*, Routledge, Abingdon

2.   M Neelen and P A Kirschner (2020) *Evidence-Informed Learning Design: Creating training to improve performance*, Kogan Page, London

3.   P C Brown, H L Roediger III and M A McDaniel (2014) *Make It Stick: The science of successful learning*, Harvard University Press, Cambridge, MA

4.   P A Kirschner and C Hendrick (2024) *How Learning Happens: Seminal works in educational psychology and what they mean in practice*, Routledge, Abingdon

5.   C Ruhl. Cognitive bias: How we are wired to misjudge, Simply Psychology, 2023. www.simplypsychology.org/cognitive-bias.html (archived at https://perma.cc/DZMII U9PW)

6.   C Nickerson. Social constructionism theory: Definition and examples, Simply Psychology, 2024. www.simplypsychology.org/social-constructionism.html (archived at https://perma.cc/VZ97-TUMR)

Let's retrieve what we explored earlier in the context of how we apply them (see what we did there?!). Table 10.1 gives just a few examples.

We invest considerable effort in understanding how others' brains work so we can help them be equipped and ready, but how often do we apply this knowledge to ourselves?

REFLECT ON YOUR INTERNAL NAVIGATION INSTRUMENTS

- Which learning science concepts (see Table 10.1) actively inform how you learn? How might you better apply these to improve your learning?
- What do you do to reduce cognitive load when you are overwhelmed?
- How has your professional community limited your perspective on what constitutes 'best practice'?

Applying insights from learning science to our own practice can help us release our own potential. They can also shed light on what might hold us back. Take cognitive bias, for example!

How cognitive bias impacts our work

Cognitive biases are an important navigational instrument which can be positive, helping us make quick decisions when needed. But they can also lead us off course when facing complex challenges that require deeper consideration.

As L&D leaders, operating with unchecked biases can result in us making poor decisions because we miss out on important signals or misinterpret those we have.

Let's examine some of these 'instrument errors' that can affect each stage of our work.

TABLE 10.2 Cognitive biases

Tuning In biases	Responding biases	Improving biases
Distance bias: Paying attention to local needs	Status quo bias: Defaulting to the familiar	Confirmation bias: Seeing evidence that supports our current approach (happy sheet), or only remembering external data that confirms we were right
Attribution bias: Misattributing causes of performance or assuming training can fix it all	Bandwagon effect: Being swayed by the latest 'trends'	Outcome bias: Overvaluing the lucky successes
Observer bias: Seeing what we expect to see	Curse of knowledge bias: Creating over-complicated solutions when all you need is a pdf	Not invented here bias: Rejecting the need for ongoing improvements
Projection bias: Assuming others think the same, projecting our preferences onto others	Planning fallacy: Underestimating implementation time	Linear thinking bias (missing feedback loops)
Disruption blindness: Missing potential disruption and underestimating change	Sunk cost fallacy: Continuing just because we spent a lot on a solution	
Cultural blindness: Failing to acknowledge cultural differences, often assuming that treating everyone the same is fair		
	IKEA bias: Placing high value on something we built ourselves	

Caught in the doldrums: The impact of limiting beliefs

While cognitive biases are universal human tendencies, limiting beliefs that we hold deeply about ourselves or others around us are more personal. The early crews of the *Hōkūle'a* found life tough when they hit the doldrums, notorious windless zones that kept them stranded for days on end. Just as they would watch their momentum gradually fade without understanding why, our limiting beliefs silently drain our professional energy and initiative.

These deeply held assumptions about ourselves and our capabilities don't announce themselves with warning flags; they simply leave us immobilized when we most need to move forward. Unlike the challenge of navigating through fog or storms – where at least there's movement and the possibility of correction – the doldrums represent a complete absence of momentum. We may be able to see where we want to go clearly enough, but find ourselves powerless to move toward it.

In L&D these limiting beliefs take various forms:

- **Others' resistance:** If we think 'People in our organization will always resist new learning approaches' then it may stop us from trying something new.

- **I don't have a voice:** If we think 'We need a seat at the table in order to be heard' then we might miss opportunities to influence change in different ways.

- **Spotlight:** If we think 'I can't suggest this innovative approach because everyone will judge me if it fails' then we might miss the opportunity to embed better business value and raise our credibility.

- **Isolation:** If we think 'No one understands what we're trying to do in L&D' then we might stop trying, and then no one will.

- **Fear/imposter:** If we think 'Other L&D professionals know more than I do, so I shouldn't challenge the status quo' then we risk being dragged back into the past with them.

When we apply some learning science to our own professional mindset, we see how limiting beliefs take root. Our mental schemas can harden into fixed frameworks that reject new approaches. The natural tendency to avoid cognitive strain leads us to label certain ideas as 'too complex' rather than worth the effort. Even our work community might normalize constraints through shared language and unchallenged practices.

Wherever they come from, our limiting beliefs can keep us stalled and immobilized – preventing us from applying what we know and exploring potentially valuable new territories.

Recalibrating our navigation instruments

How do we escape the doldrums and ensure our cognitive instruments are recalibrated for landing our business potential? The same way skilled navigators do – through regular checks, adjustments and using multiple reference points.

Cameron Hedrick's approach – learning the names of 50 biases and discussing them regularly with his team – offers one powerful strategy for being aware of how our biases may impact our decisions.

When it comes to mitigating limiting beliefs, a good coach can help! Creating new experiences, talking about them, celebrating them and challenging assumptions with evidence can all help generate the momentum needed to escape our professional doldrums.

Amplifying our L&D professional superpowers

As L&D professionals, we know the frustration. Some of us feel boxed in by expectations to churn out courses and curricula. Some struggle for credibility beyond being the 'training people'. Despite our expertise, we find ourselves sidelined in conversations about performance and business outcomes. And, with AI churning out content faster than ever, there's that nagging fear: where do we bring value? These experiences can confirm our biases and nurture our limiting beliefs.

Throughout this book, we've explored how high-performing L&D teams are working through this frustration, their success in improving business value increasing as they shift from producing interventions for the organization to enabling learning within it.

However, as L&D leaders intent on becoming enablers of workplace learning, we need to immerse ourselves in the dynamic pulse of work at every opportunity. We've deeply explored how the principles of constantly Tuning In, Responding and Improving help shape the way we support organizational learning to drive business value. As we move toward supporting common business goals, we're no longer outside of the system – we are actually part of it. Before we even do anything, our very presence changes the environment.

How we see ourselves in that new space of work matters.

As Cameron Hedrick said, 'You're not an HR person first. You're a businessperson who specializes in human capital. You're a revenue driver who specializes in humans, just like your CMO focuses on marketing and a CFO on finance.'

This perspective shift isn't just philosophical – it fundamentally changes how we operate and the impact we have.

But how do we get there? We've already seen in this book that it's not just about following a new (hopefully evidence-informed) model or methodology or getting buy-in for a new piece of tech. Our personal observations of L&D leaders who are reimagining their role as learning enablers reveals something deeper.

How we see ourselves fundamentally influences the impact we have on others. Our professional identity – who we believe ourselves to be at work – determines not just what we do, but also how others respond to us.

The shift from content creator to learning enabler isn't just about changing what we do whilst battling our biases. It's about recognizing and amplifying the professional superpowers we already possess. Let's explore three powerful capabilities that can transform our professional identity and, as a result, our impact.

Our presence superpower: How we show up and interact

The most powerful tool in our L&D toolkit isn't a learning platform or programme – it's us. Our observations, conversations and insights can spark just as much learning as any course, and sometimes more.

When embedded in the workplace – having curious conversations, noticing patterns, asking thoughtful questions – we create our own 'learning moments' that transform our interactions with others in real-time. This is what organizational theorist Edgar Schein calls 'use of self as an instrument of change' – the intentional deployment of our presence as a catalyst for development.

Many seasoned learning professionals who excel in the classroom know this intuitively as we adapt our interventions to the responses of the participants.

Dr Mee-Yan Cheung-Judge and David Jamieson's research with organizational development (OD) professionals revealed that their presence in the organization itself can be a potent catalyst for change.[7] As enablers of learning, following the TRI principles we increasingly find ourselves moving out of our safe domains into the heart of business where our very presence can influence others. Recognizing this potential 'superpower' might feel overwhelming, but their work showed that it can be cultivated through conscious self-awareness, a commitment to understanding our environment and its people, and the intentional application of our cognitive and relational capabilities in each interaction.

WHAT THIS LOOKS LIKE IN PRACTICE

- Instead of staying in our offices waiting for training requests, we regularly visit where the work happens.
- We ask questions that make people think differently about their challenges.
- We notice patterns across teams that individual managers can't see.
- Our conversations become interventions that shift thinking in the moment.

Try this: Schedule 'no-agenda' conversations with key stakeholders where you simply ask about their current challenges. Notice how your curious questions often lead to insights they wouldn't have reached alone.

Our influence superpower: How we shape systems and processes

We're not just responding to the organization – we're actively shaping it. Every time we choose to push back on a training request, suggest an alternative approach or reframe a problem, we're exercising what social scientists call 'agency' – our capacity to make choices that influence our environment.

Many of us feel trapped by how others define our role, but research on identity theory shows that professional identities are constantly being negotiated.[8] When we act as if we have the authority to guide learning approaches (even when no one has explicitly given us that authority), people begin to treat us as if we do.

One L&D leader we interviewed described this transformation: 'I was holding onto old habits until recently. When faced with a complex project without clear answers, I deliberately shifted away from jumping to solutions. Instead, I began asking what the business problem or opportunity really was, recognizing that "learning on its own is not going to solve your problem."'

This intentional shift in approach led to challenging but valuable conversations with stakeholders. 'I'm happy with that because we're having the right conversations,' they noted. 'Whereas two or three years ago, I'd have wanted to give a solution because my value was providing answers.'

This leader changed the system around them by changing their own actions first.

WHAT THIS LOOKS LIKE IN PRACTICE

- When someone requests a course, we look for ways to explore business outcomes first.
- We are comfortable sharing evidence that suggests formal learning approaches may not be appropriate.
- We initiate conversations about how different learning approaches might contribute to value rather than waiting to be included.
- We view ourselves as responsible for performance outcomes, not just training delivery.

Try this: The next time someone requests a specific training solution, respond with: 'I'd like to understand more about what you're trying to achieve so that we can get the best outcome for you. Let's explore the challenge before deciding on the approach.'

Our expertise superpower: How we apply our unique knowledge

Our understanding of how people learn and develop is specialized knowledge that most people in our organizations don't have. Building mastery and expertise in our craft gives us not just the ability but the self-confidence to recommend the most effective approaches – even when they differ from what was requested.

This is what psychologist Albert Bandura calls 'self-efficacy' – our belief in our ability to succeed in specific situations. Bandura's extensive research (spanning over 40 years and thousands of participants) shows that self-efficacy isn't just positive thinking; it's built through successful experiences, seeing others succeed, receiving encouragement and managing emotional reactions.[9]

When we build and trust our expertise about how people learn, we're more likely to speak up when a requested solution won't address the actual need. Instead of simply executing orders for courses or programmes, we can confidently suggest alternatives based on our understanding of how learning actually happens. This isn't about being difficult or contrarian – it's about honouring our professional knowledge and using it to create genuine value.

Cameron demonstrates this when he openly discusses his limitations with his team while still maintaining confidence in his expertise about learning and organizational change. This balance of humility about what he doesn't know with confidence in what he does creates psychological safety that enables experimentation and adaptation.

WHAT THIS LOOKS LIKE IN PRACTICE

- You confidently recommend approaches based on learning science, even when they're unexpected.
- You trust your assessment of a situation over assumptions in a training request.
- You speak with authority about how people actually learn and develop.
- You're willing to challenge conventional training wisdom when necessary.

Try this: Identify a situation where your expertise tells you the requested solution won't work. Practise articulating an alternative approach based explicitly on your professional knowledge. Begin with 'Based on what we know about how learning transfers to performance…' or 'The evidence on skill development suggests that…'.

FIGURE 10.1 Honing our professional superpowers

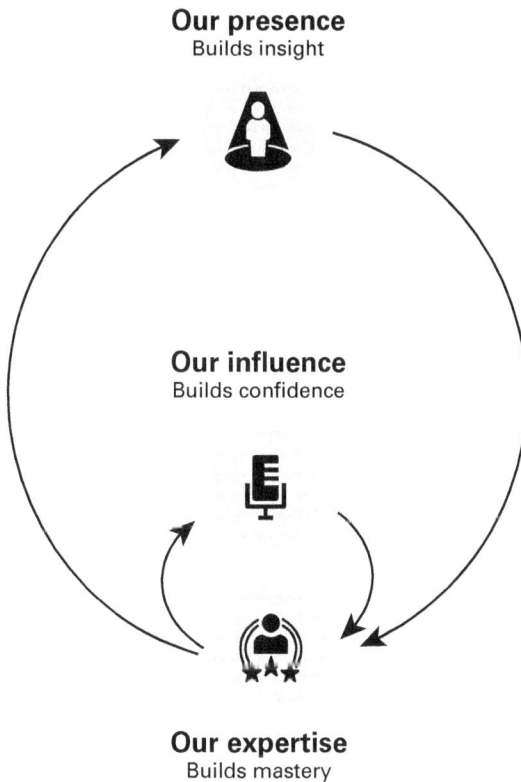

Our presence
Builds insight

Our influence
Builds confidence

Our expertise
Builds mastery

How these superpowers work together

These three superpowers work together in a powerful cycle that transforms both how we see ourselves and how others see us.

- When we use our presence in the workplace, we gain insights about how to connect shared business goals with the people we work with. Over time, this opens doors to our influence and agency in that space.

- As we start to use our influence we start to be curious, building more confidence.

- Building our expertise gives us the courage to suggest approaches that go beyond what was requested.

- Taking these actions leads to better outcomes, which reinforces both our belief in our expertise and others' willingness to value our presence.

- As others increasingly value our presence, we have more opportunities to embed ourselves in the workplace, continuing the cycle.

Each successful iteration of this cycle doesn't just change what we do – it changes who we are in the organization. We shift from being the people who create courses to the people who enable performance improvement. Our identity transforms from content producer to learning enabler.

BEING INTENTIONAL WITH IMPACT

Arun Pradhan, General Manager of Learning at ANZ bank, describes himself as a 'curious and empathetic Geek' on his LinkedIn profile.[10] But he uses this description with deliberate intent: 'That's partly a nudge for me, because no one is curious all the time. I think about when being curious is most valuable and set up cues to kick-start my curiosity.'

Arun intentionally builds curious habits, identifying cues that trigger his curiosity. 'When someone gives me feedback, that's a cue to start being curious,' he explains. 'Another nudge is when I start a new project.' Perhaps most valuably, he notes, 'When I'm absolutely certain about something, that's when I deliberately ask questions like "What would I see if I was wrong?"'

He's equally intentional about how he shows up in organizational settings. 'I might mention something from big tech early in a meeting – "Google tried this approach, but Amazon does that" – because then people start to associate you as someone who understands the broader context and brings outside perspectives. With others, I might reference an evidence-based study. You don't need much to create an impression before you can pull back and be curious.'

This balance reflects what Arun calls 'being intentional with impact'. He explains, 'Curiosity is wonderful, but there are times when you need to show you're bringing something valuable to the table. L&D leaders who aren't as impactful often aren't political enough – that sounds like a dirty word, but it's about understanding how to navigate the system to create meaningful change.'

Strengthening your L&D superpowers: A development guide

Arun has provided us with some practical insight on how to develop our presence in the workplace. As we transition from content producers to learning enablers, here are some additional suggestions about how we can strengthen our superpowers to make a bigger impact.

1. DEVELOP YOUR PRESENCE SUPERPOWER

- Practise genuine curiosity in every interaction, asking questions that help others gain insight rather than demonstrating your knowledge.
- Build trust deliberately through consistent reliability and respecting others' perspectives even when you disagree.
- Develop awareness of how your expressions, tone and reactions impact conversations, especially in challenging situations.
- Notice patterns in meetings and conversations that reveal underlying needs beyond what's being directly requested.
- Create psychological safety by managing your own reactions when facing resistance or criticism.

2. ENHANCE YOUR INFLUENCE SUPERPOWER

- Frame learning challenges in business terms, connecting solutions to measurable outcomes that stakeholders value.
- Build strategic relationships across functions before you need them, understanding others' priorities and pressures.
- Know when to challenge training requests by suggesting alternatives based on evidence, not just opinion.

- Articulate your ideas concisely, adapting your language to match stakeholders' priorities and concerns.
- Balance persistence with flexibility, knowing when to push for change and when to step back and regroup.

3. STRENGTHEN YOUR EXPERTISE SUPERPOWER

- Stay evidence-informed by connecting with research and learning science that grounds your recommendations.
- Practise explaining complex learning concepts in simple, accessible terms that non-specialists understand.
- Trust your assessment when a requested solution won't address the actual need, offering alternatives with confidence.
- Balance confidence in your expertise with genuine openness to others' perspectives and approaches.
- Continuously expand your knowledge through deliberate practice and reflection on both successes and setbacks.

These recommendations not only help us embed the TRI principles that we've been exploring but they also help transform how we show up in our organizations.

Research on professional effectiveness shows that when we harness our presence (use of self), influence (agency) and expertise (self-efficacy) intentionally we create stronger stakeholder connections, develop keener perception of organizational dynamics and build confidence to navigate complexity. This doesn't just enhance our credibility and confidence; it significantly increases our ability to create conditions where meaningful learning can flourish, ultimately driving the business value that matters most in our organizations.

From mindset to action: Preparing to be BOLD

Throughout this chapter, we've explored how our internal landscape – our biases, limiting beliefs and thinking patterns – profoundly shapes our professional impact. By developing awareness of these patterns and consciously embracing our L&D superpowers, we've begun the essential inner work that precedes effective outer action.

Like Cameron Hedrick, who in the early days of his career realized his thinking was the barrier rather than others' behaviour, many effective L&D leaders describe a similar awakening. This internal shift – from seeing oneself as a solution provider to a business partner – consistently preceded their most meaningful organizational contributions.

While mindset provides the foundation, translating awareness into consistent action requires an internal compass to guide our professional decisions. In the next chapter we'll explore how cultivating BOLD thinking habits allows L&D professionals to navigate complexity with confidence and purpose. This internal compass orients us toward **Business-First** value, keeps us **Open Minded** to multiple perspectives, encourages **Leading and Learning,** and helps us take **Deliberate** action even in uncertain conditions. These four cardinal directions create a navigational system that builds upon the mindset work we've begun here. This self-awareness will help you identify which aspects of the BOLD compass you already navigate by and which represent opportunities to lead ourselves and others in new directions.

Notes

1   Author interview with Cameron Hedrick, 27 September 2024.
2   L Overton. *Learning at Work 2023: Survey report*, CIPD, 2023. www.cipd.org/globalassets/media/knowledge/knowledge-hub/reports/2023-pdfs/2023-learning-at-work-survey-report-8378.pdf (archived at https://perma.cc/R74X-NAXE)
3   Source: Learning Performance Benchmark study, see Appendix 1.
4   Source: Learning Performance Benchmark study, see Appendix 1.
5   Dr Ina Wienbaur Heidel, 12 Levers of Learning Transfer, see overview in Appendix 2.
6   Source: Learning Performance Benchmark study, see Appendix 1.
7   M Y Cheung-Judge and D W Jamieson. Providing deeper understanding of the concept of use of self in OD practice, *OD Practitioner*, 2018, 50.
8   B E Ashforth and F Mael. Social identity theory and the organization, *Academy of Management Review*, 1989, 14 (1), 20–39.
9   A Bandura and S Wessels (1997) *Self-Efficacy*, Cambridge University Press, Cambridge, pp 4–6,
10 Author interview with Arun Pradhan, 14 October 2024.

11

Calibrating our BOLD compass

An eye for business value

James Swift never set out to be an L&D leader.[1] His sales background instilled a mindset that would transform his approach to talent development in ways traditional L&D training never could.

'I absolutely loved new business,' James reflects. But as a successful sales manager faced with an underperforming sales team, James's business-first mindset guided his response. 'I looked at my target and then I looked at my team. There was a massive disconnect.' Rather than accepting this gap, he focused on developing his people – discovering a passion for helping others succeed: 'I really enjoyed seeing other people doing well and knowing I've played a part in that.'

Working in a global and rapidly growing consultancy business, the next logical step was to apply to become sales director, but when that didn't happen the company unexpectedly offered him the head of talent development role.

James's passion for driving concrete outcomes became the foundation of his talent development philosophy. From sales, he was comfortable with measurable impact, setting ambitious targets and persistently working through challenges until results materialized. This mindset shaped his thinking in his new learning leadership role. While many L&D professionals might have focused on programme design or learning theories, James's first thought was, 'What impact am I going to be able to say I've achieved?'

He initially targeted speed-to-competence – identifying and tracking the tasks and behaviours that new joiners needed to reach revenue-generating performance. He believed in the importance of systems but wasn't constrained by them. James intentionally designed learning experiences based on what worked in real customer conversations and experimented with AI to track and improve performance. His approach helped new joiners generate an additional £1.5 million in revenue during the first year.

His pragmatic approach to talent development continues to embody this distinct mindset that blends business focus, openness to experimentation and deliberate methodology to drive value.

> There are no challenges in business that haven't been solved before. So if you've got a challenge, you either haven't spent enough time on it or you haven't got the right people in the room. *James Swift*[2]

James's approach to addressing the challenge he faced was informed by his background in sales – evidence-informed, deliberate and business-focused. It contrasts with others whose instinct might be to design a programme or a course. The difference wasn't in his technical skills or resources but in the way he thought about the problem, his role and his measurement of success.

Each of us brings unique perspectives to our work, shaping our instinctive responses. Some naturally focus on business outcomes, others excel at exploring possibilities, some embrace experimentation, while others gather extensive evidence before deciding.

What matters is whether our ingrained approaches align with what's needed in a given situation, and if we're aware enough of our patterns to adapt when necessary.

While the TRI principles provide a framework for navigating workplace learning, their application is influenced by something more personal: the mindsets and mental models that act as an internal compass. This chapter explores what shapes this compass, how to recognize its influence and how to calibrate it to navigate toward greater impact.

Our internal compass

In our exploration of the Polynesian Voyaging Society in previous chapters, we were inspired by how ancient navigators like Mau Piailug possessed an internal mental model – a star compass – that helped them navigate vast oceans without modern instruments. Sitting in the centre on their canoe, these navigators were able to look at the ocean and the circle of the horizon surrounding them. Dividing that circle into segments and memorizing how the stars would rise and set within those segments helped them to create a portable internal map that guided every decision. The star compass isn't a physical tool but a mental construct – a way of organizing and interpreting environmental cues to maintain direction even when obvious landmarks were absent.

As aspiring or seasoned L&D leaders, we need to navigate our own challenging waters. We may often feel that we are in the centre of shifting stakeholder expectations, internal politics and technological disruption whilst trying to land on business value. To do this, whether we are aware of them or not, we make decisions on a set of mental frameworks that guide our decisions and responses – our own internal compass.

In Chapter 10 we explored how our brains naturally develop those cognitive frameworks and mental models that help us make sense of the world. Our professional thinking habits – the persistent perspectives and settled tendencies that influence the way we think about our professional world of L&D work – are shaped by our experience. The schemata, frameworks of knowledge that we develop to make sense of the working world, will have developed throughout our careers, influenced by culture, events, interactions and expectations of others.[3] They influence what we notice during the Tuning In process, the solutions we consider when Responding, and what data we prioritize when Improving. When something doesn't quite fit with them, we experience cognitive dissonance – discomfort.

For instance, James is a learning leader with a strong business past and as a result might instinctively tune into operational metrics and bottom-line impacts that are uncomfortable for some others. Someone who has been operating in their role as a solutions provider might automatically feel the need to offer a programme rather than ask questions and explore.

These thinking habits influence our professional superpowers, the way we show up in our dynamic workplaces, and this in turn influences the outcomes of our work. They help us make sense of the world and respond appropriately. But as we saw in Chapter 10 they can also create limitations.

The good news is that our thinking habits are not fixed. This is where metacognition – thinking about our thinking – becomes crucial. By developing awareness of our own thinking habits, we gain the ability to adapt them when necessary. Developing this type of self-awareness isn't merely helpful – it's essential for an L&D leader navigating a changing and potentially unpredictable landscape. When we can identify and understand the thinking habits that influence our work, then we can leverage their strengths while compensating for their limitations. We can intentionally shift our perspective when a situation calls for a different approach. And, most importantly, we can expand our range of responses beyond our default patterns.

Like Mau's star compass, our professional thinking habits guide us through uncertainty. But, unlike physical tools, they operate largely beneath our awareness – until we make the deliberate choice to examine them. In the sections that follow, we'll explore a framework for recognizing these thinking habits and working out how we can change them when needed.

BOLD learning leaders

In 2020, as organizations worldwide scrambled to respond to pandemic disruption, we noticed something intriguing through our work with the Emerging Stronger project. While many L&D teams were struggling to adapt – wrestling with cancelled in-person programmes, remote workforce challenges and slashed budgets – others were thriving. These teams weren't just surviving; they were becoming more strategic, more visible and more valued by their organizations.

What distinguished these learning leaders wasn't their technology or resources. It was their approach to the challenges they faced. Before the pandemic hit they had already seen their role as one that supported business rather than learning and they had been deliberately exploring new ways to do that. Their approach to their role before the pandemic influenced the way that they showed up in their organizations during crisis.[4]

The Emerging Stronger research project, which journeyed with L&D professionals through the pandemic and beyond, revealed that those who were ready to navigate the disruption successfully shared certain thinking patterns. They approached challenges with a business-first orientation, remaining open to new perspectives while continuously learning and taking deliberate action.

Geraldine Voost exemplifies this approach.[5] She was working for a technology manufacturing business when the pandemic hit and was already guiding the training department toward a more strategic business model. 'The whole crisis has worked to our advantage,' she explained, as the disruption to classroom delivery created space to accelerate their shift from being order-takers to linking learning with strategic goals. Rather than simply moving training online, Geraldine used this opportunity to deepen their business-first orientation, ensuring every new project answered the critical question her general manager had posed: 'What changes will I see that prove this was worth the investment?'

James and Geraldine show us that how we turn up at work matters. Driving business value often requires stepping beyond conventional L&D boundaries into unfamiliar territory – becoming co-creators and change-makers rather than order-takers or service providers. This shift demands courage, particularly when it means challenging stakeholder assumptions or organizational conventions.

However, the effective learning leaders we studied weren't demonstrating what we might call 'brassy bold' behaviour – charging ahead based on ego or overconfidence. Instead, they exhibited what we term 'smart BOLD' thinking – an approach grounded in business understanding, openness to multiple perspectives, willingness to learn through experimentation and deliberate action.

Smart BOLD thinking involves being:

- **B**usiness-First: Orienting decisions around organizational outcomes rather than learning outputs.
- **O**pen Minded: Approaching challenges with curiosity and receptivity to multiple perspectives.
- **L**eading and Learning: Embracing experimentation and continuous improvement in oneself and others.
- **D**eliberate: Taking intentional, evidence-informed action rather than defaulting to convention.

This smart BOLD approach complements the TRI principles we've explored throughout this book. While the TRI principles provide the external navigation framework, BOLD thinking habits represent our navigation compass. They influence how we apply the TRI principles in practice.

For example, a learning leader with a business-first orientation will naturally excel at the **Aligning Together** aspect of Tuning In, while someone with an explorer orientation might have particular strengths in **Connecting to Individuals**. A professional comfortable with experimentation will likely embrace the **Adapting Course** aspects of Improving, while someone with a deliberate, evidence-informed approach might excel at designing rigorous feedback loops for **Monitoring Progress**.

Understanding these internal orientations helps us recognize our natural strengths while identifying areas where we might need to reorient our thinking. In the next section, we'll explore the four BOLD thinking habits in detail, examining how they influence our work and how we might develop greater awareness of our own default patterns.

Recognizing our thinking habits

The BOLD L&D compass is not like the standard compass that helps us orient through the magnetic pull of the north. We have seen throughout the book that the pull of the business value north star is critical for L&D.

Equally important for setting direction is our ability to be Open Minded enough to see that goal through the eyes of others, willing to explore alternative approaches and being deliberately intentional in our actions. All of these orientations or professional thinking habits create direction, momentum and traction in our work.

Marc Howell (Chapter 6) was deliberately intentional with his evidence-informed business case at AstraZeneca. Siva Kulasingam and Rodney Beach (Chapter 9) demonstrated an Open Minded partnership to create an innovative solution. Adam Harwood (Chapter 7) showed Leading and Learning by moving beyond classroom training to performance-focused approaches.

All three exemplify the powerful influence of the Business-First pull in action.

None of these orientations are inherently 'right' or 'wrong' and we don't need to act on them in a certain order. The value in each of these orientations is in becoming aware of our natural tendencies and how they influence our work. Like any compass, the BOLD L&D compass doesn't tell us where to go. As you stand in the centre of a web of people, politics, needs and wants, it helps you understand your current orientation so you can make the decisions needed to arrive at your business value goals.

FIGURE 11.1 BOLD L&D compass

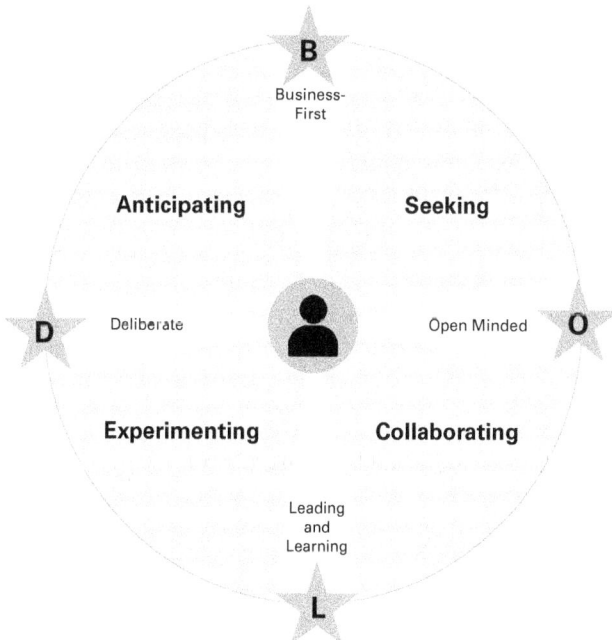

Let's explore how each of these orientations can influence our decisions and lead us to drive better business value. We'll also look back to the people we've met in the book so far to see what this looks like in practice.

Business-First: How we think about value

FIGURE 11.2 Thinking about value

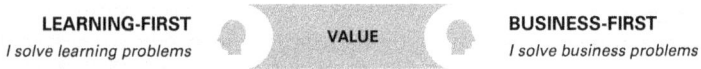

| LEARNING-FIRST | VALUE | BUSINESS-FIRST |
| *I solve learning problems* | | *I solve business problems* |

This first thinking habit reflects the L&D value spectrum introduced in Chapter 1. At one end of this continuum, we define success primarily through learning outputs – course completions, satisfaction scores or training hours. At the other end, we define value through business outcomes – operational improvements, productivity gains or revenue impact.

Marie Daniels (Chapter 5) exemplifies Business-First thinking in action. When developing a sales capability programme, she didn't rely on standard learning metrics. Instead, she created dashboards tracking sales competencies, confidence levels and customer engagement. She structured her conversations around business impact: 'What would success look like for the business?' rather than learning: 'What training content do you need?'

Our orientation on this thinking habit significantly influences how we apply the Tuning In principle. Business-First thinkers naturally excel at Aligning Together, connecting learning initiatives to strategic priorities. When Tuning In, they seek to understand business metrics and key performance indicators (KPIs) before focusing on learning needs.

When Responding, this orientation shapes how professionals evaluate options, prioritizing those with clearer connections to business outcomes. And when Improving, it influences what we choose to measure and track.

We see this thinking habit throughout the real-world examples in this book. Sebastian Tindall's resource-led approach at Vitality (Chapter 7) prioritized supporting frontline staff to stay abreast of rapid operational changes over traditional training design. Marc Howells at AstraZeneca (Chapter 6) directly linked learning transformation to the company's Great Place to Work strategic pillar, using benchmarking data to show that, despite high learning spend, impact was suboptimal.

Open Minded: How we think about our role and relationships

This dimension encompasses two related thinking habits – how we:

- View our **professional role**: Expert versus explorer.

- Approach **relationships** with others: Independent versus interdependent.

ROLE ORIENTATION

FIGURE 11.3 Thinking about our role

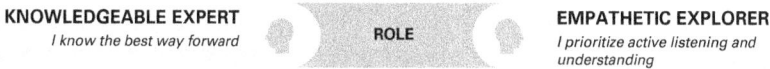

KNOWLEDGEABLE EXPERT   ROLE   EMPATHETIC EXPLORER
I know the best way forward   *I prioritize active listening and*
                                                        understanding

At one end of this thinking habit, professionals seeing themselves as experts will habitually seek and find opportunities to apply their knowledge to diagnose problems and prescribe solutions. At the other end, they operate as explorers, approaching situations with curiosity and a willingness to discover alongside stakeholders.

Annaleigh McKay and Karina Moon at Multiplex (Chapter 7) exemplified an explorer orientation in their behaviour change campaign in their Appropriate Workplace Behaviour programme. Rather than positioning themselves as experts on workplace behaviour, the L&D team created space for open discussions about sensitive topics. They collected over 3,000 ideas from participants, using these to co-create the behaviour change campaign rather than imposing predetermined solutions.

RELATIONSHIP ORIENTATION

FIGURE 11.4 Thinking about our relationships

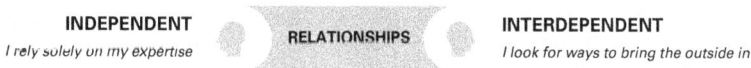

INDEPENDENT   RELATIONSHIPS   INTERDEPENDENT
I rely solely on my expertise   *I look for ways to bring the outside in*

Do we think of ourselves as independent specialists who deliver services or as interdependent partners who work across silos and create value collaboratively?

Barbara Thompson (Chapter 9) demonstrated interdependent thinking when developing a graduate programme, deliberately working with six different external partners despite management concerns about complexity.

Her perspective that 'This isn't about lobbing something over the fence. It's about collaborating to get the best possible outcome' reflects a relationship orientation focused on collective value creation rather than transactional service delivery.[6]

Again, the way we think about our relationships with others might profoundly influence our application of the Tuning In principle, particularly **Connecting to Individuals** and **Grounding in the Real World**. Interdependent thinkers might more readily work across organizational boundaries to understand context. Independent thinkers might want to be given an element of an initiative and run with it.

When Responding, those with an Interdependent orientation might amplify their work by **Engaging Influencers** in collaborative design. Similarly, when Improving, interdependent thinkers may find it easier to gather diverse feedback and act on **Adapting Course** based on multiple perspectives.

Leading and Learning: How we think about change

This dimension encompasses three related continuums – our:

- view of **technology**: fix versus enable
- **time** orientation: learning-paced versus business-paced
- approach to **risk and innovation**: hold back versus move on

TECHNOLOGY ORIENTATION

FIGURE 11.5 Thinking about technology

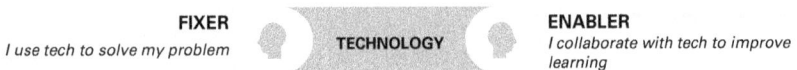

FIXER	**TECHNOLOGY**	**ENABLER**
I use tech to solve my problem		*I collaborate with tech to improve learning*

Some of us see technology primarily as a tool to fix problems or make existing processes more efficient. Others view it as enabling entirely new possibilities.

The Coles and Liberate Learning partnership (Chapter 9) demonstrates an enabler orientation. When Siva Kulasingam couldn't find a suitable existing technology to support learning for retail staff, he partnered with Rodney Beach to create something entirely new. Rather than just fixing existing problems, together they envisioned how technology could enable a completely different learning approach.

TIME ORIENTATION

FIGURE 11.6 Thinking about timeframes

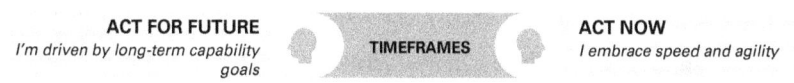

ACT FOR FUTURE
I'm driven by long-term capability goals

TIMEFRAMES

ACT NOW
I embrace speed and agility

This continuum spans from a learning-paced 'act for the future' approach that prioritizes thorough development and comprehensive rollout to a business-paced 'act now' orientation that values speed and responsiveness.

James Swift balanced these orientations at Leyton by addressing immediate client retention issues while simultaneously building long-term capability through a framework for continuous improvement.

RISK AND INNOVATION ORIENTATION

FIGURE 11.7 Thinking about risk and innovation

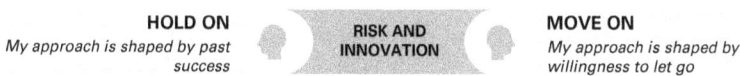

HOLD ON
My approach is shaped by past success

RISK AND
INNOVATION

MOVE ON
My approach is shaped by willingness to let go

Some of us prefer to minimize risk by implementing proven approaches, while others embrace experimentation despite uncertainty. Leading Ericsson's Learning NEXT community, Pauline Rebourgeon (Chapter 4) exemplifies a 'move on' orientation, engaging 450+ members actively experimenting with emerging technologies rather than waiting for proven solutions. Their perspective that 'The worst thing that could happen with these experiments is that people might have learned things' reflects comfort with productive failure as part of innovation.[7]

These orientations significantly influence our application of the Responding principle, particularly **Enabling Learning** and **Engaging Influencers**. Those who see technology as enabling new possibilities create more innovative learning experiences, while business-paced thinkers demonstrate greater flexibility in adjusting to changing priorities.

When Improving, a 'move on' orientation enhances our ability to be **Adapting Course** based on feedback, even when it means significantly changing direction. Experimental thinkers are often more comfortable with rapid iterations and small-scale pilots as part of continuous improvement.

Deliberate: How we think about decisions and influence

The final dimension encompasses how intentional we are, how we:

- approach **decision-making**: experience-led versus evidence-informed
- view our ability to **influence** change: service provider vs changemaker

DECISION ORIENTATION

FIGURE 11.8 Thinking about decisions

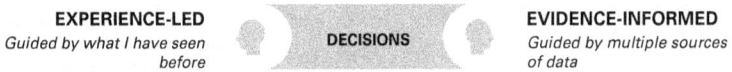

EXPERIENCE-LED
Guided by what I have seen before

DECISIONS

EVIDENCE-INFORMED
Guided by multiple sources of data

At one end of this continuum, we rely primarily on past experience and professional judgement to guide decisions. At the other end, we systematically gather and analyse diverse evidence before determining direction.

James Swift at Leyton demonstrated a strongly evidence-informed approach by customizing an AI system to analyse client calls and identify specific behaviours that appeared in successful interactions. Rather than relying solely on sales experience, he systematically collected data showing where critical skills were lacking, then used this evidence to design targeted interventions.

INFLUENCE ORIENTATION

FIGURE 11.9 Thinking about our influence

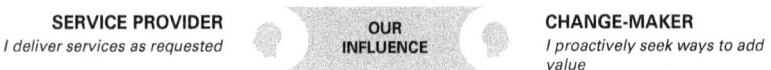

SERVICE PROVIDER
I deliver services as requested

OUR INFLUENCE

CHANGE-MAKER
I proactively seek ways to add value

This continuum spans from viewing ourselves as service providers who respond to requests, to seeing ourselves as changemakers who proactively shape organizational direction.

Marc Howells at AstraZeneca (Chapter 6) exhibited strong changemaker thinking when transforming the company's learning approach. Rather than waiting for permission, he proactively built governance structures, engaged stakeholders and created enterprise learning boards to drive transformation. By connecting learning directly to business strategy and engaging leaders at multiple levels, he positioned himself as influencing organizational priorities rather than simply responding to them.

These orientations influence all aspects of the TRI principles. Evidence-informed thinkers typically gather more comprehensive data during Tuning In, while changemakers excel at proactively engaging stakeholders when Responding. When Improving, evidence-informed professionals design more rigorous feedback loops and evaluation approaches.

In the next section, we'll see how these thinking habits operate together through Keith Resseau's example, observing how her BOLD compass influenced her approach to the role of technology in her work.

BOLD in action: Navigating the edge of innovation

Keith Resseau never planned to be an L&D innovator, but her mindset of 'equal parts evangelist and sceptic' propelled her through decades of technological experimentation.[8] From building an LMS in the 1990s to exploring AI coaching, Keith has consistently sought the intersection between emerging technology and real business problems.

'I get bored really easily,' Keith admits. 'I am at my happiest when I'm trying to pull apart a really sticky problem. There's a bit of the explorer in me who likes to take something that nobody knows what to do with yet.'

Throughout her 20 year career at a global consultancy firm, Keith's explorer mindset translated into pioneering projects like Spark, an award-winning social learning platform that modelled the very behaviours it aimed to teach. 'One of the best ways to teach someone anything is to have them experience it,' Keith explains. 'Don't just tell them about it. Don't just show it to them. Let them actually experience it.'

Her approach to innovation includes deliberately embracing discomfort: 'Being out of my comfort zone is my comfort zone. When I'm uncomfortable, it means I am learning something, so I take discomfort as a sign that I'm headed in the right direction.'

Keith's value has evolved from being perceived as a technology expert to being a translator between technical teams and business stakeholders. She encourages L&D professionals to break free from traditional paradigms when approaching new technologies.

'Stop focusing on content creation,' she advises. 'Look at how you can tackle things that have been too hard for us to do. How can you do things that just weren't possible before?'

Her recommendation for others? 'Do more "What if…" thinking. Start from a mindset of possibility rather than limitation.'

How thinking habits influence practice

Keith's story perfectly illustrates our BOLD thinking habits in action:

- The **Business-First** orientation emerges in how her role evolved from technology expert to 'translator between technical teams and business stakeholders' – focusing on business challenges rather than learning solutions.

- We see her **Open Minded** explorer approach when she describes her passion for 'pulling apart sticky problems' and exploring unknown territory.

- Her statement that 'being out of my comfort zone is my comfort zone' is an example of the **Leading and Learning** orientation, where experimentation and risk-taking drive growth.

- Her self-described mindset of 'equal parts evangelist and sceptic' reflects the balance of a **Deliberate** orientation that embraces both evidence and innovation.

REFLECT ON YOUR THINKING HABITS

Think of a situation where you have made a decision or judgement call. Plot the habits that you think influenced your decisions, feelings and actions on the thinking habit continuum outlined in Appendix 4 (see Figure A4.1).

Repeat this exercise using another decision or judgement call that you made.

- Are you spotting any patterns?
- What difference would a shift in orientation in one or more thinking habits make to your decisions?

As you reflect on these thinking habits, remember that there's no universally 'correct' orientation. Different contexts and activities call for different orientations. The key is developing:

1 **self-awareness** of your natural tendencies along each continuum

2 **contextual awareness** of what's needed in specific situations

3 **agility** to shift your orientation when circumstances require it

Knowing when to turn around

We've established that there is no right or wrong orientation across these thinking habits. However, sometimes our most comfortable direction won't get us to our goal. Occasionally, we must turn around to deliver the specific business value our organizations need.

Being aware of our preferred orientation and how it might influence our work is the starting point. This awareness helps us recognize signals in our work that indicate a need to change direction.

Table 11.1 outlines potential signals that suggest it might be time to adjust our orientation – you might add others. The table also offers some distilled wisdom from L&D leaders we interviewed that may help shift your perspective.

TABLE 11.1 Signals to turn around

Thinking about your:	Signals to turn around	Turn from	Try this approach (tips from L&D leaders)
Value	Blank faces from business leaders when presenting learning metrics	Learning to business value	Ask what impact they want the initiative to have
Role	Creating solutions that are not being used	Expert to explorer	Spend your first year (meeting/week) listening
	Stakeholders constantly seeking your direction	Explorer to expert	Once the problem is clear, pivot to the expert role where your unique L&D knowledge is most valuable
Relationship with others	Frustration with multiple teams working on the same problem	Independent to interdependent	Adopt a 'de-siloed people strategy' – work in fluid ways on cross-functional teams where people roll in and out based on their expertise
Technology	Excitement about tools without business applications	Fixer to enabler	Be clear on what you are trying to achieve and what you are trying to help people do. Then ask what tools are out there

(continued)

TABLE 11.1 (Continued)

Thinking about your:	Signals to turn around	Turn from	Try this approach (tips from L&D leaders)
	Complaints about content libraries	Enabler to fixer	Take a long, hard look at all your content, retire the least-used 30%
Time frames	Constant firefighting with no progress	Act now to act for the future	Don't get sidetracked. We're not here to put out little fires that will just spark up again
	Analysis paralysis preventing action	Act for the future to act now	Just start doing something, because not doing something is, in fact, a decision
Risk and innovation	Team avoids trying new approaches despite poor results	Hold on to move on	Create a minimum viable product that you just get out and test
	Experiments without clear outcomes to learn from	Move on to hold on	Stop and reflect. Work out what was the result of our experiment? What have we learned from it? And then take action
Decisions	Relying on experience when data contradicts instincts	Experience-led to evidence-informed	Challenge your own thinking by asking 'What biases are influencing me? Is my experience blinding me to data?'
	Paralysed by data analysis when quick decisions needed	Evidence-focused to experience-led	Stop searching for perfection; good enough is good enough
Influence	Seeking permission to implement improvements	Service provider to changemaker	Start being really bold – do something, suggest something different
	Lacking stakeholder support for new ideas	Service provider to changemaker	We needed to build a coalition of the willing that understood that where we were going would benefit everybody

Keith's advice to 'do more "What if…" thinking' and 'start from a mindset of possibility rather than limitation' demonstrates her recognition that sometimes we need to turn from a cautious orientation to a more experimental one to drive innovation.

Similarly, Cameron Hedrick's realization (Chapter 10) that 'my thinking was the barrier, not their behaviour' represents a pivotal moment when he turned from seeing himself as the expert with solutions to an explorer seeking to understand the real challenges.[9]

These orientation shifts aren't about abandoning our strengths. Rather, they help expand our ability to respond effectively to different situations. The key is developing the self-awareness to recognize when our default approaches aren't serving us well, and the flexibility to adjust our orientation accordingly.

YOUR TURN AROUND SIGNALS

Reflect on the signals available to you:

- Which of these signals do you recognize in your current work?
- What one orientation shift might most improve your effectiveness right now?

Becoming BOLDER: Your safety net

Developing BOLD thinking habits requires courage, especially when stepping outside your comfort zone to adjust your orientation. Every successful navigator needs a safety net – elements that provide security and confidence when navigating uncertain waters.

Six critical safety net elements emerged from our interviews with learning leaders who consistently demonstrate BOLD thinking and action,

- **A clear vision:** Having a compelling 'north star' provides direction when experiments fail or resistance emerges. As Pinky Thompson advised Nainoa, 'You need to know the path, where you are going and why you are going there.'[10] Define your purpose and values clearly enough that they guide decision-making even in turbulent times.
- **Strong evidence:** Data becomes a safety net when you're challenging established practices. James Swift at Leyton used AI analysis of client

FIGURE 11.10 BOLD safety net

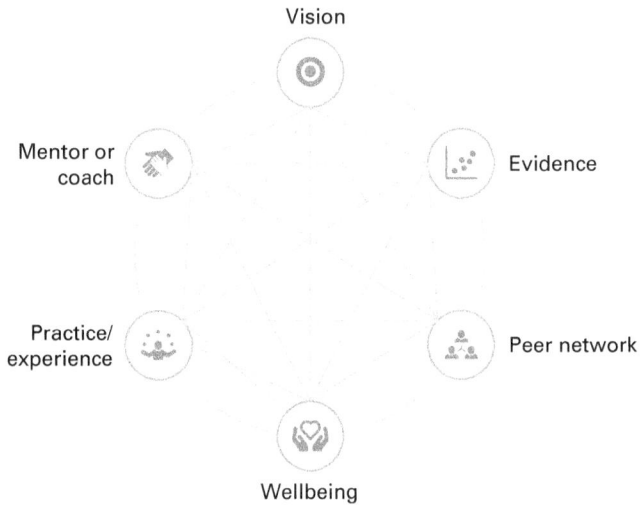

calls to identify specific behaviours that drove results. This evidence gave him confidence to implement unconventional approaches because he knew precisely what needed changing.

- **Peer network:** No navigator succeeds alone. Ericsson's Learning NEXT community of 450+ members provides collective courage through shared experimentation. Find or build your own network of trusted colleagues who can provide perspective, feedback and moral support when navigating new territory.

- **Wellbeing:** Regular reflection rituals provide the space to process experiences, learn from them and recalibrate. As one of our interviewees noted, forcing reflection time into your calendar becomes essential when navigating complexity.

- **Practice and experience:** Competence breeds confidence. Deliberately build skills in the areas where you're least comfortable. If you're business-focused but struggle with technology, invest time in understanding new platforms. If you're exploratory by nature, develop expertise in measurement and analysis.

- **Mentors and coaches:** Someone who acts as a trusted sounding board can help you navigate uncertainty and test your thinking. As Siva Kulasingam demonstrated in his relationship with Rodney Beach (Chapter 9), having someone you can call to say 'Do you hear anyone else talking about this? Do you know anyone else who's doing this?' provides crucial perspective when exploring uncharted territory.

MICHELLE'S INSIGHT: CREATING WELLBEING TO NAVIGATE BOLDLY

For years, I tuned in and made decisions primarily from my head. I didn't have a good sense of what was happening in relationships around me and I didn't pick up signals from others. This realization led me to develop intentional wellbeing practices that now form a critical part of my safety net.

Working with mentors has been a critical part of this journey. They've helped me develop practices to manage my energy and emotions.

I now create regular space for reflection – through journaling or walks in nature – to check in with myself before important engagements. I pause to sense what's happening in my body and set intentions for how I want to show up. Before mentoring someone new, speaking at an event or starting a project, I'll visualize the kind of relationships I want to create and the energy I want to bring.

This practice of 'pre-paving' – Tuning In to myself and setting intentions – helps me identify potential blockages or limiting thoughts that might affect my effectiveness. It's about slowing down just enough to catch the signals my body and emotions are constantly sending me. When I create that space, I can show up more grounded, open and ready to serve in whatever way is most needed.

These safety net elements don't eliminate risk – they make risk manageable. By strengthening these supports, you can navigate boldly, knowing you have the resources to recover when inevitable challenges arise.

Using your BOLD compass to chart your path

Like James in our opening story, each of us brings unique perspectives, backgrounds and natural orientations to our work. The BOLD compass isn't about conforming to a single 'correct' perspective. It's about expanding our awareness of how we think and developing the flexibility to adjust our orientation when circumstances require it.

What makes a navigator truly effective isn't perfect knowledge of the stars or mastery of every technique – It's the ability to adapt to changing conditions while maintaining sight of the destination. As you continue on your journey to equip others in a continually changing workplace, your greatest asset isn't what you know but how you think.

In the next chapter, we'll apply these thinking habits directly to your own career journey. We'll explore how to use the TRI and BOLD principles to chart your personal development path and build your professional capabilities, ensuring you're equipped and ready to navigate your future as a changemaking L&D leader.

Notes

1 James Swift – Human centric organizational performance, Diary of a CLO podcast, 8 January 2025.

2 James Swift – Human centric organizational performance, Diary of a CLO podcast, 8 January 2025.

3 C Nickerson. Schema Theory in Psychology, Simply Psychology, 2024. www.simplypsychology.org/what-is-a-schema.html (archived at https://perma.cc/UBS6-EMXJ)

4 L Overton. L&D thinking habits for a smarter, stronger L&D, Learning Changemakers, 2021. www.learningchangemakers.com/research_whitepapers/5-new-thinking-habits-for-a-smarter-stronger-ld (archived at https://perma.cc/6LDE-2DQ7)

5 J Arets and G Voost. How L&D can create business value – Jos Arets and Geraldine Voost, Learning Uncut Emergent Series podcast, 25 June 2020.

6 B Thompson and S Desai. Smarter working partnerships for L&D – Barbara Thompson and Shai Desai, Learning Uncut podcast Emergent Series podcast, 16 September 2020.

7 P Rebourgeon and P Sheppard. L&D innovation with AI – Pauline Rebourgeon and Peter Sheppard, Learning Uncut podcast, episode 152, 27 August 2024.

8 Laura Overton interview with Keith Resseau, 22 October 2024.

9 Author interview with Cameron Hedrick, 27 September 2024.

10 S Low (2019) *Hawaiki Rising: Hokulea, Nainoa Thompson, and the Hawaiian renaissance*, University of Hawai'i Press, Honolulu.

PART FIVE

Shaping the future

12

L&D

Equipped and ready

WRITE YOUR OWN STORY

It's five years from now. You've reached your destination of meaningfully co-creating business value. This is your story of how you've shaped your future.

....

....

....

....

Where are you on your journey? What patterns and beliefs influence how you navigate your career? How will you continue to evolve as a learning leader, and how might you guide your team through shifting waters?

Let's step into this next phase equipped and ready, prepared to shape what comes next.

By the nature of our work in L&D, we constantly think about helping others succeed in their role and careers. Yet we're often less intentional about becoming equipped and ready for success in our own careers or in building high-performing L&D teams that can adapt to changing conditions. The ability to lead ourselves and our teams to achieve our full potential is essential if we are to help others achieve theirs

In this chapter we return to the TRI principles, applying them to the way we chart our own course to our professional destination. By integrating these insights with what we've learned about BOLD, we can use TRI as a personal and team navigation system – one that helps us make intentional choices, remain adaptable and take ownership of our professional growth.

Get your bearings

As skilled navigators, both aspiring and seasoned L&D leaders need to regularly check their position. Understanding where we are and maintaining a clear vision of where we're headed increase our chances of delivering value in a changing world of work.

Distance covered

Throughout this book, we've explored how to navigate the complex landscape of workplace learning. We've seen why traditional models often fall short of what we need today and how evidence-informed principles better stand up to real-world complexity.

The TRI principles have shown us how to stay aligned, take action and adapt with purpose. The BOLD compass has helped us recognize how our thinking habits shape our effectiveness as L&D leaders.

Now it's time to apply these insights to ourselves and our teams so we can lead with clarity, courage and adaptability.

What have you observed on your journey?

Before exploring how to navigate your own L&D future, take a moment to reflect on your personal journey through this book. The Polynesian navigator Nainoa Thompson kept meticulous notes of his observations from the position of stars and the patterns of waves to the flight of birds, building his understanding of navigation with each journey – just as we've encouraged you to do in your Field Notebook.

WHERE ARE YOU NOW?

Review your Field Notebook entries from previous chapters. Look for emerging patterns, insights or recurring themes.

- What key insights from the TRI principles have resonated most strongly with you, and how are they changing your approach to your work?
- Which thinking habit shift would most transform your effectiveness as a BOLD learning leader?

- Where do you sense the greatest opportunity for your professional growth or for the development of your team?
- How have your views about L&D's role in driving business value shifted or been reinforced?

These reflections will help position you at the centre of your own BOLD compass as we move forward, providing a clearer sense of your current position and the direction you wish to navigate for yourself and with your team.

L&D's own navigation challenges

As L&D professionals, we face a unique challenge: guiding others through a changing workplace while navigating the same terrain ourselves. This creates pressures beyond just keeping up with trends.

The overwhelm factor

Our expanding role creates several challenges:

- **Growing expectations:** We're now expected to support personalized learning experiences, business transformation, culture change and innovation, all while showing business impact. This makes it hard to prioritize our own growth.
- **Shifting skills and technology:** Skills are changing rapidly both for those we support and for ourselves. New tools emerge constantly, each promising to transform learning. We juggle developing new capabilities while maintaining our core skills.
- **Competing priorities:** Daily demands consume time needed for strategic thinking and personal development. We're caught between delivering now and preparing for the future.

The uncertainty factor

Beyond immediate pressures, we face questions about the future:

- **Blurring boundaries:** Lines between L&D and other functions are increasingly fluid, raising questions about our core responsibilities and required skills. This creates opportunities to expand influence, while also challenging our identity.

- **Technological disruption:** AI and emerging technologies are reshaping what we deliver and how we work. We are grappling with which aspects of our roles to automate and how we effectively partner with AI rather than be displaced by it.
- **Evolving profession:** The nature of L&D work itself is changing. What roles will remain important? What will disappear? What capabilities will matter most? For teams, the challenge is evolving together while supporting individual paths.

The personal factor

Beneath external challenges lie internal barriers:

- **Ingrained patterns:** As explored in Chapter 10, our past successes shape our approaches, creating habits that limit adaptability. In teams we unconsciously reinforce collective routines and thinking habits, making it hard to shift direction.
- **Fear and loss of agency:** Change triggers concerns about relevance and value, sometimes leading to either paralysis or reactive mode rather than purposeful adaptation.
- **Attachment to identity:** Perhaps hardest is letting go of practices tied to our professional identity. Teams develop shared stories about their value that make shifts difficult when circumstances demand new approaches.

Understanding these barriers is the first step toward addressing them. Recognizing our personal and collective headwinds helps us chart a better course forward.

From challenge to opportunity

These challenges offer opportunities for growth. Even small shifts toward clearer choices create direction. We don't need all the answers, but we do need to know what matters most.

While we can't control the changes reshaping L&D, we can control our response. By making deliberate choices about skills, mindset, projects and networks, we take ownership of our professional path.

Adaptability itself has become an essential capability. The skills our profession requires are evolving rapidly, making the BOLD mindset crucial for helping us learn and adjust and while moving toward value.

We're all at different career stages – some new to L&D with fresh ideas but needing foundations. Others are shifting roles or guiding teams through change. Whatever your stage, the principles in this book can help you move forward.

Next, we'll explore how TRI can serve as a navigation system for both personal and team development.

TRI as a navigation system for growth

The TRI principles that have guided our approach to driving business value serve equally well as a framework for navigating our own professional growth and team development:

- **Tuning In** supports us to develop awareness of our purpose, drivers and environment. We listen deeply to ourselves, our team members and our organizational context to understand what shapes our professional journey.

- **Responding** helps us to make deliberate choices about our development. We apply evidence-informed approaches to our own growth, translating awareness into meaningful action.

- **Improving** focuses us on creating feedback loops and continually refining our approach. Development becomes an ongoing process of adaptation rather than a destination.

The L&D Sail Plan

Myron 'Pinky' Thompson advised the Polynesian Voyaging Society following a tragic capsizing of *Hōkūleʻa* and the death of a crew member: 'You need to know the path, where you are going and why you are going there… Ninety percent of success is in preparing for it. You must have a sail plan.'[1]

The canvas in Appendix 5 is your navigation sail plan. Structured around the TRI and BOLD principles, it helps you reflect on your professional destination, the course to reach it and how you'll adapt along the way. Use it to guide your own growth or for collective team development.

In the rest of this chapter we'll explore each TRI principle through the lens of personal and team development, offering practical approaches and tips to complete your sail plan effectively.

Tuning In to your opportunity

Tuning In is about becoming more aware of ourselves, our drivers and the environment we operate in. Before setting course, we need to understand what matters most and where we stand now.

For individuals, this means clarifying how you personally contribute to business value in ways that energize you. For teams, it's about building collective clarity around purpose and goals. In both cases, it's also about understanding the currents in our environment that shape what's possible. When we regularly Tune In, we ground our development choices in business reality, making them more intentional, adaptable and relevant.

CLARIFYING YOUR DESTINATION

At the heart of professional navigation lies a simple question: how will you meaningfully create business value?

This is about the deeper sense of contribution that sustains you while driving business outcomes. In Chapter 1 we explored how high-performing L&D professionals orient themselves towards business value rather than just learning activity. Your personal destination combines what energizes you with where and how you can make the greatest impact. Whether improving performance, enabling organizational agility, enhancing culture or supporting talent development, clarifying your contributions helps you stay grounded when conditions change.

For team leaders, it means surfacing a shared purpose that resonates with both organizational goals and individual aspirations. Teams with a clear sense of how they collectively contribute to business value are more resilient and focused in the face of change.

UNDERSTANDING YOUR DRIVERS

Sustainable growth starts with understanding what drives you toward creating business value. What sparks your curiosity? What pushes you to grow in ways that enhance your impact?

What if you're more passionate about creating great learning experiences or building a big team than driving business outcomes? Your technical expertise, leadership ambitions and desire to help others grow can all serve as powerful vehicles for delivering business value. The answer lies in alignment rather than choosing one over the other. When you develop in areas that both energize you personally and contribute to organizational goals, you create a sustainable path forward.

Our interviews with L&D professionals revealed that development is often triggered by moments of frustration, fresh perspectives, new responsibilities or learning from setbacks. Noticing your own growth catalysts can help you shape development that's energizing and purposeful.

As a team leader, understanding what drives each team member allows you to connect personal motivation to shared goals. When people know what motivates one another, they can offer more targeted support and harness the team's diverse energy.

SEEING YOUR ENVIRONMENT

Effective development depends on understanding the environment you're in because context shapes both opportunities and constraints. Organizational culture, systems, priorities and relationships all influence what's possible as well as what might create barriers.

Look for cultural signals: does your organization favour speed or precision? Is experimentation supported or discouraged? These unwritten norms affect which development paths are most likely to succeed in your context.

Tuning In to context as a part of team development means collectively scanning for shifts in priorities, expectations or business conditions. This shared awareness helps you align your personal or team development with the bigger picture by identifying where your growth can best align with organizational needs. It enables you to time initiatives strategically and grow in areas that will create the most value in your setting.

When you see your environment clearly, you can plan growth that's not just personally satisfying but also practically relevant and timed to maximize impact.

SAIL PLAN REFLECTIONS

Reflect on these questions to complete the Tuning In section of your L&D Sail Plan in Appendix 5:

- What aspects of your L&D work do you find most energizing and meaningful, and how do these connect to creating business value?
- When do you feel you are making your most valuable contribution to your organization's success?
- What has triggered your most significant professional growth experiences?

- What current business priorities could create opportunities to align your growth with organizational needs?
- What aspects of your organizational culture might support or challenge your development approach?

TUNING IN TIPS

Table 12.1 provides you with some practical ways to Tune In on an ongoing basis. These practices help you spot opportunities for growth by maintaining awareness of yourself, others and your environment. As you develop these habits, you'll notice patterns and possibilities that might otherwise remain invisible.

Which could you include in your sail plan? What else might work for you?

Responding to shape your growth

Responding helps us turn awareness into purposeful action. After Tuning In we're better equipped to make deliberate choices about how we grow.

Whether individually or as a team, this means aligning development efforts with our goals and our context. From what we choose to develop, to how and with whom, we can shape a meaningful, achievable journey.

LEADING WITH A LEARNING MINDSET

Eric Berger, a senior L&D leader in the financial services sector, describes both his personal and team development approach as 'operating in a mode of learning'.[2] For him, this means working in a continuous cycle of consultation, action and reflection.

'The part we often skip is reflection,' he says. 'We either move on quickly or only talk about what went well.' Eric creates space for what he calls 'spicy conversations' about what isn't working, believing they spark the greatest learning.

This mindset also shapes how he builds his team. Some of his most valuable hires have been those least like the existing group. By introducing difference, he creates 'productive friction' that challenges assumptions and fuels innovation.

For Eric, leading with a learning mindset is about curiosity, humility and a deliberate focus on growth.

TABLE 12.1 Tuning In tips

Tip	For individuals	For team leaders	BOLD alignment
Connect to your purpose	Write a personal purpose statement and review it monthly to check alignment with your actions	Facilitate a team session to co-create a shared vision that links individual values and organizational goals	Business-First: Knowing your value helps focus on impact
Clarify your contribution	Note specific times when your work made a real difference. What enabled that impact?	Invite team members to share their 'most valuable contribution' stories to spotlight diverse strengths	Business-First: Helps direct effort toward what matters most
Monitor your energy patterns	Track when you feel energized or drained across a work week. Use this to guide your planning	Discuss energy patterns within your team and shape collaboration around peak times	Deliberate: Use insight to work more intentionally
Map your personal learning network	Sketch who and what supports your learning – mentors, peers, resources and communities	Create a team network map showing knowledge flows and external connections	Leading and Learning: Awareness of networks unlocks new ideas
Observe organizational culture signals	Note behaviours, language or rituals that reflect learning norms in your organization	Guide your team to gather and discuss cultural signals. What supports or hinders learning?	Open Minded: Understanding norms helps navigate wisely
Schedule regular reflection time	Block 15–30 minutes weekly to reflect on recent experiences and lessons learned	Build reflection into your team's rhythm through retrospectives or 'learning moments'	Deliberate: Reflection sharpens decision-making
Scan for changing expectations	Review recent stakeholder interactions. What's shifting in priorities, tone or goals?	Introduce regular scanning discussions – what are we noticing that's new?	Business-First: Staying attuned ensures relevance

CHOOSING WHAT TO DEVELOP

In a fast-changing world we can't develop everything, so being intentional matters. The key isn't developing more – it's developing what matters most.

Combine broad capability with deep expertise in areas that energize you and add value. This allows you to stay adaptable while offering something distinct.

Don't just focus on skills. Mindset matters too. Reflect on your BOLD compass: which thinking habit orientations would strengthen your impact if further developed?

For teams this means aligning collective capability-building with individual aspirations. When everyone knows where to focus, development becomes more purposeful and better resourced.

SHIFTING SKILLS FOR L&D

In 2024, RedThread Research surveyed 148 L&D professionals to ask what skills they believe they will need for future success.[3] This surfaced a total of 30 skills across six categories. While core L&D skills such as learning science and learning design are viewed as table stakes (17 per cent of all the skills nominated by respondents), they are not sufficient for future success. In fact, the most often nominated category was technology skills (22 per cent of all the skills nominated), with an emphasis on using/applying AI. This was followed closely by 'power skills' (21 per cent of the skills nominated), with adaptability being the most significant of these.

This quote from a senior learning leader sums up the uncertainty about what skills will be needed in L&D, and highlights the importance of developing our capability to learn continuously:

> The problem is that we are building an airplane while flying. We have to adjust direction, bring in new technology, and revisit the skills of our own L&D teams. With this analogy in mind, the pilot and crew require upskilling and reskilling in a time of great change. This is the reality regarding the skills of L&D. Cris Bonini, *Global Head of L&D, KPMG International*[4]

FIGURE 12.1 L&D skills: What L&D pros say

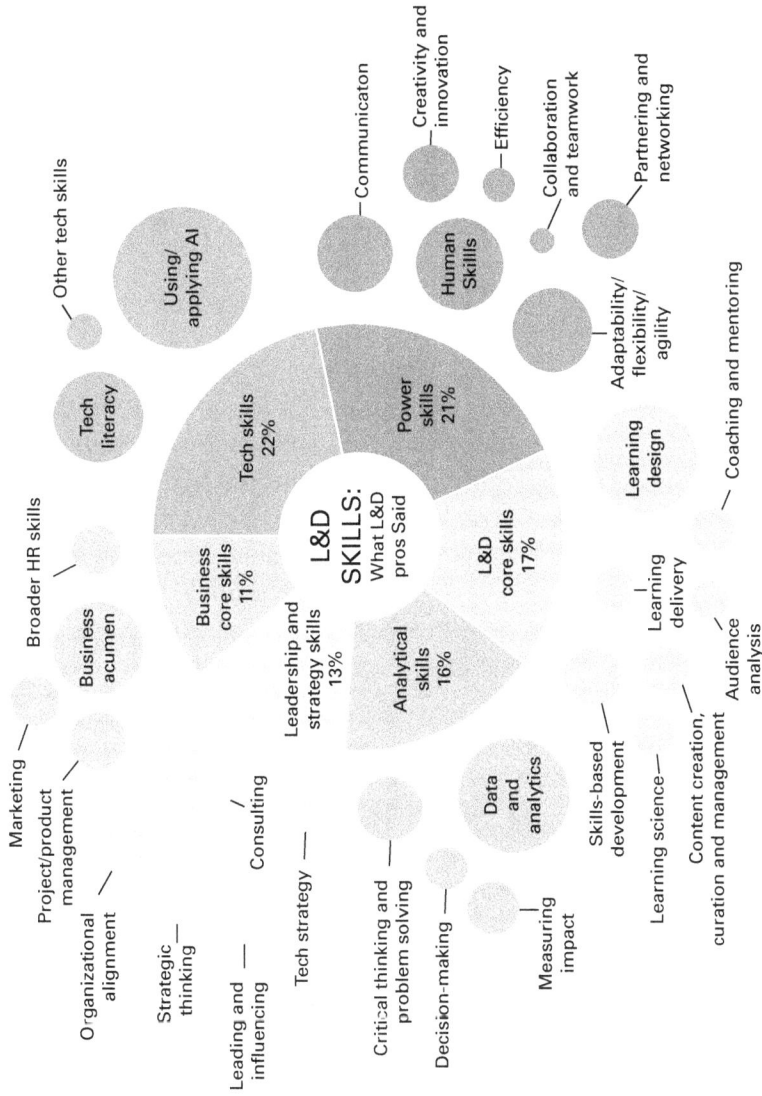

L&D SKILLS: What L&D pros Said

- Tech skills 22%
- Power skills 21%
- L&D core skills 17%
- Analytical skills 16%
- Leadership and strategy skills 13%
- Business core skills 11%

Tech skills: Using/applying AI, Tech literacy, Other tech skills

Power skills: Communicaton, Creativity and innovation, Efficiency, Collaboration and teamwork, Partnering and networking, Human Skilils, Adaptability/flexibility/agility, Coaching and mentoring

L&D core skills: Learning design, Learning delivery, Audience analysis, Content creation, curation and management, Learning science, Skills-based development

Analytical skills: Data and analytics, Measuring impact, Decision-making, Critical thinking and problem solving

Leadership and strategy skills: Tech strategy, Leading and influencing, Strategic thinking, Organizational alignment, Consulting

Business core skills: Business acumen, Project/product management, Marketing, Broader HR skills

SOURCE RedThread Research. L&D skills for the future: Leveling up, 12 December 2024, RedThread Research Community, Figure 3

APPLYING LEARNING SCIENCE AND DIGITAL CONFIDENCE

Think of your development approach as a double-hulled canoe where learning science and digital confidence provide stability in changing waters. Together these two hulls keep you learning and moving forward.

Use evidence-informed practices on yourself. Space your learning, practise deliberately and seek timely feedback. These proven strategies will work just as well for you as they do for others.

At the same time, build digital confidence. As Dani Johnson of RedThread Research puts it, 'Get your hands dirty. If someone's waiting for the IT department to hand something down, they're giving up a lot of their power – and the fun part of their job.'[5]

GROWING THROUGH WORK

Some of the best development happens through the work you're already doing – when you approach it intentionally. Turn everyday tasks into learning moments. A presentation becomes a chance to practise storytelling. A meeting becomes an opportunity to deepen business insight. Adding a learning lens to real work builds skills without needing extra time.

The same applies for teams. Allocate work and shape collaboration to provide hands-on stretch experiences. Build learning into your team's rhythm. Create safe spaces to experiment. As Pauline Rebourgeon put it, 'The worst thing that could happen... is that people might have learned something.'[6]

BUILDING YOUR NETWORK

Strong networks support growth. They offer feedback, encouragement, challenges and new opportunities.

Start by identifying people who can help in your priority areas – trusted peers or mentors who know your context and offer grounded support. Then, seek out others who think differently – people in other teams, disciplines or industries. Eric Berger calls this 'productive friction' – intentionally connecting with those who bring alternative views to spark new insight.

Both types of connections are valuable. Familiar allies help you stay steady. Diverse voices help you stretch and grow.

For teams, networks expand your capability to sense and respond to change. Map who you're connected to, both inside and outside your organization, and how knowledge flows. This kind of collective intelligence helps teams adapt faster.

SAIL PLAN REFLECTIONS

Reflect on these questions to complete the Responding section of your L&D Sail Plan

- What blend of deep expertise and broad capabilities would best serve your purpose and direction?
- Which current or upcoming work activities offer opportunities to develop key capabilities or thinking habits, and how might you allocate work to align with development goals?
- How might you embed deliberate practice into everyday work to deepen learning and growth?
- Who within your network can help accelerate growth, provide valuable feedback or stretch opportunities?
- How might you apply learning science to your development journey?

RESPONDING TIPS

Table 12.2 features practical ways to translate your awareness into action for professional development. These approaches help you implement evidence-informed choices, align work with growth and build the networks needed to thrive.

Which could you include in your sail plan? What else might work for you?

TABLE 12.2 Responding tips

Tip	For individuals	For team leaders	BOLD alignment
Apply learning science to yourself	Select one learning science principle and apply it to your own development for a month	Review team development against learning science. Improve one practice using what you learn	Deliberate: Grounding growth in evidence supports smarter decisions
Explore a digital tool	Set regular time to explore a new tool. Approach it with curiosity, not pressure	Host 'tech playgrounds' where your team explores tools in a low-risk way	Leading and Learning: Playful exploration builds digital confidence

(continued)

TABLE 12.2 (Continued)

Tip	For individuals	For team leaders	BOLD alignment
Create environmental cues	Design your workspace to prompt your development habits (e.g. visual reminders)	Shape team routines and spaces to reinforce key learning behaviours	Deliberate: Intentional design nudges useful habits
Run a small learning experiment	Try a new approach on a low-stakes task. Reflect and record what you learn	Encourage low-risk team experiments. Share learnings openly	Leading and Learning: Small tests reduce risk while sparking growth
Stretch yourself	Volunteer for a project that pushes your limits. Define what you want to learn	Assign stretch work with clear support to ensure growth, not stress	Leading and Learning: Intentional stretch supports bold learning
Partner with a learning buddy	Set up regular peer check-ins for feedback and mutual support	Pair team members for peer coaching and shared development	Open Minded: Learning with others builds perspective and confidence
Build cross-functional bridges	Connect with someone in another function and exchange ideas regularly	Create opportunities for your team to collaborate across disciplines	Business First and Open Minded: Broadens perspective and impact

Improving to continually adapt

Growth is iterative. Improving is about staying on course through small, ongoing adjustments. By regularly getting our bearings we stay on track to our goals. This continuous loop of reflection and adaptation makes development sustainable for ourselves and our teams. It helps us stay responsive and ready, even as conditions shift around us.

GATHERING MEANINGFUL FEEDBACK

Feedback powers learning, especially when we're intentional about what we seek and how we use it.

Don't wait for formal reviews. Just as McKinsey (Chapter 8) encouraged their staff to do, ask trusted colleagues: 'What's one thing I have done well? One thing I could try differently?' Make it regular and specific. Also pay attention to feedback from your work itself. Did your approach deliver the intended outcome? What positive or negative signals is the environment giving you?

Look for patterns across sources over time. Tune in to what repeats, what resonates and what genuinely helps you grow.

For teams, embed feedback into your rhythm through check-ins, retrospectives and debriefs. When shared well, feedback becomes a growth habit that strengthens the entire team.

USING EMOTIONS AS FEEDBACK

Emma Weber, a learning transfer expert, credits much of her resilience to a practice she calls 'emotional processing' – using emotions as feedback for growth.[7]

'When something triggers me, it's a signal to pause and reflect,' she explains. For example, when a colleague challenged her view on AI coaching, her defensive reaction prompted deeper inquiry. That moment of reflection led to new possibilities and ultimately reshaped her business.

Emma's process includes journaling and short daily check-ins to explore what she's feeling, the beliefs behind those feelings and whether they still hold true. She encourages others to start small: 'If you've never reflected before, try one minute a day.'

For Emma, emotions aren't barriers – they're data. Learning to work with them helps us grow with intention.

SHARING YOUR GROWTH

Sharing our development journey builds confidence and opens doors for others to do the same.

Talk about what you're learning, how and why it matters. We don't need to have everything figured out. Sharing work-in-progress invites dialogue, reflection and mutual support.

In teams, modelling this openness creates a learning-positive culture. Regularly ask: 'What have we tried? What's changed? What have we learned?' Use these moments to celebrate progress as well as surface insight. Making development visible maintains momentum.

Build stories about growth into how you share outcomes. When presenting a project, highlight not just the result, but what your team learned in getting there. This normalizes learning through doing.

Making progress public turns growth into something we lead with and that builds our credibility.

REFINING YOUR APPROACH

Learning rarely follows a straight line. Even with a clear sail plan we adapt our course based on progress and discoveries. Refining your approach means staying alert to signals (feedback, data, outcomes) and adjusting accordingly. It shows you're actively navigating rather than drifting.

Benchmarking can help when used thoughtfully. Look for patterns across time, projects or peers. What's shifting? What's improving? Where are the gaps?

Build this into your rhythm with short monthly or quarterly learning reviews. Ask: 'What's working? What needs adjusting? What's changed in my context?'

For teams, review progress collectively and update your course together. Even small changes, applied consistently, can have a big impact.

SAIL PLAN REFLECTIONS

Reflect on these questions to complete the Improving section of your L&D Sail Plan:

- What feedback and data would help you to understand your progress?
- Which parts of your work could provide meaningful signs of your growth?
- How will you make time to reflect on your progress and adjust your approach?
- How could you share what you're learning in a way that builds trust and credibility?
- How will you recognize and celebrate your growth (and that of your fellow team members)?
- How could you 'bring the outside in' to improve even further?

IMPROVING TIPS

Table 12.3 provides practical approaches to help you gather feedback, reflect on progress and refine your development journey. These practices create the continuous improvement loops that keep your growth aligned with changing needs and opportunities. Your Field Notebook can support any of these practices, serving as a central tool for capturing insights and tracking your development.

Which could you include in your sail plan? What else might work for you?

TABLE 12.3 Improving tips

Tip	For individuals	For team leaders	BOLD alignment
Establish feedback loops	Ask 2 or 3 trusted colleagues for monthly feedback on a specific aspect of your work	Set up simple, regular feedback swaps between team members	Open Minded: Seeking diverse input builds self-awareness and adaptability
Conduct personal quarterly reviews	Block time quarterly to review your progress, celebrate wins and adjust your plan	Run quarterly team check-ins to reflect on growth and update development priorities	Business-First and Deliberate: Keeps progress aligned with business needs and demonstrates intentional growth
Use emotions as signals	When triggered, pause to ask: What am I feeling? Why? What belief is behind this?	Support your team in normalizing emotional check-ins and reflection	Open Minded: Emotions are insight – not interference
Audit your assumptions	Identify one belief you hold about your role or organization. Test it through discussion or experimentation	As a team, surface assumptions about how things work. Choose one to explore or challenge together	Open Minded: Questioning assumptions helps shift perspective and unlock change
Share your growth story	Talk about how you're developing – what you're learning and why it matters	Celebrate team growth stories. Highlight what's changed and how it's helping	Leading and Learning: Makes growth visible and valued
Create a portfolio	Build a simple record of your development (projects, reflections, results) to track growth over time	Encourage the team to capture key work and lessons in a shared space to highlight impact and progress	Leading and Learning: Demonstrates commitment to continuous learning and provides a visible growth record
Create a personal improvement backlog	Keep a running list of small changes or habits you want to build, and review it regularly	Invite team members to create and share their own backlogs. Use them to guide stretch goals or peer support	Deliberate: A backlog brings structure to continuous improvement

TRI in action for team development

The TRI principles offer a powerful framework for both personal and team development. **Tuning In** creates awareness of our purpose and context. **Responding** enables intentional choices about our development. **Improving** helps us refine our approach through continuous feedback and adaptation.

Together, these principles create an integrated system for navigating professional growth in a changing landscape. They keep us connected to what matters while remaining adaptable to new opportunities and challenges.

The following example from Westpac's Consumer Banking Capability team demonstrates how these principles can be woven together in practice. Their approach shows how development can be embedded into everyday work, creating sustainable growth for both individuals and the team. As you read this example, notice how they've integrated elements of **Tuning In** (understanding individual development needs), **Responding** (allocating work strategically) and **Improving** (reflecting together in deep dive sessions) to create a holistic approach to development.

This example offers inspiration for how we might apply the TRI principles in our own context, adapting specific practices to fit our unique needs while maintaining the core philosophy of conscious, continuous growth.

AN INTENTIONAL APPROACH TO DEVELOPING AN L&D TEAM

Development is embedded into how Westpac's Consumer Banking Capability team operates. Led by Justin Sterns, the team integrates structured development into daily work to ensure continuous learning.[8]

'We consciously weave the development needs of our team into our everyday operating rhythm,' Justin explains. This starts with structured talent reviews that identify development needs and career aspirations, which in turn guide work allocation. 'We actively look for work that will support the development objectives,' says Justin. 'That might be stretch assignments or putting you on a project with somebody who's an expert in the area that you want to work in.' This ensures team members develop through hands-on experience and mentorship.

Another key practice is the team's monthly deep dive sessions, designed to sharpen critical thinking and adaptability. Each session focuses on a topic linked to talent reviews or emerging from business needs. For example, when internal clients requested a masterclass on generative AI, the team used the materials they developed in their own monthly session. 'We focus on getting down to first principles, not just taking things at face value,' Justin notes.

What makes these sessions particularly effective is their direct connection to practice. After exploring field work methodologies in a session, the team updated their playbook with new techniques for understanding customer needs. This continuous refinement of practice ensures that learning is put into action immediately.

By making development an intentional, structured and adaptive part of their operating rhythm, the team ensures they are not just keeping up with change but actively preparing for the future – both for their own growth and the organization's success.

Navigating together

We've explored how TRI can guide both personal and team development. This brings to mind the Hawaiian concept of Aloha – more than just a greeting, it's about respect, shared purpose and connection.

Our growth journeys matter beyond ourselves. When we Tune In better to our own purpose and how we create value, we become more aware of others' needs. When we Respond thoughtfully to our development needs, we show what taking ownership looks like. And when we Improve consistently, we help build a learning culture that lifts everyone up.

Your L&D Sail Plan is a tool for more purposeful, adaptable development for both individuals and teams. Like Polynesian voyagers who knew that successful journeys need both individual skills and teamwork, our professional growth is both our own responsibility and something we do together – a collaborative journey toward greater value.

In the next chapter we'll look at how being equipped and ready ourselves helps us shape the future of learning and development, moving from our own journeys to creating new paths for our profession.

Notes

1 S Low (2019) *Hawaiki Rising: Hokulea, Nainoa Thompson, and the Hawaiian renaissance*, University of Hawai' i Press, Honolulu.

2 Author interview with Eric Berger, 5 November 2024.

3 RedThread Research. L&D skills for the future: Leveling up, RedThread Research Community, 12 December 2024.

4 RedThread Research. L&D skills for the future: Leveling up, RedThread Research Community, 12 December 2024, Figure 3.

5 S Collins and D Johnson. The rise of technology and L&D – Stella Collins and Dani Johnson, Learning Uncut Emergent Series podcast, 17 August 2020.

6 P Rebourgeon and P Sheppard. L&D innovation with AI: Ericsson's community approach – Pauline Rebourgeon and Peter Sheppard, Learning Uncut podcast, episode 152, 27 August 2024.

7 Author interview with Emma Weber, 25 September 2024.

8 Michelle Ockers interview with Justin Sterns, 5 March 2025.

13

Shaping our future

Over the horizon: Getting ready

Wouldn't it be great if somebody could tell us about the future of L&D – then we could make some concrete plans! The trouble is nobody can accurately predict what is over the horizon for workplace learning.

Back in 1999, John Chambers, the former CEO of Cisco, predicted that 'The next big killer application for the Internet is going to be education. Education over the internet is going to be so big it is going to make email usage look like a rounding error.'[1] But it took until 2022 for L&D teams to be delivering more online learning than face-to-face programmes.[2]

In 2014 Clark Quinn called for a revolution in L&D – because L&D practices were becoming increasingly irrelevant.[3] He called for a shift in focus from training and events to performance and innovation. Yet in 2023 just under half of the Learning Performance Benchmark participants agreed that they analysed organizational problems before recommending a solution and only a third of the sample actually had a plan to meet those needs.[4]

The pandemic created an opportunity to get closer to the business needs,[5] but in 2024 RedThread Research flagged that L&D involvement in strategic conversations around business strategy and workforce planning had dropped by almost 50 per cent in the preceding two years.[6] Their predictions for the future looked bleak.

It's a roller coaster out there.

Whilst very few can accurately predict the future, we can learn to **anticipate** what is to come, and more importantly to prepare for it. We can anticipate that:

- if our organizations continue to rely on humans in the workplace to get things done then our work places will always be complex and interwoven
- the world is becoming more unpredictable

- technology, specifically AI (for the moment), will cause disruption to processes, roles, products, services, customer expectations and our jobs at increasing speed
- if humans are involved in work, they will need to be able to constantly adapt, to learn new approaches to work and abandon others, and
- they may need some help in doing just that!

Effective anticipation allows us to prepare for and potentially shape our future. In contrast, poor anticipation can trip us up – for example, when we suffer from analysis paralysis or an over-reliance on a single trend.

In this book we have explored 20 years of Learning Performance Benchmark evidence, not to tell us what to do next but to learn how to effectively anticipate and prepare for what is over the horizon. So far, the study has revealed principles that will help us anticipate and plan to take up a role of enabler rather than the producer of the past.

We have explored how the high-performing teams are **Tuning In** – taking notice of and anticipating what their organizations need to improve performance. They are **Responding** with intent to achieve business goals and are continually using data, connection and insight to ensure that they are **Improving**.

We have also shown how these principles are not restricted to the elite – they are a navigation framework that all aspiring and seasoned L&D leaders can embed into the smallest tasks and the broadest strategies, helping us prepare for and anticipate change.

A future of building business value

In Chapter 1 we invited you to join a journey – one where you would step into your role as an L&D leader regardless of your title, position or career stage. Now, as we approach the end of our journey through this book, it's time to recognize that **you already are that leader**.

Like Polynesian wayfinders who guided their communities across vast oceans, you've developed the navigation skills to:

- chart paths for stakeholders to reach their goals
- make small daily decisions that keep yourself and others on course
- inspire others to follow new routes, and
- create business value – and with it, a vision of what's possible

Remember the Learning Value Landscape quadrant we introduced at the beginning of our journey? Let's revisit it at Figure 13.1 with fresh eyes.

FIGURE 13.1 The Learning Value Landscape

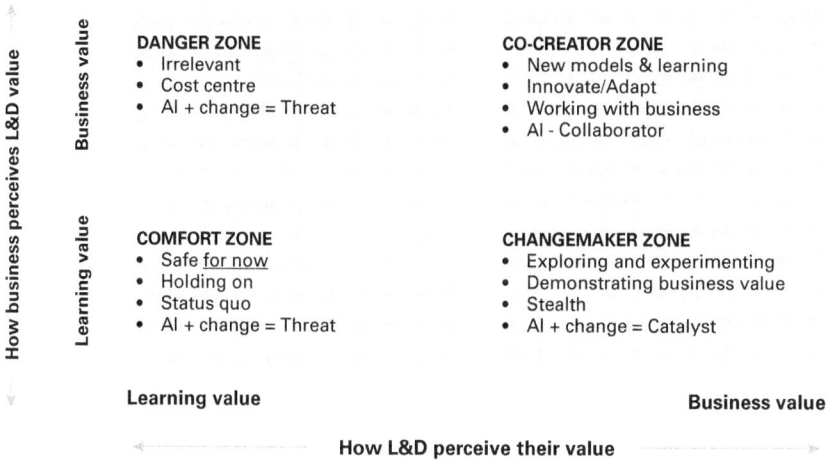

Our journey began with a recognition that many L&D professionals find themselves positioned on the left side of this quadrant – either in the **Danger Zone,** where business leaders expect strategic impact while L&D focuses on learning delivery, or in the Comfort Zone, where both sides are satisfied with the status quo of course and content creation and delivery.

But you're now equipped with the TRI navigation principles and BOLD compass to turn around. This isn't a dramatic, all-at-once transformation that requires organizational upheaval or a complete reinvention of your identity. Rather, it's about adjusting your course, sometimes subtly and sometimes in bigger steps, toward the right side of the quadrant.

The great thing about being in the **Changemaker Zone** is that we can challenge the status quo and demonstrate value stealthily. This path involves patiently demonstrating value, experiment by experiment, project by project – gradually turning stakeholders' heads by showcasing what's possible. It means looking for opportunities to step beyond traditional boundaries, using your growing fluency with the TRI principles to deliver results that matter to the business. When you're told 'We've always done it this way' you now have the tools to respectfully challenge assumptions and offer evidence-informed alternatives.

Alternatively, your journey may lead you to the **Co-creator Zone,** where business leaders actively seek your partnership in addressing strategic challenges. Here, your navigation skills help teams tackle complex problems by ensuring people are equipped and ready. You're welcomed to the table not because of your title, but because of your demonstrated ability to bring unique value that drives business results.

As Dolly Parton wisely observed, leadership is about creating 'a legacy that inspires others to dream more, learn more, do more, and become more'.[7] In L&D, this isn't reserved for those with corner offices or global teams. It's available to anyone who chooses to navigate and create value rather than simply deliver training or create content.

To navigate is to lead. To lead is to create value. And you are now well on your way to being equipped and ready to do both.

Remember, this is about turning around – shifting your orientation toward business value while bringing others with you. Sometimes this happens through quiet, persistent demonstration of new approaches (the Changemaker's path). Other times it happens through open partnership with business leaders who recognize your strategic contribution (the Co-creator's way). Both paths are valid. Both paths create value. Both paths represent true leadership in L&D.

The horizon you've been eyeing throughout this book isn't just a destination – it's a new vantage point from which to see possibilities that weren't visible before.

TRI and be BOLD: Navigating forward

Throughout this book, we've explored how the TRI principles and BOLD compass provide a navigation framework to help us create business value in a continually changing world. These principles aren't just theoretical concepts or new language for common sense practices – they are practical tools grounded in evidence that guide your decisions and L&D thinking habits regardless of what technological, environmental or organizational shifts emerge over the horizon.

We've witnessed these principles in action across remarkably different contexts – from multinational corporate environments at AstraZeneca and McKinsey to public sector settings like North Yorkshire Police; from retail operations at Coles to professional services at EPAM; in industries as varied as construction, insurance, financial services, consulting and technology. These examples demonstrate the principles in action as a reliable navigation system while allowing for adaptation to the unique characteristics of each environment.

Our TRI principles and BOLD compass align with what strategic leadership experts at Wharton have identified as essential skills for uncertain environments.[8] Their research confirms that 'the more uncertain your environment, the greater the opportunity if you have the leadership skills to capitalize on them'. These capabilities – anticipating opportunities, challenging assumptions, interpreting information, making decisions with limited data, aligning stakeholders and fostering learning – are consistent with what TRI and be BOLD help you develop as practical navigation tools.

Whether you're an aspiring L&D leader taking your first steps or a seasoned professional, these principles provide both the stability and flexibility you need. By **Tuning In** to signals in your organization, **Responding** with evidence-informed choices and continuously **Improving** through feedback, you establish a rhythm of navigation that becomes second nature.

Your BOLD compass ensures you maintain true direction even when conditions shift. Like Polynesian navigators who understood both celestial constants and changing conditions, you can hold steady to your value destination while adapting to your environment.

Continual changing is our new reality. The work of ensuring individuals, teams and organizations are equipped and ready will always be vital – but how we accomplish this will continue to evolve. As we look ahead, remember that if we are not intentional in shaping our future, others – including technology – will shape it for us.

The future may be unknown but using TRI and be BOLD as our navigation instruments, we place ourselves in a position where we are able to observe, anticipate and position ourselves to take advantage of disruption ahead to ensure that we continue to land on business value.

AI: The disruption advantage

Our content obsession over the last 30 years has ingrained habits that are hard to shift. In 1996, Bill Gates first proclaimed 'Content is king' in a famous essay.[9] In 2003, Elliot Masie expanded on this for L&D, declaring, 'If Content is King, Context is Queen.'[10] By 2021 Forbes argued that with content now so cheap, tiny and ubiquitous, it's actually context that has become king (or at least the kingmaker).[11]

Our hunger for creating content has become so ingrained that producing great 'learnings' is now part of our identity. We create microcontent accessible in the moment of need, and content in the form of games and virtual reality to help us practise. Each new technology over the last 20 years has provided new ways of developing, curating or delivering our content.

In 2025 large language models are disrupting everything. AI has got us cornered, threatening to drown our carefully produced interventions in what Donald Taylor calls a 'beige wave' of sloppy, unchecked content that pulls every well-designed piece down with it.[12]

But, for some organizations, the AI 'disruption' is quickly turning into an advantage, opening opportunities to enable performance that weren't possible before. In April 2025 Josh Bersin shared with us an example of an organization using AI to identify coaching opportunities (similar to the process James Swift used as described in Chapter 2).[13] They went on to use AI to generate personalized content for call centre agents in real-time. This time, the technology is helping learning leaders move far beyond traditional publishing models in pursuit of their business value goals.

From his latest research, Josh anticipates AI fundamentally 'blowing up' the $360 billion corporate learning market. He highlighted a significant trend where major companies aim to reduce their training departments by a third while accelerating skill development through AI integrated into the flow of work. Existing L&D roles and systems – including the chief learning officer, learning management system (LMS), instructional design and needs analysis – are being questioned. However, AI is also creating new job roles.

He believes this current AI wave is different from other technology predictions due to its sheer pervasiveness.

Marc Zao-Sanders' recent research published in the *Harvard Business Review*[14] backs up this sense of pervasiveness. In 2024 he scoured online forums such as Reddit and Quora for real AI use cases. When he repeated this research in 2025, he found that the top use cases had become deeply personal – therapy and companionship topped the list, with organizing lives and finding new purpose in second and third place. Enhanced learning jumped from eighth to fourth place. Individuals now have their own large language models in their pockets, responding in real-time to their needs.

Josh agreed that AI is now embedded in everyday work tools, leading to a more decentralized learning architecture compared to relying on learning experience platforms (LXPs) or portals.

Josh Bersin's current research confirms with even more urgency that traditional models for learning have to shift for us to restore credibility in our potential. To make this shift, Josh recommends that 'L&D professionals embrace curiosity, innovation and a growth mindset. They must focus on enabling performance, be willing to try new approaches and collaborate with operations and business leaders to be part of this transformation. Our L&D leaders need to inspire learning and be open to new technologies to avoid being left behind.'

Shaping our future together

We have learned the following four things about navigating new pathways through continual change to better business value.

Building collective courage: The power of community

Nainoa Thompson didn't navigate alone. His journey was supported by an elder navigator, fellow voyagers, astronomers and cultural practitioners who gave him the courage to venture into challenging waters. In our complex L&D landscape, we too need communities to build collective courage.

A range of forward-thinking communities are helping to shape L&D's future, including several whose leaders we spoke with as we wrote this book:[15]

- **CLO LIFT:** Unites chief learning officers from major global organizations to tackle 'wicked problems' like governance and skills acceleration through collaborative problem-solving. Their collective wisdom creates practical tools and playbooks that benefit the wider profession.[16]
- **CLO100:** Both a programme for learning leaders to build commercial awareness and business acumen, as well as a community that provides an ongoing support network where leaders can openly discuss challenges.[17]
- **Offbeat:** Supporting L&D professionals to step out of their comfort zone, shake off traditional ways of working and adopt more impactful practices. This community emphasizes bringing people together in an authentic way and embracing experimentation, practice and knowledge sharing.[18]
- **L&D Shakers:** A global community meeting locally and online to help L&D professionals connect, grow and take bold action.[19]
- **Professional Associations:** Supporting the professional development of L&D practitioners and provide opportunity to connect with peers through networking events, conferences and other activities.

What unites these successful communities is their focus on action over conversation, their embrace of honest reflection and their commitment to creating meaningful change.

These are just a handful of the many L&D communities that we can choose from. The communities that will help shape L&D's future balance supportive relationships with challenging conversations, create psychological safety while pushing boundaries and foster both learning and action.

CHOOSE YOUR COMMUNITIES WISELY

When considering which communities to invest your time in, ask:

- Does this community share a vision for shaping L&D's future that aligns with creating business value?
- Do members share evidence and practical experience, not just opinions?
- Will these relationships support me during setbacks and challenges?
- Does participation energize me and expand my thinking?
- Can I both contribute to and draw strength from this community?

As discussed in Chapter 11, communities are a critical part of our BOLD safety net. Not only are they a source of courage, they also offer us an opportunity to shape the future together with others, creating greater value together than any of us could create alone.

Crossing boundaries to co-create value

Charles Jennings shared his experience of working across boundaries with the head of customer service, Richard, when he was in a learning leadership role at Reuters.[20]

'Richard and I were spending more than a million pounds supporting global customer service at Reuters, but it wasn't having the business impact needed,' Charles recalled. 'I asked what really mattered to him, and he said, "There's only one thing that matters to me, Charles – CSAT [customer satisfaction scores]. I've got 18 per cent of my bonus on the CSAT globally moving up three points this year. Would you be prepared to put 18 per cent of your bonus on raising the CSAT?"'

Charles agreed, and they aligned everyone's incentives – from regional heads to the head of learning responsible for sales and service. 'We all had the same bonus percentage,' Charles explained, 'and we hit our target by August. It was a really basic metric – it was based on financial incentive. But it just worked.'

'What happened was my team and Richard's team and the regional heads all met every two weeks. Everyone was just focused on the number and how they could creatively improve it together. We were all just thinking, "How the hell can we get this thing moving?"'

Throughout this book we've journeyed with people who've been willing to cross boundaries in order to achieve a shared goal. The skill surge at McKinsey was a collaboration.

The external partnerships shared in Chapter 9 did not take a usual request for proposal route. Both parties were challenged. Both had skin in the game, took risks and celebrated together.

L&D leaders do not just work together with business and partners, they learn together as they deliver shared goals.

Shape tomorrow by leading differently today

The future of L&D doesn't arrive in a single transformative moment. It emerges through the daily choices and actions of L&D leaders like you who decide to lead differently today. While we can't perfectly predict what lies over the horizon, we can begin embodying the change we believe is necessary.

The most powerful shifts in our profession don't require organizational restructuring, new job titles or technological revolutions. They begin with individual leaders who choose to reorient their practice toward greater value, step by step.

Consider these transformations you can begin today:

- **From content producer to learning enabler:** When someone requests a new course, pause to ask: 'What performance outcome are we trying to achieve, and what's the most effective way to support it?'

- **From training administrator to navigator:** Observe where people struggle, what enables success and how systems help or hinder performance. Use your Field Notebook to look for patterns that reveal systemic barriers to learning, performance and creating value.

- **From best practice follower to principle-based guide:** Apply the TRI principles to your unique context. Ask: 'How can I Tune In more deeply to what's really happening here? What evidence should inform my Response? How will I know if we're Improving?'

- **From risk aversion to courageous experimentation:** Create safe spaces for experimentation – pick one of the experiments suggested in Part Three to address an immediate need while testing a new approach. Celebrate learning from both successes and failures.

- **From individual expertise to collective wisdom:** Invite diverse voices into your problem-solving process, especially those closest to the work being done. Build networks that connect people across boundaries.

- **From opinion to evidence-informed action:** Base your recommendations on the best available evidence rather than industry trends or personal preference. Be transparent about what you know, what you don't know and how you're continuously learning.

Equally important is modelling the qualities and behaviours you wish to see in your organization:

- Want a learning organization? Be visibly curious today.

- Seeking business value? Find opportunities and stretch assignments that connect directly to organizational priorities.

- Desire credibility? Demonstrate it now through evidence-informed decisions.

- Hoping to build a more adaptable function? Develop your own intentional practices for sensing change and adjusting course.

These shifts don't happen overnight, nor do they occur in isolation. Each small change in how we show up today – each conversation reframed, each assumption questioned, each experiment undertaken – creates ripples that gradually reshape the landscape around us.

As you consider the leader you want to be tomorrow, remember that the journey begins with how you choose to lead today. The principles and compass that have guided our exploration throughout this book offer a foundation from which you can confidently step into this evolving future as an active shaper of what L&D can become.

Just start

Throughout this book we have emphasized the 'ing' of our world of work – we operate in a flow of continual changing and moving that happens all around us every day. Learning to be comfortable in this world is at the heart of the TRI navigation principles. Something remarkable happens when we are consistently Tuning In to what matters, Responding with purpose and continuously Improving. We unlock a powerful virtuous cycle that strengthens relationships across the organization and builds an ecosystem that supports ongoing learning and adaptation.

High-performing teams create an environment where people appreciate the value of learning to the business, senior managers demonstrate commitment

FIGURE 13.2 L&D Value Cycle

to learning and managers recognize the value of on-the-job learning. But it is not just the high-performing teams making this connection. We noticed the pattern again when analysing the data for the CIPD Learning at Work 2021 survey.[21] When leaders value the impact of learning, the learning leaders are also likely to agree that L&D is aligned with strategic priorities, that managers see the connection between learning and team performance and that managers actively support employee development. This creates a reinforcing loop where visibility leads to value, which leads to further investment and support.

Is this a linear process? Maybe it is in some cases. In others it might be appropriate to start anywhere in the cycle. Start working with managers and see where that leads. Start working on strategies to get closer to what the business needs. Start with a coffee with someone new. Start with a chat with a busy manager who wants the best for their team. In each of these moments, *you* are representing the high-performing team.

Just start.

Shaping the future of L&D: A renaissance

As we come to the end of this leg of our journey together, we want to return to the story that has inspired us – the *Hōkūle'a*, Star of Gladness. In 2025, the Polynesian Voyaging Society celebrated their 50th anniversary, marking half a century since they set out to prove what many thought impossible. Yet what began as a mission to validate ancient navigational techniques evolved into something far more profound.

'The birthday is such an important moment for us to dream again and believe again and have courage to let go of the lines,' reflected Nainoa Thompson.[22] His words remind us that the *Hōkūle'a*'s legacy isn't measured by a single successful voyage, but by the way that they are inspiring the next generation of navigators and their communities to respect and care for themselves, for each other and for their natural and cultural environments.'[23]

For us in L&D, the journey we've outlined in this book isn't about proving our worth through learning metrics or course completions. It's about going back to the basic principles to discover how we can create a renaissance in how organizations learn, adapt and thrive in continually changing environments.

Throughout these pages, we've tried to challenge conventional thinking about what L&D is and can be. We might query whether L&D is the right label for what we do in the future. We might question the use of the word 'leader' for those who have no political clout or teams to guide. The terms we use to describe ourselves – whether learning professionals, performance consultants, capability builders, engineers or leaders – matter far less than the value we create. As L&D leaders, our identity isn't defined by our title but by our impact.

The principles of TRI and BOLD offer navigational tools, not rigid formulas. Like Nainoa's star compass, they provide orientation while honouring the uniqueness of your context and journey. They allow you to navigate with purpose and confidence even when the destination isn't yet visible on the horizon.

The journey ahead is not clear. But it is not clear for many in the organizations that we serve which is why, right now we need *you*.

We need your passion to see others learning and developing so that they are equipped and ready.

We need your leadership, your willingness to anticipate, create vision, help others make the decisions they need to make and take action that they need to take to achieve their full potential.

The future of L&D will be shaped by leaders like you who embrace complexity, navigate with principles and remain focused on raising the island of business value on the horizon – even when it can't yet be seen.

YOUR LEGACY

Take a moment to reflect: How will you start to build your legacy today? What first step will you take to create an L&D renaissance in your organization?

Notes

1   J Cross. An informal history of eLearning, *On the Horizon*, 2004, 12 (3), 103–10.
2   Source: Learning Performance Benchmark study, see Appendix 1.
3   C Quinn (2014) *Revolutionize Learning and Development: Performance and innovation strategy for the information age*, Jossey-Bass, San Francisco.
4   Source: Learning Performance Benchmark, see Appendix 1.
5   L Overton. *Learning at Work 2023: Survey report*, CIPD, 2023. www.cipd.org/globalassets/media/knowledge/knowledge-hub/reports/2023-pdfs/2023-learning-at-work-survey-report-8378.pdf (archived at https://perma.cc/LZ89-86K7)
6   D Johnson and H G Adams (2024) *Hope Isn't a Plan: Building a progressive L&D strategy – final report*, RedThread Research Community.
7   Quoted in L Adraine (ed.) (1997) *The Most Important Thing I Know*, Andrews McMeel Publishing, Kansas City.
8   P J H Schoemaker, S Krupp and S Howland. Strategic leadership: The essential skills, *Harvard Business Review*, January–February 2013, 131–40.
9   B Gates. Content is king, UNFPA Kyrgyzstan, 3 January 1996. kyrgyzstan.unfpa.org/sites/default/files/pub-pdf/content-is-king.pdf (archived at https://perma.cc/E63F-MFZ6)
10 E Masie. If content is king, context is queen! Learning Trends, 264, 2003.
11 S Padmanabhan. Why content is no longer king – and what it means for education technology, Forbes Business Council, 23 June 2021.
12 D Taylor. LinkedIn post, January 2024. www.linkedin.com/posts/donaldhtaylor_learninganddevelopment-slop-genai-activity-7274717607910338560-p_OD (archived at https://perma.cc/E6AK-K9HU)
13 Laura Overton interview with Josh Bersin, 19 April 2025.
14 M Zao-Sanders. 2025 top-100 gen AI use case report updated, Filtered, 2025. learn.filtered.com/thoughts/top-100-gen-ai-use-cases-updated-2025 (archived at https://perma.cc/ZWY5-CV76)

15   Michelle Ockers interview with Ben Campbell, CEO Australian Institute of Training and Development, 2 April 2025, and Laura Overton interview with Peter Cheese, CEO Chartered Institute of Personnel and Development, 4 April 2025

16   Author interview with Brian Hackett, 15 October 2024. CLO Lift Initiative – The Learning Forum. https://thelearningforum.org/clo-lift (archived at https://perma.cc/BM5H-YS97)

17   Author interview with Cathy Hoy, 7 October 2024. clo100.com (archived at https://perma.cc/KMQ2-4HD4)

18   Author interview with Lavinia Mehedintu, 15 October 2024. www.offbeat.works (archived at https://perma.cc/7TZE-44EX)

19   L&D Shakers. About, LinkedIn, 2025. www.linkedin.com/company/l-d-shakers/about/ (archived at https://perma.cc/BJ5Z-LQQ9)

20   Laura Overton email interview with Charles Jennings, 22 April 2025.

21   E Crowley and L Overton. *Learning and Skills at Work Survey 2021*, Chartered Institute of Personnel and Development, 2022. www.cipd.org/globalassets/media/comms/news/as2learning-skills-work-report-2021-1_tcm18-95433.pdf (archived at https://perma.cc/5KN4-DG9N)

22   Hokuleacrew. Hokulea is 50, Instagram, 15 March 2025. www.instagram.com/reel/DDv0VybxRCE/> (archived at https://perma.cc/CH59-PWTS)

23   Polynesian Voyaging Society Hōkūle'a. About, Hōkūle'a, nd. hokulea.com/about (archived at https://perma.cc/K2JM-BRLM)

APPENDIX 1

Learning Performance Benchmark

New insights for a new age

Throughout this book, we've emphasized how 'success leaves clues' and how data-informed decision-making can help us navigate the complex world of workplace learning. The Learning Performance Benchmark (LPB) study, spanning over 20 years, has been instrumental in identifying the principles that consistently correlate with business impact. Re-examining the data in the light of L&D challenges today has led us to the principles that form the foundation of the TRI framework introduced in this book.

Appendix 1 provides context on this longitudinal research that has informed our thinking and recommendations. Between 2003 and 2023, the study gathered input from over 11,000 organizations, 67,000 employees and 1,300 senior executives across 83 countries, giving us unprecedented insight into what drives effective L&D.

The evidence trail: How we discovered what works

Laura Overton established and led this research programme, initially called the Towards Maturity Benchmark, until 2019. The independent study began with funding from the UK government and evolved into a community-funded initiative. It continues through Mind Tools for Business under the supervision of Dr Gent Ahmetaj.

What makes this research particularly valuable is its consistent focus on business impact over time, even as technologies, terminologies and workplace dynamics evolved. The study has always asked: 'What behaviours and practices consistently lead to improved business outcomes?'

When we reference the data from this study throughout this book, we're drawing from an evidence base that has revealed consistent patterns despite changing workplace contexts – from pre-smartphone workplaces through economic downturns, digital transformation and a global pandemic.

In preparation for this book, Laura has explored data patterns unfolding over a 20-year period from both published and unpublished data in this study. Throughout the chapters the data and trends are referenced as follows:

Learning Performance Benchmark study, see Appendix 1

For those of you who love to dig into the data, Table A1.1 is a whistlestop tour of how we have developed the research and what we have found out in the last 20 years.

TABLE A1.1 Timeline of key reports in the Benchmark series

Learning Performance Benchmark report	What caught our eye looking back over 20 years
Linking learning to business (2004)[1]	Initial study with 16 organizations and 2,000 employees focused on e-learning. Key findings: importance of holistic learning approach, winning hearts and minds, and working with culture to drive business change.
Towards maturity (2007)[2]	E-learning success depends more on relevance, learner experience and stakeholder engagement than on specific technologies.
Driving business benefits (2009)[3]	Focus on building the business case for learning technologies, trends in their adoption, implementation strategies, barriers encountered and methods for improving their impact, all analysed through the lens of perceived organizational e-learning maturity.
Accelerating performance (2010)[4]	The Towards Maturity Index (TMI) was introduced replacing self-reported maturity levels. The TMI focuses on six interwoven behaviours operating together vs a linear approach to L&D process.
Boosting business agility (2011)[5]	Focus on learning strategies that enhance capabilities of organizations to flex with change.
Bridging the gap (2012)[6]	Exploring the impact of learning through work and learning in work.
The new learning agenda (2013)[7]	Introducing a holistic view of organizational learning and a focus on speed and agility. Behaviours of top performers were analysed, those in the top 25% of the TMI.
Modernising learning (2014)[8]	Evidence from the top deck (top 10% in the TMI index referred to as high-performing teams in this book) emphasized a significant shift calling business leaders and learning leaders to co-create value.

(continued)

TABLE A1.1 (Continued)

Learning Performance Benchmark report	What caught our eye looking back over 20 years
Embracing change (2015)[9]	Evidence to encourage business leaders to expect more, a call to learning leaders to equip the self-directed learner and to ensure that they are ready and prepared.
Unlocking potential (2016)[10]	Isolating the behaviours that influence efficiency, performing, business agility and learning culture. First report exploring AI (bots, intelligent tutors).
L&D where are we now (2017)[11]	A snapshot of trends.
The transformation curve (2018)[12]	This report took a fresh look at 15 years of data and introduced a four-stage maturity model for L&D, encompassing all organizational learning activities beyond just technology.
The transformation journey (2019)[13]	Using the maturity model to explore high-performing learning culture, identifying and overcoming barriers arising from digital disruption, cultural resistance and L&D capability.
Back to the future (2020)[14]	Exploring a rise in learning investment coinciding with decline in impact.
Innovate, dominate or decline (2021)[15]	The TMI became the Organizational Learning Index (OLI). The study warned against complacency in L&D.
Is your learning culture keeping pace with rapid digitalization? (2022)[16]	Exploring the fact that many organizations were stuck using outdated strategies and online learning overtook face-to-face learning in popularity for the first time since data collection began.
Learning and development in organizations: Reflecting on 20 years of research. Part 1: Learning and development in organizations (2023)[17]	Looking back over 20 years of Benchmark data.
Learning and development in organizations: Reflecting on 20 years of research. Part 2: Unlocking excellence (2023)[18]	This report used powerful network analysis to reveal how interconnected L&D behaviours contribute to success at different maturity stages, with strategic and business alignment being central for top performers.

(continued)

TABLE A1.1 (Continued)

Learning Performance Benchmark report	What caught our eye looking back over 20 years
Learning and development in organizations: Reflecting on 20 years of research. Part 3 Megatrends reshaping the future: The crucial role of L&D in business transformation (2023)[19]	Asking is stage 4 of maturity the only place to be? Simply copying-high performing learning teams is not a guarantee for success.

TABLE NOTES

1. L Overton. *Linking Learning to Business*, Learning Changemakers, 2004. www.learningchangemakers.com/wp-content/uploads/2003-Linking_Learning_to_Business__compressed.pdf

2. L Overton, H Hills and G Dixon. *Towards Maturity: Insights for employers and training providers*, Learning Changemakers, 2007. www.learningchangemakers.com/wp-content/uploads/2007-Towards-Maturity-1.pdf

3. Towards Maturity. *Driving Business Benefits: Towards Maturity learning technologies benchmark report*, Learning Changemakers, 2009. www.learningchangemakers.com/wp-content/uploads/2009-Driving-Business-Benefits.pdf

4. L Overton, H Hills and G Dixon. *Accelerating Performance: Towards Maturity 2010–11 benchmark full report*, Learning Changemakers, 2010. www.learningchangemakers.com/wp-content/uploads/2010_Accelerating_performance_Full_-report_.pdf

5. G Dixon and L Overton. *Boosting Business Agility: Towards Maturity 2011–12 benchmark full report*, Learning Changemakers, 2011. www.learningchangemakers.com/wp-content/uploads/2011-Boosting_Business_Agility_Full_Report.pdf

6. L Overton and G Dixon. *Bridging the Gap: Integrating learning and work*, Learning Changemakers, 2012. www.learningchangemakers.com/wp-content/uploads/2012-Bridging_The_Gap_Full_Report.pdf

7. L Overton and G Dixon. *The New Learning Agenda: Talent, technology, change*, Learning Changemakers, 2013. www.learningchangemakers.com/wp-content/uploads/2013-_New_Learning_Agenda.pdf

8. L Overton and G Dixon. *Modernising Learning: Delivering results*, Learning Changemakers, 2014. www.learningchangemakers.com/wp-content/uploads/2014-Modernising-Learning.pdf

9. L Overton and G Dixon. *Embracing Change: Improving performance of business, individuals, and the L&D team*, Learning Changemakers, 2015. www.learningchangemakers.com/wp-content/uploads/2015-Towards-Maturity-Embracing_Change_-_Full_Report-Copy.pdf

10. L Overton and G Dixon. *Unlocking Potential: Releasing the potential of business people through learning*, Learning Changemakers, 2016. www.learningchangemakers.com/wp-content/uploads/2016-Unlocking-Potential-Digital.pdf

11. L Overton, G Dixon and G Ahmetaj. *L&D: Where are we now?* Learning Changemakers, 2017. www.learningchangemakers.com/wp-content/uploads/2017-LD-Where-are-we-now_final_digital.pdf

12. L Overton, G Dixon and G Ahmetaj. *The Transformation Curve: The L&D journey to deliver lasting business impact*, Learning Changemakers, 2018. www.learningchangemakers.com/wp-content/uploads/2018-The-Transformation-Curve_digital.pdf

13. L Overton. *The Transformation Journey: Navigating uncertainty and building digital success*, Learning Changemakers, 2019. www.learningchangemakers.com/wp-content/uploads/2019-The-Transformation-Journey-FINAL.pdf

14. J Daly and G Ahmetaj. Back to the future: Why tomorrow's workforce needs a learning culture, Learning Changemakers, 2020. www.mindtools.com/thought-leadership/reports/back-to-the-future

15. G Ahmetaj. Innovate, dominate or decline, Learning Changemakers, 2021. www.mindtools.com/thought-leadership/reports/innovate-dominate-decline

16. Mind Tools for Business. Is your learning culture keeping pace with rapid digitalization? Learning Changemakers, 2022. www.mindtools.com/thought-leadership/reports/keeping-pace-with-rapid-digitalization

17. Mind Tools for Business. Learning and development in organizations, Learning Changemakers, 2023. www.mindtools.com/thought-leadership/reports/20-years-of-research

18. Mind Tools for Business. Unlocking excellence: The strategic business alignment blueprint for L&D, Learning Changemakers, 2023. www.mindtools.com/thought-leadership/reports/unlocking-excellence

19. Mind Tools for Business. Megatrends reshaping the future: The crucial role of L&D in business transformation, Learning Changemakers, 2023. www.mindtools.com/thought-leadership/reports/megatrends-reshaping-the-future

Research methodology

The LPB has always used robust research methods while maintaining community engagement and input.

Data collection

Online surveys with factual questions and likert scales, gathering perspectives from self-selected participants through industry campaigns and direct invitations.

Analysis techniques

- Initial analysis (2007) included Principal Component Analysis to identify impact-correlated behaviours. The methodology and findings were academically reviewed (2009).
- Cronbach's alpha, correlation analysis, regression, t-tests and network analysis continue to reveal useful patterns and trends in line with the earlier findings.
- Over time statistical validation has shown the Maturity Index as a reliable measure for longitudinal comparison.

Scientific validation

- Methodology peer-reviewed in academic journals (2009).
- Endorsed by learning and development professional bodies.
- Research questions developed and reviewed annually by diverse expert panels.

Community-driven approach

- Independent research programme supported by industry ambassadors.
- Fierce protection of research independence despite industry backing.
- 80–90 per cent of participants report that participation itself generates improvement ideas.
- Evolution from government-funded project to community-supported initiative.

This blend of scientific rigor and practitioner relevance has made the LPB a trusted resource for evidence-informed decision-making in workplace learning.

Additional reports investigating the Benchmark data were developed for the community and by the community and took a deep dive into themes such as impact, alignment, engagement, skill, L&D capability, learning design and learning transfer. They can be accessed here: www.learningchangemakers. com/articles/the-evolution-of-the-ld-maturity-benchmark

Since 2020 Dr Gent Ahmetaj, Head of Research at Mindtools for Business, and his team have developed the study and we acknowledge the contribution that they have made to this study and to the L&D industry. We are grateful for Mindtools for Business' permission to share and report from the latest data gathered through the current Learning Performance Benchmark.

APPENDIX 2

Tool to build your matrix of models

As we discussed in Chapter 2, L&D professionals have access to hundreds of different models and frameworks. However, no single model represents a universal 'best practice' that addresses all contexts and challenges we face. Warren Buffett's business partner Charlie Munger advocated having a 'latticework of mental models' to navigate complexity, rather than relying on a single approach.[1] This wisdom applies equally to L&D professionals working in ever-changing environments.

We established that the TRI principles – Tuning In, Responding and Improving – underpin the most useful L&D models. What makes a model useful depends significantly on your specific context and goals. Rather than prescribing a 'right way', we encourage you to use the TRI principles as a lens to evaluate which models, or combination of models, might best serve your current situation.

By developing fluency with multiple models and understanding how they connect to the TRI principles, you'll build a more versatile practice capable of navigating both familiar and uncharted waters. Table A2.1 provides a framework to help you assess models against these principles.

Working this out in practice

Below we present three widely used models in L&D. Each has been summarized by its creator, who has also analysed how their model aligns with the TRI principles, as presented in Table A2.1. This analysis demonstrates how different models may emphasize different aspects of the principles while still being useful.

5 Moments of Need

The 5 Moments of Need, developed by Dr Conrad Gottfredson and Bob Mosher, is a framework that enables learning in the flow of work, while people are doing their work. It identifies five specific times when people require learning and support to improve their performance (see figure A2.1):

1 Apply: When people have to act upon what they have learned.

2 Solve: When people have to solve a problem or resolve an issue because things don't work the way they should.

3 Change: When people have to learn new ways of doing something which requires them to change/adapt deeply ingrained practices.

4 New: When people are learning something for the first time.

5 More: When people are expanding the breadth and depth of what they have learned.

FIGURE A2.1 5 Moments of Need

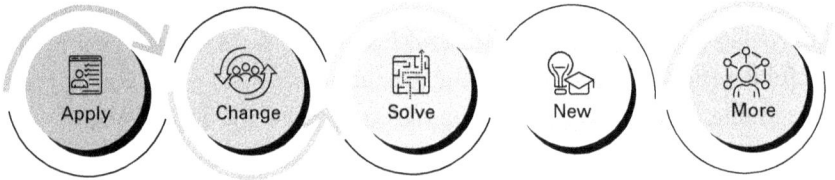

SOURCE Apply Synergies. APPLY Synergies: 5 Moments of Need, 2024. www.applysynergies.com

These moments illustrate the context in which learners must learn and what drives them to engage in learning. This model shifts the focus from learning events to developing a performance ecosystem with significant emphasis on workflow support. New and More typically benefit from formal structured learning, particularly for novices. Apply typically benefits from practice, scenarios and simulation. Change and Solve typically benefit from performance support, e.g. jobs aids, documentation, digital coaching, mentoring and other less formal approaches.

For more information see 5momentsofneed.com.

5Di

The 5Di model, developed by Nick Shackleton-Jones, is a human-centred approach to learning design based on a theory of learning – the affective context model. Instead of focusing on content and how to distribute it, the model places the intended audience at the heart of the process and can be thought of as similar to applying design thinking to learning and development. 5Di is a process comprising Define, Discover, Design, Develop, Deploy and Iterate (see Figure A2.2).

The Define stage requires us to identify performance outcomes in terms of how people will be thinking, feeling and behaving differently – rather than learning objectives. This is essential if a return on investment is to be measurable. In the Discovery stage the challenges and concerns of the intended audience are analysed – rather than a 'training needs analysis'. This is important in designing learning that either helps people with existing tasks or presents them with new ones. The model creates two distinct outputs: resources (point-of-need performance support that reduces learning requirements) and experiences (transformative activities that increase the extent to which an audience 'cares' about and adopts a behaviour). In practice, this means all discussion of 'content' is avoided and the risk of merely communicating content is largely mitigated.

For more information see shackleton-consulting.com/5di-toolkit

12 Levers of Transfer Effectiveness

12 Levers of Transfer Effectiveness, developed by Dr Ina Weinbauer-Heidel, is a framework designed to maximize the application of training and learning back to the workplace. This model helps learning and development professionals ensure that investments in training translate into actual business impact (see Figure A2.3).

Based on transfer research, the model focuses on managing three areas crucial for transfer effectiveness: trainees, training design and organization. Within those three areas, different factors can be found on which successful transfer of what has been learned into everyday work life depends.

12 Levers of Transfer Effectiveness represent the gist of scientific research for HR practitioners. They show human resource managers, L&D managers and trainers what determines transfer success and how it can be managed.

For more information see transfereffectiveness.com

FIGURE A2.2 5DI© model

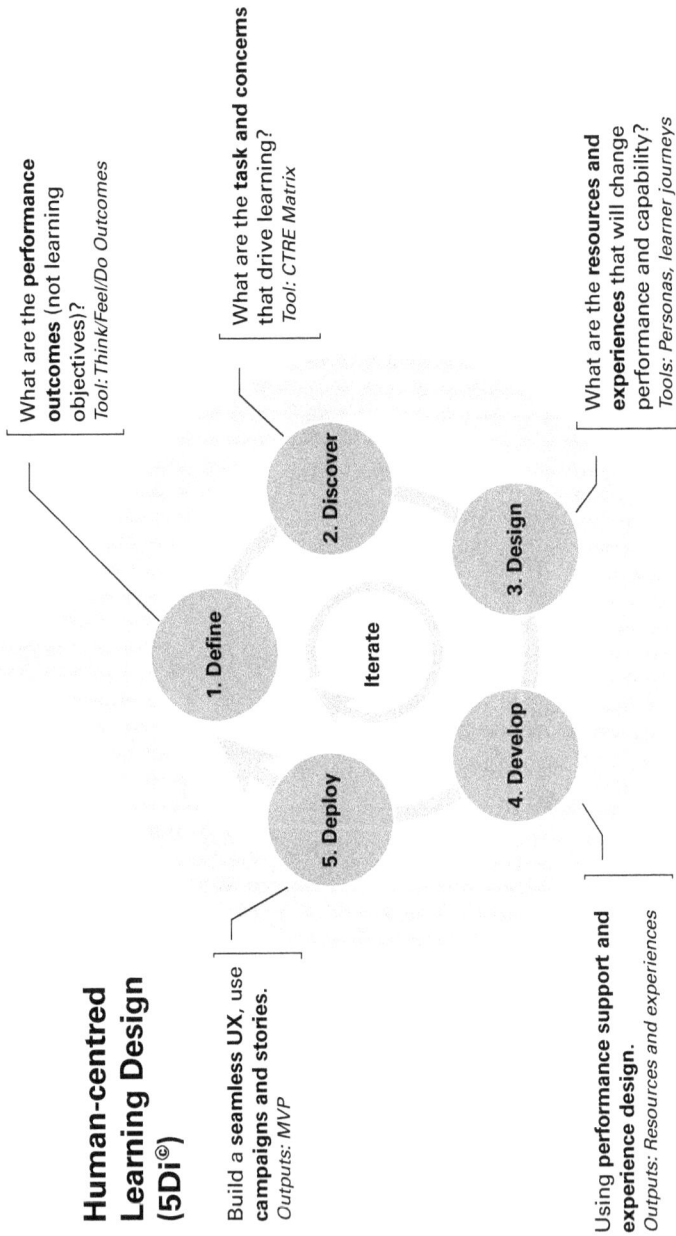

Human-centred Learning Design (5Di©)

What are the **performance outcomes** (not learning objectives)?
Tool: Think/Feel/Do Outcomes

What are the **task and concerns** that drive learning?
Tool: CTRE Matrix

What are the **resources and experiences** that will change performance and capability?
Tools: Personas, learner journeys

1. Define

2. Discover

3. Design

4. Develop

5. Deploy

Iterate

Build a **seamless UX**, use **campaigns and stories**.
Outputs: MVP

Using **performance support and experience design**.
Outputs: Resources and experiences

SOURCE Interview with Nick Shackleton-Jones

FIGURE A2.3 12 Levers of Transfer Effectiveness

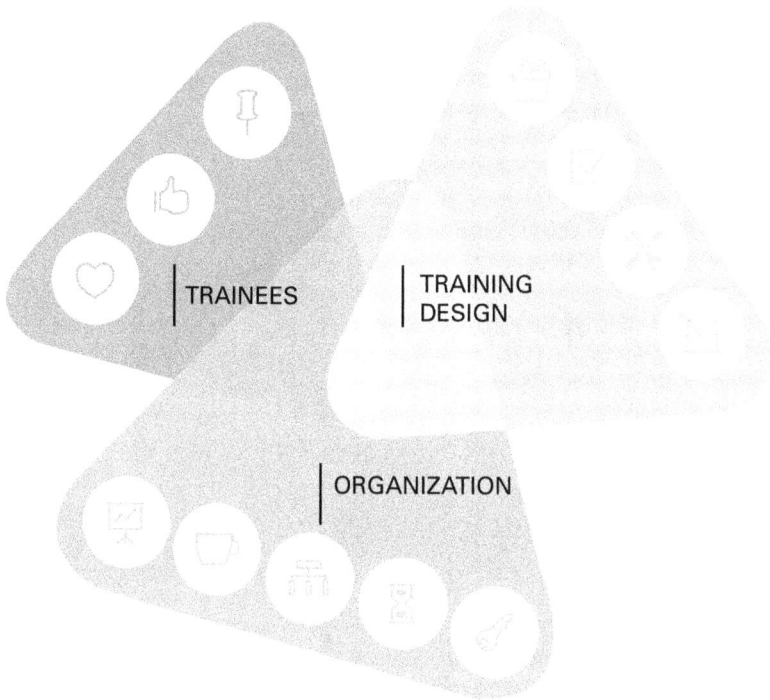

TRAINEES	TRAINING DESIGN	ORGANIZATION
01 Transfer motivation	**04** Clarity of expectations	**08** Application opportunity
02 Self-efficacy	**05** Content relevance	**09** Personal transfer capacity
03 Transfer volition	**06** Active practice	**10** Support from supervisor
	07 Transfer planning	**11** Support from peers
		12 Transfer expectation in the organization

SOURCE Dr Ina Weinbauer-Heidel

We asked the originators of each of these models to give us their view of how their model deliberately helps L&D professionals to apply the TRI principles in their own context. Table A2.1 details what they said.

TABLE A2.1 Model alignment with principles: originator's view

Principle	5 Moments of Need	5Di	12 Levers of Transfer Effectiveness
Tuning In – Aligning Together	Provides a framework for discussing performance support/ workflow learning needs with stakeholders. Workflow-oriented approach naturally aligns with business timing and priorities as it focuses on supporting the actual work done on the job.	Uses structured interviews with stakeholders and explicitly requires project definition in terms of business impact expressed in terms of 'think/feel/do' changes. Involves stakeholders and end-users in the design stage, and thereafter through pilot and MVP reviews.	Transfer Expectations in the Organization (#12) requires stakeholder collaboration to establish a clear transfer goal that helps achieve a specific organizational result and jointly aligning on how to measure this goal.
Tuning In – Connecting to Individuals	The model requires understanding how workers currently work, learn, where they find information and what they need at each moment of need. By addressing 'More' moments of need the model connects to supporting ongoing professional development, and by first pivoting on 'Apply' the deliverables you create will be performance focused.	Adopts human-centered approach using focus groups to actively listen to individuals in the Discover phase and continually refers back to the 'voice of the audience' in subsequent phases. Outputs 'emotional curves' that identify factors that enhance or depress motivation and performance. Lists audience top concerns and tasks.	Multiple levers (#1, #2, #3, #5) support active listening to individuals by highlighting the importance of relevance, confidence and application. It encourages practitioners to understand what individuals need for their jobs, how they learn and the conditions that support learning transfer – like motivation, self-efficacy and volition. This insight enables more personalized, effective support for learning and career progression.

(continued)

TABLE A2.1 (Continued)

Principle	5 Moments of Need	5Di	12 Levers of Transfer Effectiveness
Tuning In – Grounding in the Real World	The model is naturally focused on the workplace environment and the workflow. Therefore it would naturally consider cultural factors. It also necessitates engagement with stakeholders to create an effective performance support ecosystem.	Discover phase usually surfaces aspects of the operating environment and systems in addition to the concerns and tasks that contribute to day-to-day performance. Engages a wide range of stakeholders across all phases and seeks to share the load for some aspects of the work, e.g. creating resources and experiences.	Key players in ensuring transfer success are trainees, peers, supervisors and the company's culture in the form of transfer expectations within the company. Effective transfer is a joint effort. It relies on collaboration, with each stakeholder playing their part, with our support to enable them to play their role in making transfer happen.
Responding *Choosing Well*	Grounded in cognitive science principles related to learning and performance support including spaced practice, learning in context and experiential learning. Explicitly expands beyond traditional formal learning to include performance support tools and workflow resources, particularly for the Apply, Solve, and Change moments.	5Di is the only learning design model grounded in a general theory of learning – the affective context model. The affective context model provides an explanatory framework for learning research ranging from comparative psychology (such as conditioning) through to contemporary neuroscience. Shifts away from course-centric thinking to resources (point-of-need support) and experiences (challenges, stories), supporting workflow learning, as well as considering process changes.	The model is grounded in transfer research – an interdisciplinary field that integrates insights from learning science, organizational studies, motivation research, behavioural science and neuroscience, applying them to the specific context of adult learning and application within corporate training and development.

(continued)

TABLE A2.1 (Continued)

Principle	5 Moments of Need	5Di	12 Levers of Transfer Effectiveness
Responding *Enabling* *Learning*	Provides framework for blending formal learning (New, More) with application support (Apply, Solve, Change). Explicitly focuses on supporting skills application in the workflow. Social support can be incorporated across all moments, especially Solve moments.	Solutions include resources (e.g. one-page guides, checklists, short-form video) and/or experience to address audience concerns and tasks, helping people to perform work at point of need and promoting skills application. Experiences may include approaches that connect people, e.g. action learning, shadowing, coaching, mentoring.	Active Practice (#6) ensures realistic skill rehearsal during training. Transfer Planning (#7) helps learners prepare to apply new skills. Opportunities for Application (#8) and Transfer Capacity (#9) ensure learners have time, tasks and support to embed behaviours. Support from Peers (#11) encourages collaboration and shared learning – essential for sustaining change and improving performance.
Responding *Engaging* *Influencers*	Managers play a critical role in supporting Apply, Solve and Change moments, and must be equipped with the resources and guidance to support performance in the workflow. They don't carry the burden of coaching and 'knowing everything'. The performance support does that. It's an enablement model. The model can be extended to include roles for various performance supporters.	Marketing and communication campaigns are used to launch and raise awareness. Managers often play a key role in promoting learning, and resources and experiences aimed at managers are identified during the define and discovery stages.	Transfer goals (i.e. desired behaviours) are aligned in advance with all key stakeholders, including participants, their supervisors, trainers and others who are engaged to support learners based on targeted behaviours and context. Manager Support (#10) acknowledges manager importance in supporting transfer and tools are provided to equip them. Peer Support (#11) addresses peer influencers.

(continued)

TABLE A2.1 (Continued)

Principle	5 Moments of Need	5Di	12 Levers of Transfer Effectiveness
Improving *Monitoring Progress*	The model shifts the focus of evaluation from learning completion to performance outcomes, and naturally connects to performance data through its focus on workplace application.	Tests MVP solution(s) during iterative design and development, using feedback to improve the solution. Encourages ongoing use of audience and business data to gather feedback and monitor impact-linked initial hypotheses and target outcomes. Brings business stakeholders into process from the beginning, making it natural to involve them in evaluation.	Follow-up and Accountability (#12) is about measuring transfer effectiveness, based on the philosophy that what gets measured gets done.
Improving *Sharing Progress*	Performance focus aligns with business language and helps to communicate impact in terms of performance improvement. No explicit guidance on recognition strategies.	Establishing clear business outcomes in the Define phase positions you to communicate impact in business language. Focus on performance change creates opportunities to celebrate tangible successes.	Progress is measured and communicated in terms of behaviour change and desired business impact. The model allows not only assessment of whether change occurred, but also analysis of why it has or hasn't. Positive Personal Outcomes (#3) touches on recognition but focuses more on anticipated benefits than celebration of successes.

(continued)

TABLE A2.1 (Continued)

Principle	5 Moments of Need	5Di	12 Levers of Transfer Effectiveness
Improving *Adapting Course*	Supports continuous improvement of work and performance across all moments of need using workflow data and business metrics. It builds self-confidence in the learner and teaches them how to own their professional development.	MVP approach explicitly encourages experimentation and iteration during solution development. Feedback loops are built into the process, including post-deployment and supporting adaptation.	The model assesses not only whether change has occurred, but also why it has or has not. This enables continuous optimization and sustainable, transfer-effective development. The 12 levers are used at many points in a project to monitor progress and decide on how to improve transfer.

Note

1 C Munger. A lesson on elementary, worldly wisdom as it relates to investment management and business, 1994: Charlie Munger's famous talk at USC Business School, FS, 2025. https://fs.blog/great-talks/a-lesson-on-worldly-wisdom (archived at https://perma.cc/Q62Q-QNUH)

APPENDIX 3

Learning science checklist

This concise checklist brings together key concepts from learning science to help you design more effective learning experiences (Table A3.1). Before finalizing your next learning solution, review these principles and assess how well your approach incorporates them.

TABLE A3.1 Learning science checklist

Learning science concept	Description	Application question
Content Relevance	People learn best when content directly addresses their needs and accurately reflects workplace realities.	Have you provided content that directly aligns with learners' goals and real-world applications?
Retrieval Practice	Pulling information from memory deepens understanding and improves retention.	Have you included opportunities for learners to recall and apply knowledge without immediate prompts?
Spaced Practice	Spreading learning across time is more effective than concentrated exposure.	Have you included well-spaced practice opportunities?
Elaboration	Connecting new knowledge to existing understanding creates stronger neural pathways.	Have you prompted learners to relate new concepts to prior knowledge and experiences?
Varied Repetition	Multiple exposures to content in different contexts strengthens learning.	Have you designed various ways to encounter and work with key concepts?
Timely Feedback	Specific, constructive feedback helps correct misconceptions and guide improvement.	Have you built in mechanisms for learners to receive timely, actionable feedback?
Reflection	Metacognitive practices help learners assess understanding and take ownership.	Have you created structured opportunities for learners to reflect on their learning?

(continued)

TABLE A3.1 (Continued)

Learning science concept	Description	Application question
Social Learning	Learning is enhanced through observation, modelling and interaction with others.	Have you incorporated opportunities for collaborative learning and knowledge sharing?
Emotional Engagement	Emotional connections to content enhance attention, motivation and retention.	Have you considered how to create meaningful, emotionally resonant learning experiences?
Cognitive Load Management	Learning is optimized when cognitive load is appropriate – not too high or too low.	Have you structured content to manage complexity and avoid overwhelming learners?

When using this checklist, remember that not every principle needs equal emphasis in every solution, but consciously considering each one will help you make evidence-informed choices about your design.

Use the following AI prompt if you'd like to explore these principles further:

Help me understand the learning science principle of [XXX]. Share the key findings from authoritative research papers (ensure these are real papers and give me links). Speak in plain English. I'm an [XXX role] so help me understand how I could apply these lessons in my world.

APPENDIX 4

L&D thinking habits continuum

A quick reference guide to BOLD L&D thinking habits as described in Chapter 11.

FIGURE A4.1 L&D thinking habits continuum

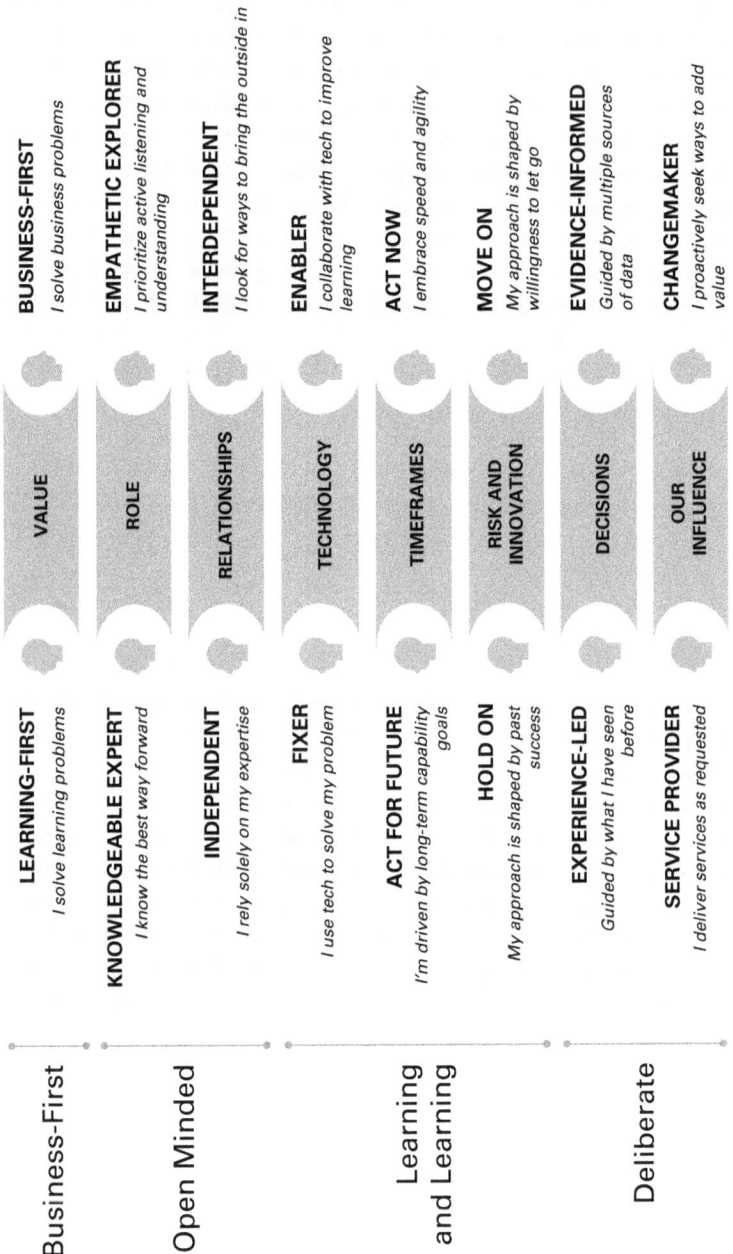

Continuum		Left habit			Right habit

Business-First

LEARNING-FIRST
I solve learning problems

VALUE

BUSINESS-FIRST
I solve business problems

KNOWLEDGEABLE EXPERT
I know the best way forward

ROLE

EMPATHETIC EXPLORER
I prioritize active listening and understanding

Open Minded

INDEPENDENT
I rely solely on my expertise

RELATIONSHIPS

INTERDEPENDENT
I look for ways to bring the outside in

FIXER
I use tech to solve my problem

TECHNOLOGY

ENABLER
I collaborate with tech to improve learning

ACT FOR FUTURE
I'm driven by long-term capability goals

TIMEFRAMES

ACT NOW
I embrace speed and agility

Learning and Learning

HOLD ON
My approach is shaped by past success

RISK AND INNOVATION

MOVE ON
My approach is shaped by willingness to let go

EXPERIENCE-LED
Guided by what I have seen before

DECISIONS

EVIDENCE-INFORMED
Guided by multiple sources of data

Deliberate

SERVICE PROVIDER
I deliver services as requested

OUR INFLUENCE

CHANGEMAKER
I proactively seek ways to add value

APPENDIX 5

L&D Sail Plan

Refer to Chapter 12 for guidance on completing your L&D Sail Plan.

FIGURE A5.1 L&D Sail Plan prompters

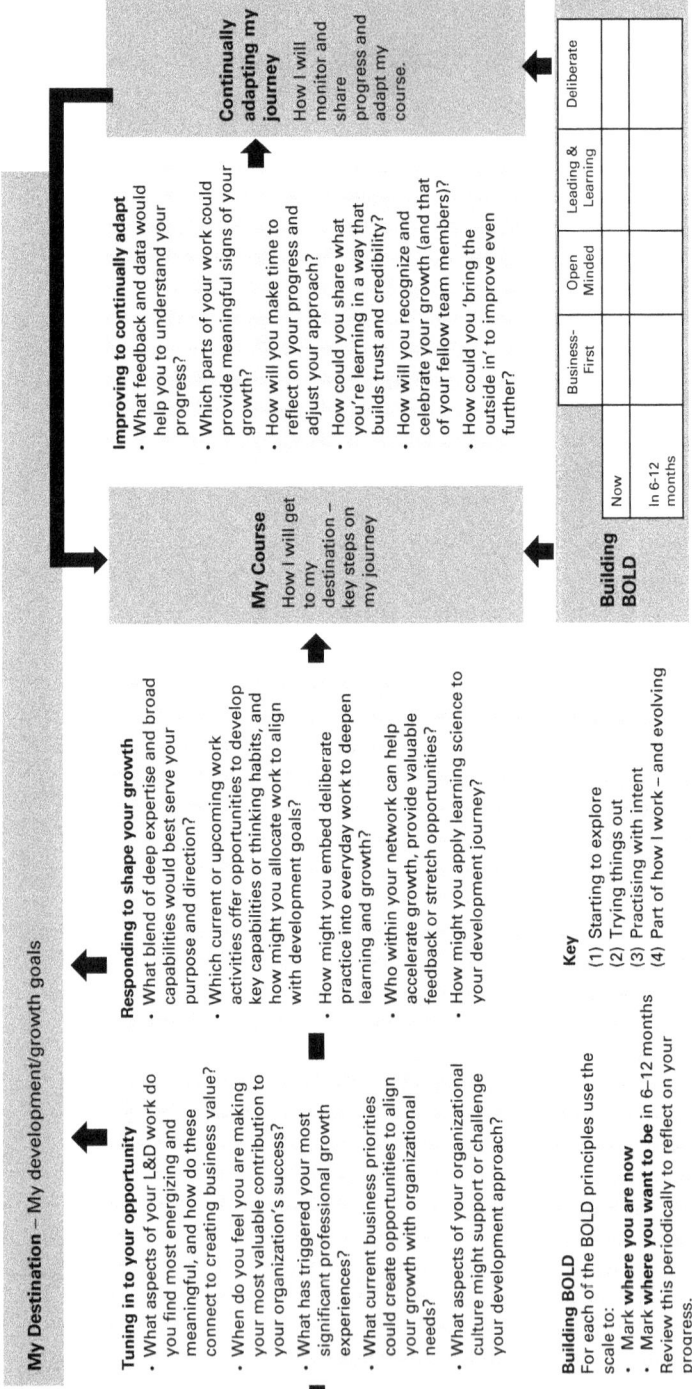

My Destination – My development/growth goals

Tuning in to your opportunity
- What aspects of your L&D work do you find most energizing and meaningful, and how do these connect to creating business value?
- When do you feel you are making your most valuable contribution to your organization's success?
- What has triggered your most significant professional growth experiences?
- What current business priorities could create opportunities to align your growth with organizational needs?
- What aspects of your organizational culture might support or challenge your development approach?

Responding to shape your growth
- What blend of deep expertise and broad capabilities would best serve your purpose and direction?
- Which current or upcoming work activities offer opportunities to develop key capabilities or thinking habits, and how might you allocate work to align with development goals?
- How might you embed deliberate practice into everyday work to deepen learning and growth?
- Who within your network can help accelerate growth, provide valuable feedback or stretch opportunities?
- How might you apply learning science to your development journey?

My Course
How I will get to my destination – key steps on my journey

Improving to continually adapt
- What feedback and data would help you to understand your progress?
- Which parts of your work could provide meaningful signs of your growth?
- How will you make time to reflect on your progress and adjust your approach?
- How could you share what you're learning in a way that builds trust and credibility?
- How will you recognize and celebrate your growth (and that of your fellow team members)?
- How could you 'bring the outside in' to improve even further?

Continually adapting my journey
How I will monitor and share progress and adapt my course.

Building BOLD

	Business-First	Open Minded	Leading & Learning	Deliberate
Now				
In 6-12 months				

Key
(1) Starting to explore
(2) Trying things out
(3) Practising with intent
(4) Part of how I work – and evolving

Building BOLD
For each of the BOLD principles use the scale to:
- Mark **where you are now**
- Mark **where you want to be** in 6–12 months
Review this periodically to reflect on your progress.

FIGURE A5.2 _&D Sail Plan

My Destination – My development/growth goals

My Course – How I will get to my destination: key steps on my journey

Continually adapting my journey – How I will monitor and share progress and adapt my course

Building BOLD

Key
(1) Starting to explore
(2) Trying things out
(3) Practising with intent
(4) Part of how I work – and evolving

	Business-First	Open Minded	Leading & Learning	Deliberate
Where am I now?				
Where do I want to be in 6–12 months?				

Key mindset shifts I will create:

INDEX

NB: page numbers in *italic* indicate figures or tables

5Di 63
   see also Appendix 2
5 Moments of Need 87
   see also Appendix 2
7-Step Performance Consulting 63
9/11 terrorist attacks, New York 15
9 Events of Instruction 87
12 Levers of Transfer Effectiveness 87
   see also Appendix 2
70:20:10 model 78

action bias 49, *61*
Action Learning 110
Action Mapping 87
active listening 53–54
Adaptive Humans + AI Agents 20
affective context model 53
agency *see* influence, using your
Ahmetaj, Gent 33
Aikau, Eddie 2–3
analysis paralysis 49, *62*
anti-fragility, building 96
ANZ Bank 208
APAC 92–93
artificial intelligence (AI) 11, 23, 29, 80, 257–59
   access to knowledge 194
   'beige wave' 258
   disruption caused by 19, 20–21, 254, 258
   generative AI 19, 20, 72, 75, 148
   for Improving 106–07
   personalized experiences 30, 194, 258
   for skills analysis 159, *166*
   'technology trap', the 72
   and uncertainty 236
Aster Group 82
AstraZeneca 103, 112, 114–15, 116–21, 217, 218, 222, 256
   democratization of learning 117
   executive support 116–17
   metrics 118–19
   micro learning 118
   technology use 117
   TRI principles 119–20

attribution bias *201*

Bandura, Albert 206
bandwagon effect *201*
Barnardo's 45–46, 48, 65
Beach, Rodney 173, 174, 175, 217, 220, 228
behavioural science 73, 74
benchmarking 103–04, *104*
Berger, Eric 240, 244
Bersin, Josh 23, 58, 258–59
BOLD mindset 40, 120–21, 128, 211, 215–30, 236, 256–57
   BOLD L&D compass 217, *217*
   Business-First 216, 218
   Deliberate 216, 222
   Leading and Learning 216, 220–21
   Open Minded 216, 219–20
   orientation, adjusting your 225, *225*–26
   Resseau, Keith 223–24, 227
   safety net elements 227–29, *228*
   'smart BOLD' thinking 216
   and uncertainty 257
   see also Appendix 4
Bonini, Cris 242
'box ticking' 127, 130
Boyd, John 39
Brann, Amy 74
Brinkerhoff, Robert 17, 110
Buglass, Dave 51
ByteDance 17, 51

Chambers, John 253
champions 81–83
Chartered Institute of Personnel and Development (CIPD)
   Learning at Work study 2021 18–19, 263
   Learning at Work study 2023 195–96
ChatGPT 46, 80
Christensen, Lisa 154
churn 38
Cisco 253
Citibank 193
CLO100 259
CLO LIFT 259

cognitive bias 193–94, *199*, 200, *201*
cognitive load *198*
cognitive science 73–74
Coles Group 105, 173–77, 220, 256
   custom LMS development 173–74
   tech integration 174
   TRI principles 176–77, *184–86*
Collins, Stella 74
COM-B model 87
confirmation bias *201*
'conspiracy of convenience' 170
content, reliance on 126, 257–58, 261
Cook, James 1
Covid-19 pandemic 15, 18–20,
      179, 183, 253
   Emerging Stronger 215
cultural blindness *201*
cultural resistance 149, *163*
Culture Map 63
Curious Advantage, The 75
curse of knowledge bias *201*

Daniels, Marie 92–93, 94, 95, 98,
      100, 112, 218
data protection 127
Deciem 60
decision orientation 222, *222*
   adjusting your *226*
Design Thinking 63
Dirksen, Julie 74
disruption blindness *201*
distance bias *201*
Dixon, Genny 33
Domain 58
Drive 54

Ebbinghaus forgetting curve 67
e-learning 22
Emerging Stronger 215
'emotional processing' 247
EPAM Systems Inc (EPAM) 53, 147, 150,
      156, 157–62, *163–64*, 166, 256
   AI use 159
   empowerment of learners 158
   skills ontology 157–58
   TRI principles 160–62, *163–64*
Ericsson 75, 221, 228
evaluation paradox 97, *107*
expertise, using your 206–07, *207*, 208, 210

feedback, gathering 246–47, *249*
Ford 29

Gates, Bill 257
global recession, 2008 15

Harwood, Adam 125, 217
Hawaiian Star Compass 3, 213, 264
Hedrick, Cameron 193–94, 203, 211, 227
Hōkūle'a 2–3, 4, 5, 50, 194, *201*, 263–64
Howells, Marc 116, 118, 119, 120, 217, 222

IKEA bias *201*
imposter syndrome 202
Improving (TRI principle) 92–113
   Adapting Course 103–05
   for aspiring leaders 109–10
   barriers to 97–98, *107–09*
   Daniels, Marie 92–93, 94, 95, 98,
      100, 112, 218
   defining 95
   for growth 237, 246–48, *249*
   Monitoring Progress 98–100
   for seasoned leaders 110–11
   Sharing Progress 101–03
   what it isn't 96
influence orientation 222, *222*
   adjusting your *226*
influence, using your 205–06, *207*, 208,
      209–10
information overload 127, *141*, 195
intentional, being 208–09
internal compass, your 213–15

jargon 38
Jennings, Charles 260–61, 23
Jobson, Simon 67–68, 89
Johnson, Dani 244

Kettleborough, Jonathan 51
Kirkpatrick-Katzell Four Levels 110
Kirschner, Paul 74
KPMG International 242
Kulasingam, Siva 173, 174, 175,
      217, 220, 228

L&D communities 259–60
L&D, purpose of 28
L&D Sail Plan 237, 251
   Improving section 248
   Responding section 245
   Tuning In section 239–40
   see also Appendix 5
L&D Shakers 259
L&D Value Cycle 263
L&D Value Landscape 17–18, *18*, 255–56
   Changemaker Zone 18, 255
   Co-creator Zone 17, 255–56
   Comfort Zone 17, 255
   Danger Zone 17, 255
L&D Value Spectrum *15*, 15–16, 98, 99

Leadership in Complexity and Change 37
learning culture 147–48, 165
'learning in the flow' 22
learning management systems 30
Learning Performance Benchmark 14–15,
         16, 38, 46, 68, 93, 162, 254
    and alignment with business goals 51
    and benchmarking 104
    and change 23
    and demonstrating achievement 102
    and evaluation 100
    and feedback loops 105
    and individuals 53
    and L&D maturity 35
    and managers 81, 101
    and overwhelm 30
    and planning 253
    and technology 75, 81
    see also Appendix 1
learning science 73–74, 75, 79, 244
    applying insights *198–99*
    behavioural science 73, 74
    cognitive bias 193–94, *199*,
             200, *201*, 203
    cognitive science 73–74
    in action 84
    limiting beliefs 201–02, 203
    neuroscience 73
    social science 73, 74
    see also Appendix 3
learning technology 75, 76
Learning-Transfer Evaluation Model
         (LTEM) 110
Learning Uncut 36
Leyton 106–07, 221, 222, 227
Liberate Learning 105, 173–77, 220
linear thinking bias *201*
LinkedIn
    2022 Workplace Learning Report 19
Loughlin, Sandra 53, 160

Masie, Elliot 257
McDonald's 146, 148, 166
McKay, Annaleigh 131, 219
McKinsey & Company 147, 150, 151–56,
         162, *163*, 166, 246, 256, 261
    feedback in 151–52, 153
    local leadership 152–53
    metrics dashboard 153
    TRI principles 154–56,
             162, *163*
metacognition *198*
micro-learning 22, 118, 174
mobile learning 22, 30

Model Evaluation and Threat Research
         (METR) 20
Moon, Karina 219
Mosher, Bob and Gottfredson, Conrad 78
Multiplex 129–34, 140, 145, 219
    box ticking, avoiding 130
    co-creating learning 131
    psychological safety 130
    TRI principles 132–34, 140, *141–42*
Munger, Charlie 77

National Australia Bank (NAB) 16
neuroscience 73
Norman, Jennifer 181
Northern Land Council 57
North Yorkshire Police 177, 178–83,
         188, 256
    continuous improvement 179, 181
    Covid-19, impact of 179
    student journey 179, *180*
    TRI principles 182–83, *184–86*
not invented here bias 39, *201*

observer bias *201*
Offbeat 259
'once and done' mindset 49, *61*
OODA loop 39
Open University 177, 178–83, 184–86, 188
outcome bias *201*
Overton, Laura 30–31, 33, 34
overwhelm 39, 235

Paine, Nigel 147
Parton, Dolly 11, 256
peer-to-peer learning 22
Perkins, David 53
personalization 235
    AI for 30, 194, 258
    scaling, challenges of 127, *141*
PESTLE analysis 63
Piailug, Mau 2–3, 4, 5, 40, 50,
         213, 214
Pink, Daniel 54
Plan, Do, Check, Act (PDCA) 110
planning fallacy *201*
Polynesian Voyaging Society 2–5, 213, 237,
         263–64
Pradhan, Arun 208–09
presence, using your 204–05, *207*, 208, 209
Pritchard, Jodie 45–46, 48, 65
'productive friction' 244
projection bias *201*

Quinn, Clark 23, 74, 253

Rebourgeon, Pauline 75, 221, 244
reductionism vs simplification 35
relationship orientation *219*, 219–20
    adjusting your *225*
remote working 127
Responding (TRI principle) 67–89
    for aspiring leaders 87
    barriers to 71–72, *85–86*
    Choosing Well 73–77
    defining 69
    Enabling Learning 78–80
    Engaging Influencers 80–83
    for growth 237, 240, 242–45, *245–46*
    for seasoned leaders 88
    Sydney Trains 67–68, 71, 79, 81, 89
    vs Reacting 69, *70*
    what it isn't 71
Resseau, Keith 223–24, 227
retrieval practice *198*
Reuters 82
risk and innovation orientation *221*, 221
    adjusting your *226*
Robbins, Tony 30
role orientation *219*, 219
    adjusting your *225*

Schein, Edgar 204
schema theory *198*
Schneider Electric 21
'self-efficacy' *see* expertise, using your
Shackleton-Jones, Nick 53, 74, 78
Shank, Patti 74
Shea, Peter 19
short-term thinking 149, *163*
'silver bullet', the 38
skills, most important
    for employees 148, *149*
    for L&D practitioners 242, *243*
social constructivism *199*
social science 73, 74
Spark 223
status quo bias *201*
Stefanski, Heather 150
Sterns, Justin 250
Stockland 55
storytelling 79
Success Case Method 110
sunk cost fallacy *201*
Swift, James 106–07, 212–13, 215, 221,
    222, 227–28, 229, 258
Sydney Trains 67–68, 71, 79, 81, 89
Systemic HR™ 58

Taylor, Donald H 75, 258

technology orientation *220*, 220
    adjusting your *225*
Thalheimer, Will 74
'Theory One' 53
Thomas Cook 125
Thompson, Barbara 168, 169, 171, 219–20
Thompson, Myron ('Pinky') 3, 4, 227, 237
Thompson, Nainoa 2–5, 40, 50, 70, 96, 194,
    227, *259*, 264
time orientation *221*, 221
    adjusting your *226*
Tindall, Sebastian 52, 135, 136, 137, 218
Towards Maturity Benchmark *see* Learning
    Performance Benchmark
'trained incapacity' 49
Training Needs Analysis 22
Transformation Curve Maturity Model *32*,
    33–34
TRI principles 36–38, *37*, 39–40, 197, 213
    for collaboration 171–72
    and complexity 195
    for continuous adaptation 150, *151*
    real world examples 256
        AstraZeneca 119–20
        Multiplex 132–34, 140, *141–42*
        Vitality 138–39, 140, *141–42*
        Coles Group and Liberate
            Learning 176–77, *184–86*
        EPAM Systems Inc 160–62, *163–64*
        McKinsey & Company 154–56,
            162, *163*
        North Yorkshire Police and Open
            University 182–83, *184–86*
        Westpac 250–51
    for today's needs 128–29
    and uncertainty 257
    see also Improving; Responding;
        Tuning In
Tsiriotakis, Kristina 60
Tuning In (TRI principle) 45–65
    Aligning Together 50–52
    for aspiring leaders 60–63, *61–62*
    Barnardo's 45–46, 48, 65
    barriers to 49, *61–62*
    Connecting to Individuals 53–56
    defining 47
    Grounding in the Real World 56–59
    for growth 237, 238–40, *241*
    for seasoned leaders 63–64
    what it isn't 48

Uber 54
Uhl, Trish 20, 146, 148, 166
urgency trap 97, *109*

'use of self' *see* presence, using your
user generated content 22

value orientation *218*, 218
    adjusting your *225*
Varney, Sharon 36–37
Vitality 52, 134–39, 140, 145, 218
    resource-led approach 135, 136
    simplification of processes 136
    TRI principles 138–39, 140,
        141–42

Voost, Geraldine 72, 80, 215

Waldman, Lauren 74, 82
Weber, Emma 247
Westpac 250–51
Woods, Damien 16
Woods, Russell 82
World Economic Forum (WEF) 148
    Future of Jobs Report 2025 149

Zao-Sanders, Marc 258

Looking for another book?

Explore our award-winning
books from global business
experts in Human Resources,
Learning and Development

Scan the code to browse

www.koganpage.com/hr-learning-
development

More from Kogan Page

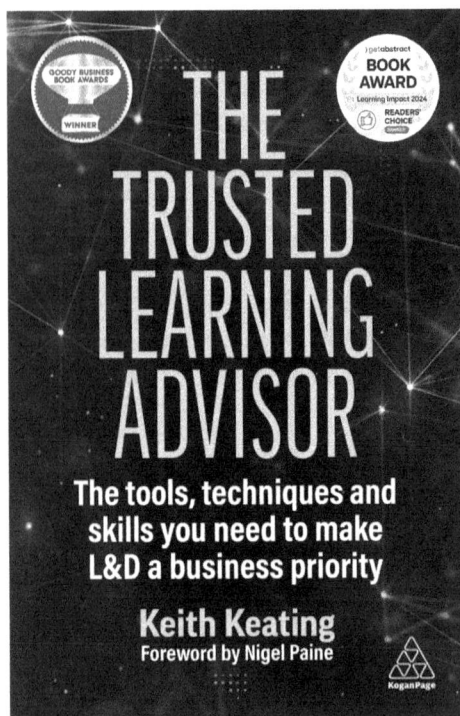

THE TRUSTED LEARNING ADVISOR

The tools, techniques and skills you need to make L&D a business priority

Keith Keating

Foreword by Nigel Paine

ISBN: 9781398612457

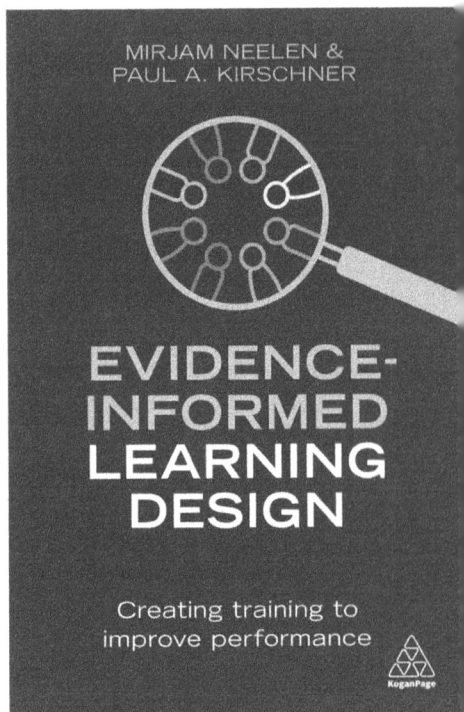

MIRJAM NEELEN & PAUL A. KIRSCHNER

EVIDENCE-INFORMED LEARNING DESIGN

Creating training to improve performance

ISBN: 9781789661415

www.koganpage.com

From 4 December 2025 the EU Responsible Person (GPSR) is:
eucomply oÜ, Pärnu mnt. 139b – 14, 11317 Tallinn, Estonia
www.eucompliancepartner.com

www.ingramcontent.com/pod-product-compliance
Lightning Source LLC
Chambersburg PA
CBHW071542210326
41597CB00019B/3090